STUDIES
ON PROPHECY

SUPPLEMENTS

TO

VETUS TESTAMENTUM

EDITED BY

THE BOARD OF THE QUARTERLY

VOLUME XXVI

LEIDEN
E. J. BRILL
1974

STUDIES ON PROPHECY

A COLLECTION OF TWELVE PAPERS

LEIDEN
E. J. BRILL
1974

ISBN 90 04 03877 9

PRINTED IN THE NETHERLANDS

TABLE OF CONTENTS

PREFACE

The reason for the publication of this collection of papers in the series *Supplements to Vetus Testamentum* is shortage of space in the journal itself. The articles are arranged in more or less chronological order, with those on general topics at the end.

Although the reader cannot expect to find here a systematic treatment of prophecy, we venture to hope that these studies of texts from both the pre-exilic and the post-exilic periods, together with discussions of important terms and ideas, will make a contribution to the understanding of the prophets.

THE EDITORS

LA VIGNE ET LE DOUBLE JE

Exercice de style sur Esaʿïe V 1-7

PAR

DANIEL LYS
Montpellier

I.

La traduction qui suit s'efforce de conserver la cohérence de l'hébreu tant dans le vocabulaire que dans la position des mots, afin que l'on puisse faire sur le français la même travail que sur l'original. On a aussi essayé de garder jeux de mots et connotations.

I 1. Je m'en vais chanter pour qui je chéris
la chanson de mon chéri pour sa vigne:

La vigne existait pour qui je chéris
en côteau de terre fertile.
2. Il l'avait défoncée, il l'avait épierrée,
il l'avait plantée d'un rouge muscat.
Puis il avait bâti une tour en son centre;
et aussi une cuve il a creusé en elle.
Il avait espéré produit de raisins doux,
mais son produit a été dégoûtant.

II 3. Et maintenant,
habitant de Jérusalem,
homme de Juda,
faites droit entre moi et ma vigne.
4. Que produire encor pour ma vigne
que je n'aie pas produit en elle?
Pourquoi ai-je espéré produit de raisins doux,
et son produit a été dégoûtant?

III 5. Et maintenant
je m'en vais vous faire connaître
ce que moi je produis pour ma vigne!

Arracher sa haie — elle existera pour brûler!
Abattre son mur — elle existera pour piétinement!
6. J'en ferai un endroit saccagé,
objet ni de taille ni de sarclage,
montant en épines et en piquants,
et aux nuages commanderai:
„Ne pas faire pleuvoir sur elle de la pluie!"

IV 7. Car
la vigne du Seigneur des Puissances
c'est la maison d'Israël,
et c'est l'homme de Juda
qui est le plant de ses délices.
Il espérait l'éthique,
et voici la clique;
le droit,
et voici le cri d'effroi.

II. Les Marques d'Articulation

A

1. Formule volitive à la 1ère personne du singulier aux v. 1 et 5, marquant le passage de la chanson à la révélation („faire connaître"). Le seul autre volitif est l'impératif 2ème personne du pluriel au v. 3.

2. Passage à la 3ème personne du singulier pour le description impersonnelle du v. 2.

3. Récurrence de 2b en 4b, chaque fois suivi par „et maintenant" en 3 et 5.

4. Interpellation au v. 3, reprise au v. 5 dans le „vous" qui est l'unique emploi de ce pronom personnel séparé en face de „moi" lui aussi unique.

5. „Car", suivi au v. 7 d'une description impersonnelle n'utilisant plus ni la 1ère ni la 2ème personne, à la façon du v. 2.

B

1. Il y a un lien logique entre 1b et 2a, 3b et 4a, 5b et 6a: chaque fois l'idée du premier verset est continuée dans le verset suivant. Par contre il y a rupture en 3a, 5a et 7a. On a donc quatre strophes: 1-2, 3-4, 5-6, 7.

2. La strophe II est liée à la strophe I par la fin (4b reprend 2b) et à la strophe III par le début (5a reprend 3a). De plus les v. 4 et 5a contiennent cinq fois la racine „produire"; on peut laisser de côté le premier emploi qui est impersonnel; les quatre autres sont disposés en chiasme, le cinquième (au v. 5a) étant lié au second (au v. 4a) comme concernant l'orateur, par-dessus les deux autres (en 4b) qui concernent la vigne. Enfin en hébreu „pourquoi" au v. 4 est de la même racine que „connaître" au v. 5.

3. La strophe I est description du passé; la strophe III est description de l'avenir, chacune commençant par une formule de décision de communication („je m'en vais chanter/(vous)faire connaître"). La strophe II fait le lien entre les deux, reprenant la fin de la strophe I pour introduire la strophe III dont la première formule est la même qu'au début de la strophe II. La strophe II est donc comme une parenthèse, reprenant au v. 4 de façon interrogative le contenu du v. 2 à propos des actes et du résultat, et préparant le dévoilement du v. 7 par l'interpellation de Juda au v. 3.

4. La strophe IV est liée à la strophe III par le dévoilement au v. 7a de l'identité du celui qui agit au v. 6 (on était déjà sur la voie par le fait qu'il commande aux nuages, et le „car" est un „oui"). Elle est liée à la strophe II par l'identification de Juda (interpellé au v. 3 à propos de la conduite de la vigne) avec la vigne elle-même. Elle est liée à la strophe I de diverses manières: le v. 7 est description impersonnelle (ni „je" ni „tu") comme les v. 1b-2; le v. 7a explicite l'imagerie du v. 1a (la vigne), tandis que le v. 7b explicite celle de 1b-2 (les actes et le résultat, tant espéré que réel); noter la récurrence de „plant(er)" et d'„espérer", tandis que „délices" reprend sémantiquement „chéri" (on verra plus loin qu'il s'agit des deux partenaires qui s'aiment).

III. Récurrences verbales et (en italiques) sémantiques

verbes à la 1ère personne sing.	1			4bis	5	6bis	
volitif 1ère personne	1				5		
pronom personnel 1ère personne					**5**		
suffixe 1ère personne	1ter		3bis	4	5		
verbes 3ème personne sing.	1	2septiens		4	5bis	6ter	7(bis)°
suffixe 3ème personne	1	2quinquiens		4	5bis	6bis	7
verbe 2ème pers. plur. volitif			**3**				
pronom personnel 2ème pers. pl.					**5**		
participe					**5**		
infinitifs		2		4bis	5ter	6	
exister	1				5bis		
planter		2					7
bâtir/creuser-*arracher/rbattre*		2bis			*5bis*		
espérer		2		4			7(bis)°
produire		2bis		4quater	5		*7(bis)*
chanter	1bis					(6)°°	
chanter chanson/pleuvoir pluie	1					(6)°°°	
pour	1ter	2°°°°		4ter*	5ter		7bis**
en	1	2bis		4			
sur						6(bis)***	
et maintenant			3		5		
pourquoi				**4**	(5)****		
car							**7**
chéri/*délices*	1ter						*7*
vigne	1bis		3	4	5		7
raisins doux		*2bis*		4			
dégoûtant		2		4			
homme de Juda			*3bis*				*7bis*
(faire) droit			3				*7bis*
Seigneur des Puissances							**7**

Les chiffres en caractères gras indiquent les non-récurrences.

° Le second emploi de „il espérait" est sous-entendu.

°° Connotation de „taille" (voir plus loin).

°°° Récurrence structurelle (redondance verbe + substantif de même racine).

°°°° Sous-entendu en français. Littéralement: „il avait espéré pour faire des raisins".

* Seul le second apparaît en français. Littéralement: „quoi pour faire encor", „ai-je espéré pour faire des raisins".

** Littéralement: „il espérait pour l'éthique/pour le droit".

*** Un seul emploi de „sur". Mais le verbe „monter" a même sonorité et même racine.

**** Un seul emploi de „pourquoi". Mais le verbe „connaître" a même racine. On notera les emplois parfaitement symétriques de l'expression „et maintenant", ainsi que du terme „vigne".

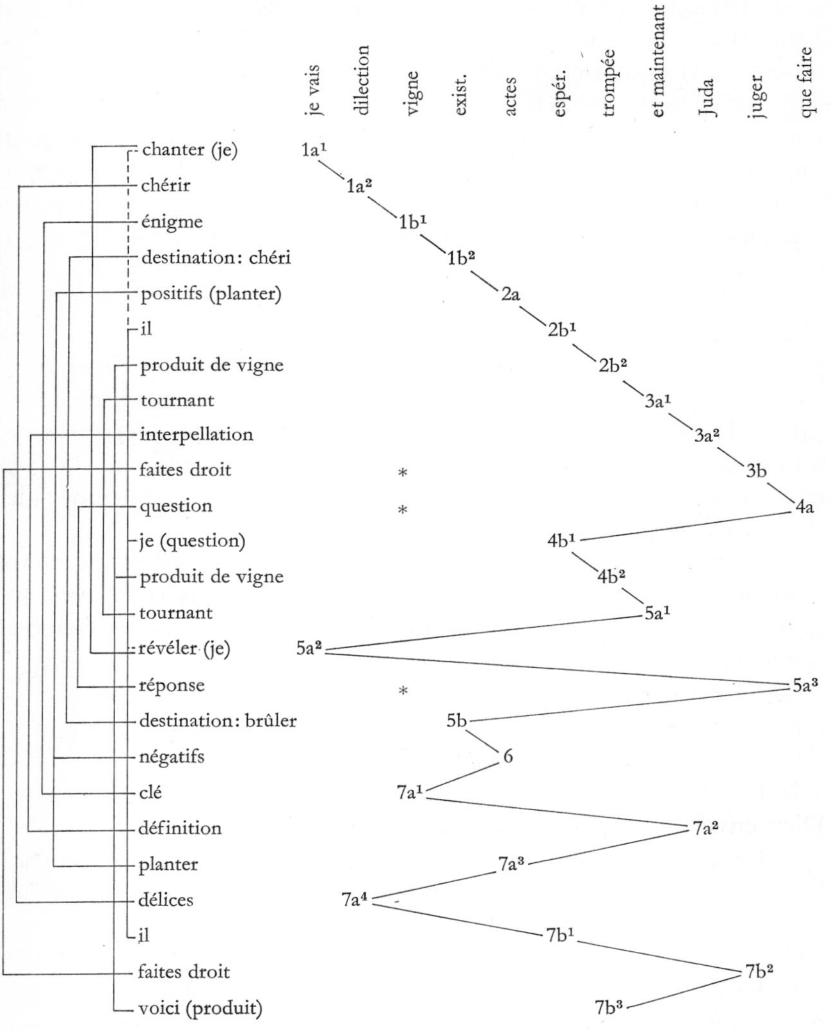
je vais
dilection
vigne
exist.
actes
espér.
trompée
et maintenant
Juda
juger
que faire
chanter (je)
chérir
énigme
destination: chéri
positifs (planter)
il
produit de vigne
tournant
interpellation
faites droit
question
je (question)
produit de vigne
tournant
révéler (je)
réponse
destination: brûler
négatifs
clé
définition
planter
délices
il
faites droit
voici (produit)
1a¹
1a²
1b¹
1b²
2a
2b¹
2b²
3a¹
3a²
3b
4a
4b¹
4b²
5a¹
5a²
5a³
5b
6
7a¹
7a²
7a³
7a⁴
7b¹
7b²
7b³
*
*
*

V. Remarques

1. Tout fait l'objet de récurrences sauf sept éléments: (*a*) le volitif 2ème personne du pluriel au v. 3b; (*b*) „pourquoi" à 4b (mais en hébreu c'est la même racine que „connaître" au v. 5 qui annonce la réponse à la question); (*c*) dans le seul verset 5, le pronom 1ère pers. sing. et le pronom 2ème pers. plur., plus un verbe au participe commandé par le pronom 1ère pers. sing.; (*d*) au v. 7, „car" qui qui introduit le dévoilement, et „le Seigneur des Puissances" qui est la clé des pronoms (voir plus loin). Le v. 5a est le pivot autour duquel s'organisent l'interpellation et le dévoilement des v. 3 et 7 qui par ailleurs ont „Juda" et „droit" comme éléments communs.

2. La première récurrence qui apparaisse est „il" ($2b^1$) - „je" ($4b^1$) - „il" ($7b^1$), à laquelle on peut aussi attacher les deux volitifs à la 1ère pers. sing. ($1a^1$ et $5a^2$). Ce „il-je-il" est par trois fois lié à l'espérance trompée, qui est l'objet de la deuxième récurrence exprimée par le „produit". Ces deux récurrences sont les seules à être ternaires, si à propos des actes on distingue entre ceux qui sont positifs (2a et $7a^3$) et ceux qui sont négatifs (6). — La dernière récurrence concerne „le droit", et, implicitement, le „produit".

3. A propos des occurrences de la première et de la dernière colonne, on notera que le premier „je vais" n'est pas la réponse au „que faire" mais y conduit; et que le second „je vais" détermine immédiatement „que faire".

4. Le dernier mot exprime l'espérance trompée, qui a trois occurrences. Chacune des deux autres occurrences introduit immédiatement un tournant décisif „et maintenant" ($3a^1$ et $5a^1$). On attendrait aussi à la fin un „et maintenant" pour le dévoilement de la décision de Dieu envers Juda, mais le poème finit sans cela.

5. Le développement est continu de 1 à 4a. $4b^1$-$5a^1$ est au centre: l'espérance trompée conduit au grand tournant; la révélation de $5a^2$ reprend le point de départ de $1a^1$. Par contre $2b^1$-$3a^1$ qui correspond à $4b^1$-$5a^1$ restait de l'ordre du questionnement.

6. La décision (5b-6) est ramassée en un point. Au contraire l'explicitation de l'ensemble (v. 7) couvre le maximum de surface en un zig-zag qui lie le tout: le v. 7 s'étale pratiquement dans toutes les colonnes, sauf la première et la dernière (c'est le cadre: $5a^2$-$5a^3$) et le „et maintenant" ($5a^1$); la colonne absente à l'intérieur du v. 7 est celle de l'„existence" qui définit la „destination" de la vigne ($1b^2$: pour le chéri; 5b: pour brûler et pour piétinement): on peut penser qu'il convient de bloquer cette colonne avec celle des „actes" (présente

en 7a[3]), à moins qu'on n'estime plutôt que l',,existence-pour" est exprimée au v. 7 dans l'appropriation de l'état construit ,,la vigne *du* Seigneur".

7. Au v. 7, si le contraste est marqué non seulement sémantiquement mais phonétiquement (rime) entre ce que Dieu espérait et ce qu'il a obtenu de la part de son peuple, par contre les actes de Dieu sont décrits seulement de façon positive: il faut rapprocher 7a[3] de 2a et non de 5b-6; ,,l'éthique" et le ,,droit" qui viennent en 7 comme récurrence de ,,faites droit" en 3 décrivent ce que Dieu espérait, et non le jugement définitif auquel le v. 3 faisait appel. L'issue reste en suspens.

VI. Quelques connotations

V. 1. ,,Vigne/côteau" ne rend pas en français l'assonance hébraïque *kèrèm/qèrèn*.

L'association ,,vigne/chéri" relève de la poésie amoureuse où la vigne désigne la fille, qui appelle le garçon ,,mon chéri": cf plus tard Ct. i 6 (viii 11-12) et i 13. Mais on verra plus loin qu'ici précisément ce n'est pas la vigne qui appelle son amoureux ,,mon chéri".

Les deux termes proches en hébreu traduits par ,,mon chéri" et ,,qui je chéris" évoquent respectivement le nom de David (*dwd*) et l'autre nom de Salomon selon 2 Sam. xii 25 (*yâdhîdh*). Ailleurs ce dernier mot s'applique essentiellement à celui que Dieu chérit: Dt. xxxiii 12, Jr. xi 15, Ps. lx 7, cviii 7, cxxvii 2 — sauf Ps. lxxxiv 2 pour les demeures de Dieu qui sont chéries des hommes. Voir plus loin ,,délices".

V. 2. ,,Raisins doux": c'est le simple mot hébreu pour ,,raisins", *ʿanâbhîm*. On a ajouté ,,doux" dans la traduction non pas tant pour marquer le contraste avec le verjus que cette vigne produit (pour cela il a suffi de rendre au v. 1 le cépage vermeil par ,,rouge muscat"), mais pour indiquer la connotation des ,,pauvres du Seigneur", les *ʿanâwîm*. La prononciation de ce terme est très proche de celui qu'on a au v. 2 (*bh* = *v*). Ce sont les humbles, les débonnaires, les doux (alors que, au moins à l'origine, *ʿanîyîm* désigne les pauvres au sens social). Voir aussi ci-dessous à propos des ,,nuages"du v. 6.

,,Dégoûtant": on comprend d'ordinaire ce terme comme désignant du raisin acide, du verjus. Cependant la racine exprime ce qui sent mauvais, ce qui est infect, d'où ce qui devient odieux (Ex. vii 18, 1 Sam. xiii 4). Et le *Lexicon* de Koehler-Baumgartner traduit le terme d'Es. v par ,,raisin pourri, putride" — mais le 3ème édition de

Baumgartner en revient aux raisins verts et acides tout en gardant au verbe le sens de „sentir mauvais". „Dégoûtant" essaie d'exprimer cela tout en connotant l'idée de „honte", dont la racine *bwsh* est très proche de *b'sh* ici utilisé.

V. 4. „Pourquoi" peut être exprimé par deux mots hébreux. Celui qui a été choisi ici est de la même racine que „connaître" qui vient tout de suite après au v. 5a comme la réponse aux deux questions du v. 4: „produire" correspond à „produire" et „faire connaître" correspond à „pourquoi".

V. 6. „Taille": il est évident qu'il s'agit d'émondage, en parallèle à „sarclage". Mais la racine *zmr* désigne aussi le chant et la louange: il est difficile de choisir entre les deux à Ct. ii 12. On suggère ici cette connotation par le mot „taille", lointainement associé en français à la voix et à la musique. Ce terme est différent de la chanson du v. 1 (*shîr*) mais l'évoque sémantiquement, alors que les „épines et piquants" qui suivent l'évoquent en hébreu phonétiquement (*shâmîr wâshâyith*).

„Nuages": *'âbhîm* rappelle en hébreu les raisins *'anâbhîm* des v. 2 et 4.

„Monter" et „sur" (français: „aux") ont même racine et même sonorité (voir plus loin).

VII. Etude des pronoms

V. 1. „Je" est différent du „chéri", puisqu'il dit: „mon chéri". La vigne est vigne du chéri, puisqu'à son sujet „je" parle de „*sa* vigne". On s'attendrait, du fait de la symbolique amoureuse (cf ci-dessus), à ce que ce soit la vigne qui dise: „mon chéri". Mais la vigne ne le dit jamais dans ce poème. En un sens „je" prononce les paroles qu'on attend de la vigne: il est distinct de la vigne mais de la sorte il s'identifie à elle.

V. 2. „Il" est différent de la vigne qui est l'objet de son amour et de ses soins, et différent de „je" dont il est le chéri. „Je" raconte l'histoire de „il".

V. 3-4. „Je" parle comme celui qui s'est occupé de cette vigne: „il" en 2b = „je" en 3b. Avons-nous ici simplement une citation du „je = il" par le „je"-poète?

V. 5. „Vous" = , habitant de Jérusalem, homme de Juda" du v. 3. C'est le seul emploi du pronom 2ème personne du pluriel, et il joue le rôle d'un pronom séparé (même si en hébreu il a la forme d'un suffixe après la particule de l'accusatif). Il est opposé à „moi", unique emploi du pronom séparé 1ère personne du singulier. ,,Vous" reprend l'interpellation du v. 3, mais pour préciser ensuite que celui qui fait le droit réclamé au v. 3 est finalement "moi".

,,Je" est le même qu'à 3-4. Comme indiqué plus haut, il y a dans les v. 4-5 cinq emplois de ,,produire": le premier est impersonnel (,,que produire"), les quatre autres sont disposés en un chiasme dont les deux éléments centraux désignent le produit (espéré puis réel) de la vigne tandis que les deux éléments extrêmes concernent le produit (passé puis à venir) de ,,je". C'est donc bien d'un seul et même ,,je" qu'il s'agit dans les v. 3 à 5.

Or, si l'articulation ,,et maintenant" est la même au début de 3 et de 5, la structure du début du v. 5 juste après cette articulation est semblable (à ,,vous" près!) à celle du début du v. 1. Ceci suggère que le ,,je" = ,,il" des v. 2-5 (cf ci-dessus v. 3-4) n'est pas simplement l'auteur d'une citation que ferait le ,,je"-poète: en fait le ,,je"-poète s'assimile au ,,je" = ,,il".

Ainsi donc le poète, qui au v. 1 s'identifiait avec la vigne tout en s'en distinguant, s'identifie aussi avec l'amoureux, le ,,chéri" dont il s'est distingué au v. 1.

V. 6. La fin de ce verset laisse deviner que ce ,,je" de 3-5 est Dieu, qui seul, en plus du saccage de la vigne, peut commander aux nuages.

V. 7. Ceci est confirmé par le dévoilement du nom, ,,Le Seigneur des Puissances", dont c'était le pronom. La vigne c'est le peuple d'Israël, précédemment interpellé au v. 3 (noter la récurrence de ,,homme de Juda"). Ainsi la vigne était alors à son insu interpellée pour juger la vigne, pour se juger elle-même (un peu comme David en 2 Sam. xii 1-7), même si c'est finalement ,,moi"= Dieu qui juge.

Conclusion: le poète s'est discrètement identifié à Israël en appelant Dieu ,,mon chéri", et à Dieu lui-même dans le jeu des ,,je". Israël est concentré dans le poète, et non dans le roi comme il serait normal. Et le vrai Dôdh ou Yâdhîdh n'est pas (le successeur de) David ou Salomon-Yedidyah, mais Dieu. Or la vigne ne dit pas ,,mon chéri" à Dieu (est-ce parce qu'elle le dit au roi? ou à un faux-dieu, qu'on retrouve par conjecture en Am. viii 14?). Le prophète-poète est le seul à reconnaître le vrai Dôdh: le vrai dieu et le vrai roi. Le refus de la vigne produit une mauvaise fertilité: pas de *ʿᵃnâbhîm* sans les *ʿâbhîm* dont Dieu est le commandant, mais pas de *ʿâbhîm* pour la fertilité sans les *ʿᵃnâbhîm* comme bon produit de la vigne.

VIII. Etude des prépositions

1. *Pour*. Le tableau (III) montre que c'est le terme le plus employé: 12 fois. Il y a bien 16 fois un verbe à la 3ème pers. sing., mais ce n'est pas tout le temps le même verbe. Par ailleurs le verbe le plus employé le sera 7 fois: „produire" (voir plus loin). Et s'il y a 12 suffixes 3ème pers. sing., 2 concernent Dieu (v. 1 et v. 7) et 10 la vigne. C'est dire l'importance de „pour" dans ce poème.

V. 1. Le premier „pour" peut indiquer le destinataire (cf Koehler-Baumgartner, *Lexicon*, *s.v.*, 9) mais aussi signifier „à la place de" (KB 11, cf Es vi 8). Cet indice est convergent avec l'assimilation du „je"-poète au „je"-amoureux. Le deuxième „pour" peut désigner le destinataire (KB 9) ou exprimer „au sujet de" (KB 7). Le poète chante à la place de son chéri, à qui il destine cette chanson, la chanson de son chéri au sujet de sa vigne mais aussi destinée à sa vigne. Le chéri destinataire est finalement le destinateur; et la vigne, objet du poème, est le destinataire ultime. Mais au v. 3 (qui ne contient pas de „pour"!) le destinataire, auquel est adressé le poème, et qui est interpellé, c'est Juda. Ceci laisse deviner déjà l'identité de Juda et de vigne à l'instant même où Juda est invité à juger la vigne.

Le troisième „pour" du v. 1 fait du chéri le destinataire de l'existence de la vigne. Mais c'est le poète, et non la vigne, qui l'appelle „chéri", et qui est donc le vrai destinateur existant pour son chéri, pour qui il chante au début du v. 1 (KB 9) tout en s'identifiant à lui (KB 11).

V. 2. „Pour" introduit comme but visé l'infinitif „produire", dont le sujet implicite est explicité dans la suite immédiate comme le producteur de verjus = la vigne.

V. 4-5. Sur ces six emplois, „pour" indique la vigne comme destinaire de l'action (respectivement passée et à venir) de Dieu, en deuxième et quatrième occurrences, chaque fois comme datif suivant le verbe conjugué „produire". Les première et troisième occurrences le placent devant l'infinitif "produire" ainsi souligné comme le but. La cinquième occurrence remplace dans ce paradigme „produire" par „brûler" qui sera maintenant le but de l'action, et sur ce modèle la dernière occurrence remplace le verbe par le substantif „piätinement". Soulignons en ces deux dernières occurrences la récurrence du verbe „exister" qu'on avait précédemment, avec „pour", au v. 1b: le destinataire de la vigne n'est plus le chéri mais le feu (cf plus loin). Ainsi le v. 4 décrit la „production" passée de l'amoureux, le v. 5 sa „production" à venir, encadrant la „production" de la vigne d'abord espérée (à venir) puis réalisée (passée). D'où l'effet de chiasme: je + passé / vigne + avenir // vigne + passé / je + avenir. Ceci se double d'un effet de parallélisme: je + bon / vigne + bon // vigne + mauvais / je + mauvais. Par ailleurs au v. 4 „pour" est employé deux fois devant l'infinitif „produire" (première et troisième occurrences dont le premier implicitement a pour sujet „je" (cf le parallélisme du deuxième stique, verbe à la première pers. sing.) et dont le second a pour sujet la vigne (cf le parallélisme du quatrième stique, verbe à la troisième personne, littéralement „et elle a produit des raisins pourris (ou acides)").

Il faut revenir sur les deux derniers emplois de „pour" au v. 5, indiquant la destination de la vigne: „brûler", "piétinement", c'est-à-dire, comme le précisera encore le v. 6, la non-vigne. Si la vigne est le destinataire de l'amoureux, étant l'objet de son amour, réciproquement l'amoureux devrait être l'objet de l'amour de la vigne et le destinataire du chant de la vigne à son égard. Cette réciproque n'est pas vraie. La vigne n'a pas ici de destinataire, mais elle a une destination.

V. 7. En contraste viennent les deux „pour" du v. 7 indiquant l'objet de l'espérance de Dieu: „éthique" et „droit", reprenant l'objet de l'espérance de l'amoureux exprimé aux v. 2 et 4 par „pour" + infinitif „produire" + complément d'objet „raisins doux" (le stique suivant précisait chaque fois que le résultat décevant a été du mauvais raisin, et donc que le sujet implicite était bien la vigne).

2. *En*. Au v. 1 cette préposition introduit „côteau" comme localisation de la vigne. En 2bis elle introduit la vigne comme localisation du travail de l'amoureux. Au v. 4 le parallélisme des deux premiers stiques montre l'équivalence de „pour" et „en": ce que l'amoureux fait en elle est fait pour elle. Cette équivalence est confirmée par l'étude des variantes: au v. 4 deux manuscrits hébreux et les versions anciennes ont lu „pour elle" au lieu de „en elle"; par contre 1QIsA dit „en ma vigne" au lieu de „pour ma vigne" (signalons au passage que 1QIsA au v. 5 supprime „pour" devant „brûler" tout en le maintenant devant „piétinement", tandis qu'au v. 7 il l'ajoute devant „clique" mais pas devant „cri d'effroi").

Noter que le „en" français du v. 6 n'est pas préposition mais pronom.

3. *Sur*. N'intervient qu'au v. 6. On a d'abord le verbe „monter", qui a même racine et même sonorité. Son sujet est la vigne, avec comme complément „épines et piquants" désignant le produit final —

plutôt que de considérer que ces mots sont eux-même le sujet: voir la même construction à Prv. xxiv 31 où le sujet est exprimé par ailleurs, ce qui montre que „orties" ne l'est pas mais est bien le complément (curieusement la *Konkordanz* de Lisowsky classe la plante comme sujet à Es. v et non à Prv. xxiv). Mais l'„élévation" de la non-vigne est sous-mise à celle de la pluie, qui ne tombera plus „sur" elle, car les nuages eux-mêmes sont sous-mis à l'amoureux (se dévoilant ainsi déjà comme Dieu) qui commande „sur" eux. Le v. 6 remplace le vocabulaire de destination („pour"), qui s'était précisé en localisation („en") c'est-à-dire en union, par un vocabulaire de distanciation et de domination.

IX. Remarques sur les autres récurrences

Suffixes 3ème personne du suinglier: tous désignent la vigne, sauf aux v.1 et 7 (Dieu).

Verbes 3ème personne du singulier: a) le sujet est „vigne" (masculin en hébreu) au v. 1, au dernier emploi du v. 2 (littéralement „elle a produit", rendu en français par „son produit"), au v. 4 (idem), à 5bis (reprise du v. 1 avec le verbe „exister"), à 6ter (deux fois pour dire ce qu'elle ne sera pas — „ni taillée ni sarclée" — et une fois pour dire ce qu'elle fera mais qui est sémantiquement tout aussi négatif — „monter en épines").

b) Le sujet est „il" (Dieu) au v. 2 (cinq actes, couronnés par l'acte d'espérer) et au v. 7 („espérer", exprimé une fois et une fois sous-entendu). Tous les actes de la vigne sont encadrés par l'espérance de Dieu. La première occurrence de cette espérance était précédée des actes bienfaiteurs de Dieu (v. 2). La dernière espérance (v. 7) devrait être suivie de nouveaux actes de Dieu, ce qui serait formellement excellent, encadrant les actes de la vigne par un chiasme, et ce qui est attendu (comme en 5-6) après la déception de 7b. Mais on reste en suspens, comme on l'a vu aux points 4 et 7 des remarques sur le schéma (V), peut-être pour laisser le peuple tirer les conséquences (cf l'interpellation du v. 3); en tout cas le caractère boiteux de la structure souligne que le poème n'est pas fermé: quelque chose devra déboucher.

Suffixes 1ère personne du singlier: au v. 1ter c'est le poète, tout de suite et définitivement relayé par l'amoureux aux v. 3bis (après les douze emplois de la 3ème pers. au v. 2), 4 et 5.

Verbes 1ère personne du singulier: au v. 1 c'est le poète, relayé par l'amoureux aux v. 4 bis, 5 (//1) et 6bis.

Participe: un seul cas à 5, associé au pronom personnel séparé 1ère personne du singulier, sans doute pour exprimer décision et imminence.

Infinitifs: aux v. 2 et 4bis c'est toujours le verbe „produire" précédé de „pour". Au v. 2 le sujet implicite est la vigne, cette production étant l'objet de l'espérance de l'amoureux. De même au v. 4b. A 4a le sujet implicite est l'amoureux, comme le prouve le second stique, et ceci concerne ce qu'il aurait dû encore faire (objet de l'espérance de la vigne?). La réponse implicite est: rien; tout ce qu'il pourra faire aux v. 5-6 sera simplement l'inverse de ce qu'il a fait précédemment.

Au v. 5 en hébreu „je m'en vais faire connaître" est une forme conjuguée (comme „je m'en vais chanter" au v. 1). „Arracher" et „abattre" sont en parallèle et indiquent ce que l'amoureux va encore produire (réponse à la question du v. 4a). Le second infinitif, précédé de „pour", est le résultat du premier; on attendrait donc un quatrième infinitif avec „pour" comme résultat du troisième, mais on a à sa place „pour" et un substantif.

Au v. 6 l'infinitif exprime également la réponse à la question du v. 4a. Contrairement aux infinitifs du v. 5 il désigne une production utile et non pas nuisible, mais il est précédé d'une particule d'exclusion qui annule cette action.

Produire: tout ceci souligne l'importance de la récurrence du verbe „produire", qui apparaît 7 fois, C'est le terme le plus employé, sauf „pour". Cette quantité n'est sans doute pas due à la banalité du verbe „faire", mais souligne le sens de l'existence (que faire?) et des relations (faire pour). On l'a traduit plus fortement par „produire". Récapitulons ses emplois en spécifiant le sujet de cette production:

la vigne:	2b (bis)	4b (bis)
l'amoureux:	4a (bis)	5a plus 7 (bis) de façon implicite („voici").

Sans intérêt est la leçon de 1QIsA au dernier emploi de 4b, lisant *wysh* (de *nś'*?).

Exister: v. 1 et 5bis, chaque fois suivi de „pour". La vigne n'est vigne que si sa destination est l'amoureux. Sinon sa destination est feu et piétinement, auquel cas elle devient non-vigne.

Espérer: v. 2, 4 et 7. Le seul sujet en est non pas la vigne qu'est l'ensemble des hommes de Juda, mais l'amoureux qu'est Dieu. Il y a renversement de l'anthropocentrisme de ce qu'on appelle les vertus chrétiennes (de même que, sans employer les verbes correspondants, il est clair que Dieu est le seul à aimer et à croire); et il y a aussi renversement de l'anthropomorphisme dans la mesure où on ne décrit pas Dieu sur le modèle de l'homme puisque précisément ce ne sont pas là des attitudes humaines.

Juger//jugement/justice: v. 3 et 7*bis*. En hébreu le jeu de mots est entre le premier et le second terme, alors qu'en français il s'est déplacé sur le troisième qui est synonyme du deuxième, à cause de l'exigence des rimes du v. 7b pour rendre les assonances hébraïques: „droit// éthique/droit". Ici encore il y a renversement, puisque cet acte est attendu, contrairement à ce qu'on pouvait supposer, non pas de Dieu mais des hommes: au v. 7 comme conduite dans l'alliance, au v. 3 comme sanction de la situation entre l'amoureux et sa vigne. Même si c'est l'amoureux qui décide en 5-6, les hommes sont interpellés à cet effet au v. 3, un peu comme en 2 Sam. xii. Mais on n'entend pas de réponse par laquelle, comme David, ils se condamneraient eux-mêmes. Le v. 5 contient un grand renversement, avec les deux pronoms „vous" et „moi" (uniques emplois). Le „vous", destinataire implicite de la chanson (il n'est pas exprimé au v. 1 mais c'est bien devant lui que le poète chante), est destinataire explicite de la révélation du v. 5. Et le v. 7a, reprenant l'interpellation du v. 3, montrera que ce „vous" est le destinataire du jugement au sujet duquel il avait été interpellé. Mais, s'il est vrai que c'est „moi", et non pas „vous", qui juge la vigne en 5-6, le jugement reste ouvert au v. 7: celui dont on attend en vain le droit peut-il faire droit à la réclamation de Dieu contre lui? Le „moi" est le „je"-amoureux (auquel s'est identifié le „je"-poète: cf supra): le destinateur des productions en faveur de la vigne, qui est le destinataire de ses produits (bons ou mauvais), est le destinateur (producteur) du jugement dont la vigne destinateur de ses produits est le destinataire. Cependant le comparaison n'est pas complétée dans son application à Juda.

Chanter/chanson—pleuvoir/pluie: cette construction redondante n'intervient qu'au début (v. 1) et à la fin (v. 6, juste avant le dévoilement de l'énigme), comme une récurrence structurelle. Le sujet de la dernière action est en dernier ressort le „je"-amoureux (Dieu) qui commande aux nuages de pleuvoir ou non. Le sujet de la première action est en dernier ressort le „je"-amoureux auquel s'identifie le poète. Si le poète et les nuages sont, respectivement, les sujets de ces verbes, c'est Dieu qui est le sujet effectif.

Délices (cf „chéri" au v. 1, supra VI): détermine l'objet de la dilection de Dieu à Jr. xxxi 20 (le peuple, parallèle à „fils cher", ce dernier mot venant d'une autre racine qu'ici „chéri"), Prv. viii 30 (la sagesse, aussi considérée comme une enfant); tandis qu'à Prv. viii 31 la sagesse elle-même trouve ses propres délices parmi les humains. Par contre ce terme s'applique à l'objet de la dilection des hommes (à savoir, les commandements de Dieu) selon Ps. cxix 24, 77, 92, 143, 174.

Le verbe correspondant indique le jeu eschatologique du bébé avec le serpent à Es. xi 8; la délectation des hommes dans la loi ou les consolations de Dieu selon Ps. cxix 16, 47, 70, cj 117, Ps. xciv 19. A Es. lxvi 12 l'acte de Dieu envers son peuple est semblable à l'acte de cajoler un enfant.

Il est clair d'après le v. 7 que le „chéri" du v. 1 est Dieu. A côté des textes de l'Ancien Testament où la révélation fait les délices de l'homme, les autres emplois de ce terme montrent que le peuple élu fait les délices de Dieu comme un petit enfant. Ici au „chéri" qu'est l'amoureux correspond l'objet de „ses délices", la vigne. L'image enfantine a cédé la place à l'image amoureuse, mais il s'agit toujours de la relation entre Dieu et son peuple. Ceci est souligné par le fait que le verbe „planter", ici présent aux v. 2 et 7, est utilisé pour la plantation du peuple de Dieu en Canaan selon Ex. xv 17, 2 Sam. vii 10, 1 Chr. xvii 9, Ps. xliv 3, Jr. xi 17, xii 2, et pour sa restauration selon Am. ix 15, Es lx 21, lxi 3, Jr. xxiv 6, xxxii 41, xlii 10, Ez. xxxvi 36; et Jr. ii 21 (postérieur à notre texte) précise que Dieu a planté son peuple (comme) un excellent cépage, utilisant le terme traduit à Es. v ii par „rouge muscat" aussi après „planter", tandis que Ps. lxxx 9 emploie la même image avec un autre mot pour désigner la vigne, de même que l'allégorie d'Ez. xvii 7.

Jamais ailleurs qu'ici le terme „délices" n'est appliqué à la vigne. En fait à Es. v 7 ce n'est pas directement la vigne qu'il caractérise, mais le plant, ce qui a été planté. On vient de voir d'une part que ce verbe peut désigner la fondation du peuple de Dieu, indépendamment même de l'image de la vigne, d'autre part que le terme „délices" peut décrire le peuple comme faisant la dilection de Dieu indépendamment de toute idée de fruit savoureux. En sorte que l'idée de „délices" ne vient pas de l'excellence des raisins pour être ensuite appliquée au peuple: c'est plutôt l'inverse.

On a noté plus haut que ce poème finit mal et en un sens ne finit pas. Que sera le sort de cette vigne qui devait faire les délices de ce chéri qu'elle ne reconnaît pas? Faut-il conclure par l'échec de l'amour de Dieu? On notera en tout cas deux choses dans l'Esaïe postexilique. Le texte le plus tardif reprend l'idée de la chanson de la vigne et invite le peuple eschatologique à la chanter (Es. xxvii 2ss); cette vigne est délectable (autre terme qu'ici); le Seigneur lui-même en prend soin, lui qui l'a réduite à n'être qu',,épines et piquants'' (même expression qu'à Es. v 6) et exige qu'elle ,,produise'' la paix avec (,,pour'') lui. Or cette paix, la dernière page du livre en parle (Es. lxvi 12), mais c'est le Seigneur lui-même qui la dirige (*nṭh*, proche de *nṭ'* ,,planter'') vers Jérusalem, en nourrissant, portant et ,,délectant'' ses enfants. Ici, comme pour ,,espérer'', il y a un grand renversement. C'est seulement par la grâce de Dieu que le dernier mot peut revenir à ,,délices''.

ṬÂBE'ÉL EN IS. VII 6 ET LE ROI TUBAIL DE TYR

PAR

ANTOINE VANEL

Paris

Une note récente de L. D. LEVINE [1]) nous livre une nouvelle liste de rois tributaires trouvée sur une stèle de Téglath-Phalasar III, de provenance iranienne. La date retenue pour cette stèle, 737, me paraît bien assurée: la campagne orientale dont elle témoigne et que nous connaîtrons mieux quand le texte sera intégralement publié doit être postérieure aux premières campagnes occidentales de Téglath-Phalasar III (de 743 à 738) puisque les territoires mentionnés sont tous situés à l'ouest de l'Assyrie [2]). LEVINE remarque que ces territoires, à l'exception de Hamath [3]), sont les mêmes que ceux de la liste de tributaires déjà connue par les annales de Téglath-Phalasar III et antérieure à la 9° campagne [4]), liste qu'il faut probablement dater de 738 [5]). Le seul royaume qui n'ait pas le même roi sur les deux listes est celui de Tyr: à *Hiram* qui figurait sur la liste des annales a succédé *Ṭubail* sur la stèle iranienne de 737.

Or, c'est au plus tard à la fin de 735 [6]) que la *coalition syro-éphraïmite* (Damas et Samarie) essaye de mettre sur le trône de Jérusalem le „fils

[1]) L. D. LEVINE, *Menahem and Tiglath-Pileser: a new synchronism*, in *BASOR* 206 (avril 1972) pp. 40-42.

[2]) Ils s'échelonnent des bords de la Mer Noire (Kaskéens) au centre de la Palestine (Samarie), le long du cours supérieur de l'Euphrate, en Cappadoce orientale, en Cilicie, en Syrie du Nord et du Sud, en Phénicie. L'Arabie mentionnée en fin de liste est également à l'Ouest de l'Assyrie, comme le soulignent les annales (ROST, pl. XXIII, cf. p. 37, l. 221; LUCKENBILL *AR* I, 778; *ANET*, p. 283-2).

[3]) Hamath, l'actuelle Hama, sur l'Oronte, est mentionnée sur la liste des annales (dont référence à la note suivante), mais pas sur la stèle iranienne récemment identifiée.

[4]) Cf. P. ROST, *Die Keilschrifttexte Tiglat-Pilesers III*, Leipzig, 1893, pl. XV (3 dernières lignes) et XVI (2 premières lignes), transcription p. 26, l. 150-154. LUCKENBILL, *AR* I, 772; *ANET*, p. 283-1.

[5]) Cf. L. LEVINE, o.c., p. 42. L'énumération des tributaires soumis au cours des campagnes de 743-738 y semble en effet complète, telle qu'on la retrouvera plus tard, en 737 et encore en 728 (cf. infra, p. 19, n. 5).

[6]) Téglath-Phalasar, en effet, arrive dans la région et descend jusqu'en Philistie dès 734, cf. Eponymes, Canon C^bI, *rev.* 40: *ana* (*mât*) *pilista* (*Reallexicon der Assyriologie*, II, art. „*Eponymen*", p. 431).

de *Tâbe'él*" (Is. vii 6). Il est donc fort probable que Tubail de Tyr, intronisé depuis deux ans seulement, est encore en place: n'est-ce pas par son fils que Raṣôn et Péqaḥ veulent remplacer Achaz? C'est très possible, d'autant plus que d'éventuelles prétentions d'un prince tyrien au trône de Juda pouvaient s'appuyer sur l'ancienne alliance entre Tyr et les Omrides et le pouvoir jadis exercé par Athalie [1]). La preuve de la participation de Tyr à la coalition de 735 et d'un lien privilégié, dans cette coalition, entre Tyr, Damas et Samarie permettrait d'aller plus loin et rendrait très vraisemblable l'identité de Tâbe'él et de Tubail: or, nous avons cette preuve.

Si, en effet, les textes de l'Ancien Testament ne nous en disent rien, les documents assyriens de l'époque sont ici plus intéressants. Dans une inscription fragmentaire de Nimrud, *ND. 4301+4305*,[2]) la partie qui concerne les campagnes de Téglath-Phalazar III en 734-732 et plus précisément, sans doute, la campagne de 734 [3]) mentionne à la l. 5 du revers „Hiram de Tyr qui avec Raṣôn . . ." (*ḫi-*]*ri-mu* (*mât*) *ṣur-ra-a-a ša it-ti* (*m*) *ra-ḫi-a-ni*): plus de la moitié de la ligne manque et nous aimerions en connaître le contenu, mais comme le note D. J. Wiseman [4]) nous avons là la trace d'une alliance entre Tyr et Damas. Ajoutons que le royaume de Samarie (Bît-Ḫumria) est mentionné à la ligne précédente, en liaison avec celui de Damas (Bît] Ḫazaili), qui apparaît à la l. 3. Le texte, cependant, ne nous parle pas de Tubail, mais de Hiram et malgré l'absence du premier signe, cette lecture est bien assurée [5]). S'agit-il du Hiram de la liste

---

[1]) Sur l'alliance entre Tyr et les Omrides, cf. 1 Reg. xvi 31-33; Fl. Josèphe, *Ant.* viii 317, 324. Le règne d'Athalie (cf. 2 Reg. xi 1-3; 2 Chr. xxii 10-12) pouvait donner aux prétentions tyriennes un prétexte d'autant plus plausible si celle-ci, mère d'Ochozias, était la fille (cf. 2 Reg. viii 18 et 2 Chr. xxi 6) et non pas la belle-sœur (cf. 2 Reg. viii 26 et 2 Chr. xxii 2) de Jézabel, fille du roi-prêtre Ittobaal de Tyr.

[2]) Cf. D. J. Wiseman, *A fragmentary inscription of Tiglath-Pileser III from Nimrud*, in *Iraq* XVIII-2 (aut. 1956) pp. 117-129 et pl. XXII-XXIII.

[3]) Le revers (pl. XXIII et transcription, pp. 125-126) où la dernière ville citée est (l. 13, 14) Gaza, cf. indications du canon des éponymes sur la date de la campagne en Philistie (supra, p. 17, n. 6) et aussi, à propos de Gaza, le fragment *ND 400* (D. J. Wiseman, *Two historical inscriptions from Nimrud*, in *Iraq* XIII-1 (pr. 1951) pp. 21-24 et pl. XI, l. 14) et *III R, 10, 2*, l. 8 et 9 (Rost, o.c. *Kleinere Inschriften* I, pl. XXV et pp. 78-79, l. 8 et 9; Luckenbill, *AR* I, 816; *ANET*, p. 283-2). Le passage correspondant des grandes inscriptions d'annales (Layard 68, 69) ne mentionne pas Gaza, mais Ascalon (ROST, o.c., pl. XVIII, 21 et pp. 38-39, l. 235; Luckenbill, *AR* I, 779; *ANET*, p. 283-2).

[4]) o.c. in *Iraq* XVIII, p. 121. Cf. aussi S. Mallowan, *Nimrud and its remains*, London, 1966, pp. 238-239.

[5]) D'après la copie de D. Wiseman (o.c. in *Iraq* XVIII, pl. XXIII, début de la

de 738, nommé ici par erreur [1])? C'est peu probable. Il se peut alors que le Hiram de 734, compromis avec Raṣôn, soit le „fils de Tubail", celui même qu'on voulait installer à Jérusalem. Son père est-il mort en 735, au début de la coalition, comme Jotam de Juda? Etait-il seulement associé au trône? Il faudrait d'autres documents pour le savoir. En tous cas, il semble bien avoir été destitué par Téglath-Phalazar III car une tablette de la fin du règne [2]) nous apprend qu'en 728, le roi de Tyr s'appelle Mitinna [3]).

Sur le fragment *ND. 4301* (rev. l. 3-5), nous venons de noter la séquence Damas, Samarie, Tyr et son intérêt pour notre propos. Il n'est pas inutile de remarquer que la même séquence se trouve au début de la liste de tributaires datée de 738 [4]) et sur celle de la stèle iranienne de 737 [5]): alors que seuls les six premiers rois sont cités dans le même ordre par ces deux documents, on trouve effectivement de part et d'autre après Kushtashpi de Kummuḫ, Raṣôn de Damas, Menaḥem de Samarie et le roi de Tyr (Hiram, puis Tubail). A vrai

---

l. 5), la lecture du signe *ri* ne fait guère de doute (il n'en manque que le clou horizontal antérieur) et celle du signe *mu* encore moins.

[1]) Il n'est pas du tout impossible que le Hiram de 734 soit le petit-fils du Hiram de 738: les cas de papponymie ne manquent pas dans les dynasties royales phéniciennes, notamment à Sidon, avec ses deux Ešmun'azar (cf. H. DONNER-W. RÖLLIG, *Kanaanäische und aramäische Inschriften*, Wiesbaden, 1964, II, p. 22) et ses deux Baalšillem (cf. M. DUNAND, *Nouvelles inscriptions phéniciennes du temple d'Echmoun*, in *Bulletin du Musée de Beyrouth*, XVIII, pp. 105-109). Cependant, on peut se demander si *Hiram* n'était pas une sorte de nom commun des rois de Tyr, un peu comme *David* à Jérusalem d'après les psaumes bibliques: en tel cas, Tubail serait le roi de Tyr (ou *Hiram*) tributaire en 738 (sous son nom 'générique') et en 737 (sous son nom propre), révolté en 735-734 et allié à Raṣôn de Damas pour placer son fils sur le trône de Jérusalem, enfin remplacé lors de la campagne assyrienne par le Mitinna attesté en 728 (cf. note suivante).

[2]) *II R 67*, cf. ROST, o.c., *Thontafelinschrift*, pl. XXXV-XXXVIII et pp. 48-77. A la l. 5 de l'avers, cette tablette est datée de la 17° année de Téglath-Phalasar III (cf. ROST, o.c., pp. 54-55) qui a régné de 745 à 727. Cf. aussi LUCKENBILL, *AR* I, 787-804.

[3]) *II R 67* (= K 3571) citée à la n. précédente, *revers* (cf. ROST, o.c., pl. XXXVII et pp. 72-73), l. 16.

[4]) Cf. supra, p. 17, n. 4, lignes 150-151.

[5]) Cf. supra, p. 17, n. 1, lignes 4-6. Les annales fournissent en plus une liste lacunaire où sont détaillés les tributs et où Raṣôn de Damas, probablement suivi de Menaḥem de Samarie (l. 83-85), précède Kushtashpi de Kummuḫ (l. 86) qui vient lui-même avant le roi de Tyr (l. 87) dont le nom manque. Dans cette liste qui ne comportait certainement pas tous les noms communs à celles citées plus haut, l'ordre commun aux listes de 738 et 737 pour les quatre premiers noms est donc modifié par le déplacement de Kushtashpi de Kummuḫ, qui passe du premier au second rang (cf. H. TADMOR, *Azriyau of Yaudi*, in *Scripta Hierosolymitana* VIII, Jérusalem 1961, p. 255-256, colonne B; ROST, o.c., pl. XIII et pp. 14-17, lignes 83-88).

dire, ce groupement n'est guère étonnant puisqu'il s'agit de trois des principaux tributaires de l'Ouest avant les campagnes de 734-732 et de trois royaumes voisins, situés au sud des autres. Mais la comparaison des listes de 738 et 737 avec celle de 728, trouvée sur une tablette de Nimrud datée de la 17° année du règne [1]), permet de voir que cette dernière, postérieure aux campagnes de 734-732 après lesquelles Téglath-Phalasar III ne reviendra plus dans l'Ouest, omet les rois de Damas, de Samarie et de Tyr et que cette omission ne saurait être accidentelle. Dans la première partie de cette liste, en effet (l. 7-9), on ne trouve que des rois déjà mentionnés dans les annales en 738 et, sauf celui de Hamath, sur la nouvelle liste iranienne de 737: tous sont des tributaires soumis entre 743 et 738. L'ordre suivi est celui de la liste des annales [2]) si l'on met à part l'interversion des noms de Shipitbaal de Byblos et d'Urik de Que, qui pourrait bien être liée à l'omission de Damas, Samarie et Tyr [3]). Les trois lignes sont tronquées, mais on peut remarquer que chacune commence par un nom de roi (ce qui n'est pas le cas dans la liste des annales) et qu'il y a place à la fin de chacune, au-delà de la restitution de la mention amorcée avant la cassure, pour dix signes environ, soit une autre mention [4]): la comparaison avec les annales impose alors de

[1]) *II R 67* = Rost, Thontafelinschrift, cf. supra, p. 19, n. 2. La liste de tributaires s'y trouve au revers, l. 7-12 (Rost, o.c., pl. XXXVII et pp. 70-73; Luckenbill, *AR* I, 801; *ANET*, p. 282).

[2]) Il s'agit de la liste de 738, cf. supra, p. 19, n. 2, dont l'ordre est d'ailleurs le même que celui de la stèle iranienne pour les six premiers rois.

[3]) L'absence de Tyr, en effet, rompt la séquence Tyr-Byblos et il devient sans doute plus normal de citer la Cilicie aussitôt après la Commagène. Cependant, il se pourrait que l'ordre *Damas*, *Samarie*, Kummuḫ, *Tyr*, Cilicie, Byblos, Karkémish, où se retrouve la séquence Kummuḫ, Que, Byblos quand on retire Damas, Samarie et Tyr, ait été celui de la liste lacunaire citée ci-dessus, p. 19, n. 5, si du moins il faut restituer dans cette liste Samarie après Damas (à la l. 84 ou à la l. 85) et Byblos après Que (à la l. 87). Notons en passant que le roi Urik de Que, quatre fois, cité par Téglath-Phalasar III dans ses listes de tributaires, est probablement le ʿWRK mentionné par le bilingue de Karatepe (cf. H. Donner, *KAI*, cité ci-dessus à la p. 19, (n. 1, n° 26, 2).

[4]) Une „mention" (nom de roi suivi du nom du royaume) comporte environ 9 ou 10 signes (moyenne effective des mentions attestées par cette liste). *Pisiris de Karkémish* (également attesté par la liste lacunaire citée ci-dessus à p. 19, n. 5. ligne 88) est régulièrement écrit avec 10 signes, ce qui correspond aux indications données par Rost à la fin de sa transcription de la l. 7. Dadilu de Kaska s'écrit avec 7 ou 8 signes: il y a effectivement un peu moins de place à la fin de la l. 8 qu'à la fin de la précédente, bien que Rost y indique l'espace de dix signes, et on notera aussi que les fins de ligne visibles plus bas sur *II R, 67* (Rost, o.c. pl. XXXVIII) sont parfois assez espacées. Urimmi de Hubishna s'écrit avec 10 signes alors que Rost ne signale que sept espaces libres à la fin de la l. 9 mais les mesures prises sur *II R, 67* m'ont montré que les dix signes pouvaient parfaitement y tenir.

restituer Pisiris de Karkémish à la fin de la l.7, Dadilu de Kaska à la fin de la l. 8 et Urimmi de Hubishna à la fin de la l.9 [1]) Il n'y a donc pas place, dans les lacunes de fin de ligne, pour Damas, Samarie et Tyr. La seconde partie de cette liste en quelque sorte récapitulative de 728 (l. 10-12), avec les rois d'Arvad, Ammon, Moab, Ascalon, Juda, Edom, Gaza, correspond de toute évidence aux territoires devenus tributaires en 734-732, mais on n'y trouve pas non plus les rois de Damas, Samarie et Tyr, tandis que les lacunes de fin de ligne pourraient tout au plus laisser place à l'un des trois [2]). L'omission des trois royaumes, aussi bien dans la liste des anciens tributaires (où ils avaient leur place) que dans celle des nouveaux s'explique probablement par le statut particulier qui est le leur à la fin du règne de Téglath-Phalasar III et nous savons que deux d'entre eux au moins ont fait l'objet d'un démembrement total ou partiel en 732 [3]). Au

---

[1]) Urimmi de Hubishna est d'ailleurs nommé aussitôt après les quatre rois de Tabal, Atuna, Tuhan et Ishtundi aussi bien dans la liste des annales (pl. XVI et ll. 153-154) que dans celle de la stèle iranienne de 737 (ll. 10-14). Avec les trois noms ainsi restitués, il ne manque plus sur la liste de 728, à part les rois de Damas, Samarie et Tyr, que la reine d'Arabie et on sait qu'une expédition importante en Arabie fait l'objet de plusieurs lignes dans la partie des annales consacrée aux campagnes de 734-732 (Rost, o.c., pl. XXII-XXIII et pp. 36 ss., l. 210 ss., cf. 240; Luckenbill, *AR* I, 778; *ANET* 283-2) et dans un fragment complémentaire (Rost, o.c., „Kleinere Inschriften" I, pl. XXV-XXVI, et pp. 80-83, l. 19 ss.; *ANET* p. 284-1).

[2]) A la fin de la l. 10, après la mention de Salamanu de Moab, il y a place pour 15 signes au maximum, ce qui suffit largement au nom d'un autre tributaire avec celui de son pays, même si l'ensemble est assez long, mais peut difficilement permettre d'en citer deux. A la fin de la l. 11, il faut compléter le quatrième nom royal (commencé par les syllabes *mu-uṣ*) et laisser place au nom de pays correspondant: l'espace disponible (5 ou 6 signes au maximum) ne permet plus alors la mention d'un autre tributaire (tous les autres s'écrivent avec au moins 7 ou 8 signes et la plupart avec 9 ou 10). Il semble donc bien que les lignes 10 et 11 aient cité chacune quatre tributaires et au début de la l. 12, Hanno de Gaza clôt la liste. Le quatrième roi de la l. 11, nommé après ceux d'Ascalon, Juda et Edom et avant celui de Gaza, est un prince du Sud, arabe ou philistin, dont le début du nom exclut aussi bien Tyr que Samarie. Il n'est pas exclu que le quatrième roi de la l. 10 soit Osée de Samarie (ou „de la maison d'Omri", cf. Rost, o.c., pl. XXV et pp. 80-81, l. 15-17) dont le territoire réduit à la Palestine centrale n'est plus celui que gouvernaient ses prédécesseurs: il serait alors nommé après Moab, ancien vassal d'Israël, ce qui montrerait assez qu'il ne s'agit plus de l'ancien royaume de Samarie.

[3]) Cf. annexions mentionnées par *III, R 10, 2* (Rost, o.c., *Kl. Insch.* I, pl. XXV et pp. 78-79 = Luckenbill, *AR* I, 815 = *ANET*, p. 283-2), l. 4-8 et par *ND 4301* (D. Wiseman, o.c. in *Iraq* XVIII, pl. XXIII et pp. 123 et 125), rev. l. 2-4. Le royaume de Damas semble avoir été intégralement annexé (cf. „le vaste pays de Bît-Ḫaza'ili en son étendue" en *ND 4301*, rev., 3, complété par *III R, 10, 2*, l. 7, où il faut abandonner la restitution de *[Nap-ta]li* au profit de *[Ḫa-za-'a-i-li]*

contraire, les royaumes mentionnés dans les l. 10-12 sont ceux qui se sont ralliés à la coalition sans en être les instigateurs [1]) ou ceux que les armées assyriennes ont soumis au passage ou encore ceux qui, comme Juda (cf. 2 R xvi 7) ont fait appel au roi d'Assyrie contre les menaces de la coalition.

En résumé, la mention de Tyr en relation avec Damas et Samarie sur *ND. 4301* et leur omission sur la liste de 728, compte tenu des listes antérieures et de ce que nous savons sur les campagnes de 734-732, sont deux faits très significatifs. Tyr a pris une part assez importante à la coalition de 735 pour être considérée par Téglath-Phalasar III de la même manière que les alliés syro-éphraïmites et traitée à peu près comme Samarie sinon comme Damas [2]). Si Isaïe

---

comme l'a noté D. Wiseman, o.c., pp. 120-121) et Téglath-Phalasar III y reçoit les tributaires (ainsi Achaz de Juda d'après 2 Reg. xvi 10-12). Les territoires enlevés à Israël sont ceux de Galaad, de Galilée et de la région côtière (cf. 2 Reg. xv 29 complété par Is. viii 23, selon les remarques déjà faites par E. Forrer, *Die Provinzeinteilung des assyrischen Reiches*, Leipzig 1920, pp. 63 et 69 et reprises par A. Alt, *Kleine Schriften* II, München 1953, pp. 210-211).

[1]) Ainsi probablement Arvad, sûrement Gaza (mentionnée dans trois textes, avec un certain nombre de détails, cf. supra, p. 18, n. 3) et Ascalon (dont le roi tombe (?) en apprenant la défaite de Raṣôn, selon le récit des annales, Rost, o.c., pl. XVIII et pp. 38-39, l. 235-236), peut-être Ammon, Moab et Edom, qui ont pu être simplement ravagés par les armées assyriennes descendant vers le Sud après la conquête des provinces damascènes et de la région transjordanienne de Galaad.

[2]) Tyr, cependant, n'a pas été annexée, pas plus que Samarie elle-même. Les territoires qui en dépendaient ont été ravagés (ainsi la ville de Maẖalab, située au Nord de Tyr, sur la route de Sidon, cf. E. Vogt, *Die Texte Tiglat-Pilesers III über die Eroberung Palästinas*, in *Biblica* 45 (1964), p. 351 et n. 1: d'après *ND 4301*, rev. 6, cette ville fortifiée fut conquise avec d'autres, ce qui obligea le roi de Tyr à se soumettre). Un lourd tribut lui a été imposé: 20 talents (d'or) et beaucoup d'autres prestations de toutes sortes selon *ND 4301*, rev. 7, mais il faut y ajouter les 150 talents d'or perçus un peu plus tard par le *rabshâqu* sur le roi Mitinna (*II R 67*, rev. 16, cité ci-dessus à p. 19, n. 3). Enfin, une partie de la Phénicie méridionale, comprenant des dépendances de Tyr, semble avoir été placée directement sous l'autorité de gouverneurs assyriens, au moins jusqu'au paiement de l'énorme tribut acquitté par Mitinna. D'une part, en effet, les six gouverneurs mis en place dans des villes de la côte d'après *III R 10, 2* (Rost, o.c., *Kl. Inschr.* I, pl. XXV et pp. 78-79; Luckenbill *AR*, 815), 4-5 semblent distincts de celui de la province de Ṣimirra (près d'Arvad, cf. E. Forrer, o.c., p. 63, ville nommée à la l. 2 avec d'autres qui en dépendent) et de celui de la province de Dûru (Dôr) (à laquelle il faut rattacher Rashpûna de la l. 5 si c'est bien l'ancienne Apollonia et l'actuelle Arsûf, comme le soutient E. Forrer, o.c., p. 60), les deux provinces côtières constituées par Téglath-Phalasar III. D'autre part, le fragment *ND 400* (*Iraq* XIII-1, pl. XI et pp. 21-24, cité ci-dessus à la p. 18, n. 3), où on retrouve K/Rashpûna (avec l'indication „qui est sur la côte", comme en *III R 10, 2*, 5 et *K 2649* = Rost, o.c., p. 86, et quelques lignes avant la mention de Hanno de Gaza, comme en *III R 10, 2*, 5 et 8), mentionne en son début (l. 4-5 et peut-être aussi 6-7) la soumission d'un roi „du milieu de la mer" (l. 4) qui pourrait bien être celui de Tyr

ne la mentionne pas explicitement, c'est qu'elle n'intervient pas sur le plan militaire dans l'expédition contre Juda [1]), mais c'est aussi-semble-t-il, parce qu'il en a assez dit en nommant le „fils de ṬB'L" que les coalisés veulent faire roi à Jérusalem. Ce personnage est assez connu de ses contemporains pour qu'ils n'aient pas besoin des précisions qui nous ont manqué jusqu'ici. Mais nous connaissons maintenant le roi Tubail (probablement Ṭōb'el) de Tyr, au règne probablement fort court, et son successeur Hiram, destitué par le roi assyrien [2]). Le prétendant au trône de Jérusalem est-il ce Hiram ou l'un de ses proches parents (frère ou neveu)? On l'affirmerait sans hésitation si les données de l'onomastique ne soulevaient pas ici plus de difficultés que celles de l'histoire [3]).

---

plutôt que celui d'Arvad (cf. E. Vogt, o.c., p. 350); s'il en est ainsi, le début de la l. 9 (après un espace sans écriture qui continue probablement celui de la fin de la l. 8) parle sans doute du pouvoir donné au gouverneur assyrien de la ville de *Ṣi-[du-nu]* (Sidon) et non pas de la ville de *Ṣi-[mir-ra]* (qui irait mieux avec Arvad), selon la restitution proposée par D. Wiseman, qui signale cependant la possibilité de *Ṣidunu* (o.c. in *Iraq* XIII, p. 24, note ad l. 9). Il est peu probable, en effet qu'on passe aussi vite de Ṣimirra à Gaza, compte tenu de l'ordre suivi par les autres textes cités et surtout si Rashpûna est bien Arsûf-Apollonia. Sidon ne seraitelles pas l'une des villes aux „six gouverneurs" de *III R 10, 2*, l. 3-4? (cf. annales, Rost, o.c., pl. XXI et l. 126, où il faut sans doute restituer *Ṣ[i-du-nu]* plutôt que *Ṣ[i-mir-ra]*, cette ligne semblant correspondée à *III R 10, 2*, l. 3-5 comme la l. 125 à *III R 10, 2*, l. 2, où est mentionnée *Ṣimirra*).

1) Cf. Is. vii 1 et 8-9; 2 Reg. xvi 5.

2) Il faut donc sans doute renoncer à voir dans *Ṭâbe'él* un toponyme à rapprocher de *Tôphel* de Deut. i 1 (W. F. Albright, in *BASOR* 140, p. 34ss., cf. H. Cazelles, „Tophel" in *VT* IX (1959) p. 413) et qui serait la région de la mère du prétendant qu'on veut substituer à Achaz (E. Vogt, in *Biblica* 37 (1956), p. 263 ss.).

3) Au moment de mettre sous presse, nous avons pu prendre connaissance de la publication intégrale de la stèle iranienne de 737: L. D. Levine, *Two Neo-Assyrian Stelae From Iran*, Royal Ontario Museum, 1972. L'auteur signale le rapprochement possible entre Tubail et Is.vii 6, mais ne le retient pas (p. 23).

Il faut reconnaître que l'interprétation la plus vraisemblable de *Tubail* est celle qui l'identifie avec **'Ittoba'al* ('TB 'L), attesté dans l'Ancien Testament (1 Reg. xvi 31), dans les écrits de Fl. Josèphe (*Ant.* 8, 317 et 324; 9, 138; 10, 228; *Ap.* 1, 123 et 156) et sous la forme *Tu-ba-'-lu* dans les annales de Sennachérib (*Taylor Prism*, 2, 48, cf. notamment M. Weippert, *Menahem von Israel und seine Zeitgenossen*, in Zeitschr. des Deutschen Palästina Vereins LXXXIX-1 (1973) p. 47 et n. 86, qui soutient sans hésitation cette identification), d'autant plus que ce nom désigne des rois de Tyr ou de Sidon (et aussi un roi de Byblos, cf. Donner-Röllig, *o.c.*, n°1). Sur la stèle iranienne elle-même, les deux dernières syllabes du nom de *Sipiṭbail* (dont l'interprétation est incontestable et qui suit immédiatement le nom du roi de Tyr) sont d'ailleurs écrites exactement comme celles de *Tubail*. Ajoutons que le nom *Ṭōb'il* ou *Ṭōb'el* ne semble attesté ni en phénicien ou punique (cf. F. Benz, *Personal Names in the Phoenician and Punic inscriptions*, Rome, 1972, p. 126), ni en ugaritique (cf. F. Gröndahl, *Die Personennamen der Texte aus Ugarit*, Rome, 1967, p. 202), tandis que son équivalent akkadien est rare (cf. *Ṭāb-ilum*: E. Weidner,

Aus den Tagen eines assyrischen Schattenkönigs, in Archiv für Orientforschung X (1935-1936), p. 48, n° 50, 9 et 61, 6, cité par J. Stamm, *Die akkadische Namengebung*, Leipzig, 1939, p. 296, parmi plus de trente noms où entre l'adjectif *ṭābu*, cf. pp. 79, 84, 85, 188, 224, 234-236, 285, 294-296, 317, 370). De plus, dans le passage de *Ṭōb'el* à la graphie *Ṭú-ba-ìl* (le signe *tu* pouvant fort bien etre lu *ṭú*), la présence du *a* est difficile à expliquer.

Il est cependant possible de relever quelques indices favorables à *Ṭōb'el* et donc à l'identification qui conviendrait le mieux aux circonstances historiques d'Is. vii 6. Tout d'abord, le signe *ba* pouvant être lu bi_6, une lecture *ṭú*-bi_6-*ìl* n'est pas exclue et éliminerait la difficulté de l'*a*, signalée ci-dessus. D'autre part, le nom divin *Baʿal* dans les noms propres est habituellement rendu par *bi-'-il* (ainsi *Si-pi-it-ti-bi-'-il*, le même nom que sur notre stèle, en *II Rawl. 67*, 57, et *Ma-ta-an-bi-'-il* en *II Rawl. 67*, 60) dans les textes de Téglath-Phalasar III (noter cependant *Ba-'-li-ṣâ-pu-na*, nom de montagne, en *III Rawl. 9*, 3, 27), donc avec l'indication du hiatus et en employant *il* et non *ìl* (*ìlu*), tandis que le nom divin *El* y est rendu par *ìl* (*ìlu*) dans le nom théophore *E-ni-ìl* (ou *E-né-él*) (*III Raw. 9*, 3, 51) comme ici dans *Tu*/*Ṭú-ba*/bi_6-*ìl* (*u*) (et il n'est pas impossible que la graphie de *Si-piṭ-ba*/bi_6-*ìl*(*u*) ait été ici „contaminée" par celle du nom royal précédent; l'autre graphie du même nom *Šp*ṭ*b*ʿ*l*, indiquée ci-dessus, pourrait d'ailleurs correspondre à une sorte d'étymologie „populaire", cf. M. Weippert, *o.c.*, p. 48 et n. 90).

Pour finir, signalons l'hypothèse, évidemment fragile, d'une réinterprétation phonétique (certainement pas graphique) dans le livre d'Isaïe, d'un **Tobaʿal* (prononcé sans l'aleph initial?) en *Ṭâbeʿél*, et ceci avant 1*Q Is a*. La vocalisation *Ṭâbe'al* du texte massorétique (que l'on corrige habituellement en fonction des versions et d'Esd. iv 7) en serait-elle un indice? Serait-on passé d'une interprétation de **Tôbaʿal* par **Ṭôbbaʿal* (*Ṭôbiyyâh* étant attesté dans l'Ancien Testament en Zach. vi 10, 14; Esd. ii 60; Neh. ii 10, 19, etc. ... et dans l'ostracon n°3 de Lakish, l. 19, sous la forme *ṬBYHW*) déformé ensuite en *Ṭâbe'al* (Is. vii 6, TM) avant d'aboutir à la lecture araméenne *Ṭâbe'él*? Cela paraît bien difficile à démontrer.

Supplements to Vetus Testamentum, Vol. XXVI

GLAUBEN UND BLEIBEN

Zur Denkschrift Jesajas Kapitel vi 1 - viii 18

VON

HANS-PETER MÜLLER

Münster

Die folgenden Marginalien zu einem der meistkommentierten Abschnitte des Prophetenkanons tragen eine Reihe philologischer, formkritischer sowie traditions- und redaktionsgeschichtlicher Beobachtungen zusammen, die für das theologische Verständnis des Textes von Bedeutung zu sein scheinen. Dabei sind alle seine Einzelworte aus einer doppelten Perspektive zu sehen: aus dem Blick auf die mündliche Verkündigung und aus der Rückschau auf diese, in der der Prophet seine Denkschrift verfaßt oder verfassen läßt. Deren Mittelpunkt aber macht die Dialektik des Glaubensbegriffes aus (vii 9b), der hier, wie vermutet wird [1]), zum ersten Male und sogleich programmatisch formuliert ist.

I

1. Die Schilderung der Theophanie (vi 1-4) zerfällt nach ihrer bislang wenig beachteten syntaktischen Struktur in fünf Teile:

(a) V. 1a führt Jahwe im Akkusativ mit Partizip (A c.p.) und Lokalbestimmung zu einer finiten Form von *R'H* ein; die Exposition der Vision Michas ben Jimla 1 Kön. xxii 19 bα ist dabei nur geringfügig weiterentfaltet.

	Fin. Verbum	Akkusativ	Part.	Lokalbestimmung
1 Kön. xxii	*ra'îtî*	*'ät-YHWH*	*yošeb*	*'ăl-kis'ô*
Jes. vi	*wa'är'ā*	*'ät-ha'adôn* [2])	*yošeb*	*'ăl-kisse'* *ram weniśśa'* [3]).

---

[1]) Vgl. R. Smend, „Zur Geschichte von האמין", *FS W. Baumgartner*, *SVT* XVI 1967, 284-290.

[2]) Da *'adonay* nicht nur anstelle des Jahwenamens, sondern auch neben ihm gebraucht wird (Jes. vii 7; xxii 12, 14; xxviii 16), wird man hierin eine Besonderheit der Sprache Jesajas sehen können, die auf seine Beheimatung in Jerusalemer Tradition zurückgeht; *'adonay* ist in dem Jerusalemer Ps. lxviii 21 Epithet des auch als El benannten Jahwe (vgl. Ps. xvi 1 f.). Vermutlich ist aber statt des frühjüdischen *'adonay* durchweg *ha'adôn* zu lesen; vgl. *ha'adôn YHWH ṣeba'ôt* Jes. i 24; iii 1; x (16), 33 neben *'adonay Y.ṣ.* iii 15.

(b) Aus dem A.c.p. werden in V. 1b. 2a eigenständige Nominalsätze, die das Bild der thronenden Gottheit in statisch-unbewegter Weise ausführen.

A.c.p.	*ra'îtî*	*'ät-YHWH*	*yošeb*	*'ăl-kis'ô*
1 Kön. xxii	19bβ	*w^{e}kål-ṣ^{e}ba' hăššamăyim*	*'omed*	*'alâw*
Jes. vi	1b	*w^{e}šûlâw*	*m^{e}le'îm*	*('ät-hăhêkal)*
	2 aa	*ś^{e}rapîm*	*'om^{e}dîm*	*mimmă'ăl lô* [1]).

Von ähnlicher Struktur ist die Einführung des thronenden Gottes Nergal, des "Königs der Erde" (*šàr erṣeti^{tim}* Z. 38. 56), innerhalb der um 670 vor Chr. abgefaßten Unterweltsvision eines assyrischen Kronprinzen [2]) Z. 51 ff. Dem Verb *ra'îtî* (*wa'är'ä̅*) entspricht die Wendung „Als ich meine [Au] gen aufhob". Darauf folgt elliptisch die Exposition des Visionsbildes mit einer stativischen Verbform anstelle der hebräischen Partizipien: „... saß (*a-ši-ib*) der kriegerische Nergal auf dem (seinem?) Thron (*ina ^{iṣ}kussî šarru-ú-ti (-šú?)*)". Auf die gleiche Weise sind die folgenden beschreibenden Sätze strukturiert: „Mit der Königstiara war er be[de]ckt (*a-[p]i-ir*), mit seinen beiden Händen hielt er (*ṣa-bit*) zwei grimme ... -Waffen, je zwei Köpfe ... ... sind sie niedergeworfen (*kam-ru*)". 1 Kön. xxii 19bß (und mittelbar auch Jes. vi 2a) aber hat im übernächsten Satz eine weitgehende Entsprechung: „Die Anunnaku, die großen Götter, standen gebeugt zur Rechten (und) zur Linken ".

(c) Jes. vi 2b bringt danach drei gleichgeordnete Sätze mit finiten Verben:

bištăyim	*y^{e}kăssä̅*	*panâw*
ûbištăyim	*y^{e}kăssä̅*	*răglâw*
ûbištăyim	*y^{e}'ôpep.*	

[3]) Vergleichbar sind:

Ex. xxiv 10	*wăyyir'û*	*'et 'ä̈lohê yiśra' el*		
11	*wăyyäḥ^{ä}zû*	*'ät-ha'ä̆lohîm*		
Gen. xxviii 13	*w^{e}hinnē*	*YHWH*	*niṣṣab*	*'alâw*
Am. ix 1	*ra'îtî*	*'ät-ha' adôn (?)*	*niṣṣab*	*'ăl-hămmiṣbe^{a}ḥ*

[1]) Der Übergang von der finiten Form von *R'H* zum Nominalsatz, der den Inhalt des Gesichts exponiert, kann auch durch *w^{e}hinnē* vermittelt werden, z.B. Ex. iii 2b: *wăyyăr' w^{e}hinnē hăss^{e}nä bo'er ba'eš*, ferner Gen. xxviii 12; Hes. i 4, 15; Sach. i 8; Dan. vii 2, 6, 8, 13.

[2]) W. von Soden, „Die Unterweltsvision eines assyrischen Kronprinzen", *ZA* XLIII, 1936, S. 1-31; vgl. A. Heidel, *The Gilgamesh Epic and Old Testament Parallels*, 1970^{7}, S. 132 ff.

Dabei durchbrechen die Pi'el- und Polelformen die statische Struktur der bisherigen Schilderung nur um eine Nuance; denn sie entsprechen einem mutmaßlichen altwestsemitischen Durativ **yaqattal(u)*, der im Präsens-Futur, ursprünglich aber ohne Rücksicht auf den Zeitstellenwert eine fortwährende Handlung bezeichnet. Als der Durativ einerseits verschwand, andrerseits aber das Imperfekt *yaqtul(u)* den ihm ehemals eigenen Charakter einer präteritalen Punktuals verlor und die Funktion des Durativs übernahm, wurden dessen Reste bei Verben von vorwiegend durativer Bedeutung wie *BRK*, *DBR* und den an unserer Stelle verwendeten Verben *KSH* und *'ŪP* dem ebenfalls durch Verdoppelung des mittleren Radikals gebildeten Intensivstamm eingegliedert, der dabei durch Analogiebildungen ergänzt wurde und dann das Qal oft weitgehend verdrängte [1]). Wenn nun in Jes. vi 2b die Intensivformen *yᵉkăssā* und *yᵉ'ôpep* vorangehende Nominalsätze aufnehmen, so ist wahrscheinlich, daß deren ursprünglich durative Funktion noch empfunden wurde, zumal V.6 als Punktual das Impf. cons. Qal *wăyya'åp* verwendet.

Ein Durativ folgt auch den oben zitierten Sätzen der akkadischen Unterweltsvision: *i*[-]? *te? i?-di-šú birqu*(*NIM-GÍR*) *i-bar-ri-iq* „. ? . seiner *Arme* blitzte (ständig) ein Blitz."

(d) Auch die Perfekte *wᵉqara'* und *wᵉ'amăr* Jes. vi 3a haben durative (besser: frequentative) Funktion [2]); wahrscheinlich wurden sie

---

[1]) Vgl. B. Landsberger, *OLZ* XXIX 1926, S. 972², O. Rößler, „Verbalbau und Verbalflexion in den Semitohamitischen Sprachen", *ZDMG* C, 1951, S. 461-514 (§ 15 f.), W. von Soden, „Tempus und Modus im Semitischen", *Akten des* 24. *internationalen Orientalisten-Kongresses München*, ed. H. Franke, 1959, S. 263-265, wo speziell auf das Pi *yᵉkăssā* neben den Qal-Part. *kosā* und *kasûy* verwiesen wird, und verschiedentlich R. Meyer, zuletzt in: *Hebräische Grammatik* I, 1966, § 3, 2d; 4, 3c, II, 1969, § 63, 2, III, 1972, § 100, 2, der auf das Fortleben der Durativformen im altwestsemitischer Substrat der Maritexte, in den kanaanäischen Amarnaglossen, im Qumranhebräisch und im Hebräisch der Samaritaner verweist. Kritisch bleibt T. L. Fenton, „The Absence of a Verbal Formation **yaqattal* from Ugaritic and North-West Semitic", *JSS* XV, 1970, S. 31-41, der nur mit der Existenz der Form im Akkadischen, Äthiopischen und in verschiedenen hamitischen Sprachen rechnen will. Weniger skeptisch ist die neue umfassendere Studie von S. H. Siedl, *Gedanken zum Tempussystem im Hebräischen und Akkadischen*, 1971, bes. S. 17-19.

[2]) Zur Funktion des Perf. cons. als „tempus frequentativum zum Ausdruck vergangener, resp. in der Vergangenheit wiederholt beendigter Handlungen usw., nach Temporibus oder Tempusäquivalenten, welche in der Vergangenheit andauernde oder wiederholte Handlungen darstellen", vgl. W. Gesenius- E. Kautzsch, *Hebräische Grammatik*, 1909²⁸, § 112e (-l), auch P. Joüon, *Grammaire de l'Hébreu biblique*, 1923, § 119, und Meyer, *op. cit.* III, § 101, 4b, wo von der Funktion des Perf. als „Durativ der Vergangenheit" gesprochen wird.

gewählt, weil ein Pi'el der Wurzeln ungebräuchlich war oder nicht als Durativ erkannt worden wäre Erst *wăyyanu'û* (V. 4a) ist ein Punktual, bezeichnet also ein Geschehen einmalig-dramatischer Art und damit den ersten Höhepunkt der Szene.

(e) V. 4 b kehrt mit der Voranstellung des Subjekts zum Stil von 1b. 2a zurück; syntaktisch handelt es sich um einen syndetisch nachgestellten Zustandssatz [1]): „. . . während das Haus voller Rauch war".

Der Satz hat wieder in der o.g. Unterweltsvision seine Parallele: *a-ra-al-lu ma-li pu-luḫ-tu* „die Unterwelt war voll der Furchtbarkeit".

Die weitgehende (stativisch-durativische) Unveränderlichkeit des Geschilderten scheint für die Erzählung einer Anwesenheitsvision [2]) im Gegensatz zu den meisten Berichten vom Kommen des in die Geschichte eingreifenden Gottes [3]) charakteristisch zu sein: Jahwe wohnt in seinem *hêkal*. Insbesondere die Nominalsätze solcher Erzählungen mögen, was die sich in dieser Form ausdrückende Erlebnisweise anbetrifft, allgemein an den Expositionen von Traum- und Visionsschilderungen [4]), was aber den Erlebnisinhalt angeht, spezieller an uralten kultischen Beschreibungshymnen [5]) ihr Analogon haben.

Der Stimmungsgehalt von Jes. vi 1-4 ist durch Macht- und Hoheitsbegriffe wie *kabôd* und *qadôš*, *ram wenišša'* und die Bildungen der Wurzel *ML'* (V 1, 3f.) bestimmt; der begegnenden Macht entspricht das Erbeben des angetroffenen Stücks Welt (V. 4a) und das Schuldbekenntnis des Propheten mit dem ursprünglich ebenfalls dynami-

---

1) C. Brockelmann, *Hebräische Syntax*, 1956, § 139 b.

2) Von den S. 26 Anm. 3,1 genannten Texten gehören Gen. xxviii, Ex. iii; xxiv 9-11 und Am. ix 1 hierher.

3) Zwar können auch da Nominalsätze mit part. Verb gebraucht werden (1 Kön. xix 12; Jes. xxx 27; Hes. i 4; Mi. i 3a); aber das Adäquatere ist in der Erzählung das Perfekt (Ex. xv 21; Jes. lxvi 16 MT; Ps. xlvi 7b; 12; lxxvi 9) oder das Impf. cons. (Ex. xiv 19a, 24; Ps. xviii 10-12) bzw. in der Ankündigung das Impf. (Jes. xxxi 4; xl 10; xlii 13; Am. i 2; Hab. iii 3; Mal. iii 1b).

4) Vgl. W. Richter, „Traum und Traumdeutung im AT", *BZ* N. F. VII, 1963, S. 202-220, wo auf S. 204 f. ausgeführt wird: „Jeder Traum beginnt mit einem Nominalsatz. Bleibt es bei dem einen Bild, das nur in Einzelzügen fortgeführt wird, dann werden weitere Nominalsätze angereiht . . . alles entfaltet sich aus beschreibenden Nominalsätzen, die einen Zustand schildern". Zum Problem zuletzt B. O. Long, „Prophetic Call Traditions and Reports of Visions", *ZAW* LXXXIV, 1972, S. 494-500.

5) Zu kultischen Beschreibungshymnen aus Ägypten vgl. A. Hermann, „Beiträge zur Erklärung der ägyptischen Liebesdichtung", *Ägyptologische Studien*, Berlin 1955, S. 118-139, bes. 127 (Lit!); ein akkadisches Beispiel ist der Ninurtahymnus KAR 102 + 328 (A. Falkenstein- W. von Soden, *Sumerische und akkadische Hymnen und Gebete*, 1953, S. 258 f.). Hinter der Statik der Schilderung steht dabei letztlich die Anschauung des Gottesbildes.

stischen Unwertbegriff *ṬM'* (5). — Die Vorstellung von Jahwe als König gehört im besonderen der Zionsmythologie zu, die den Ankündigungen Jesajas in vielfältiger Weise Modelle lieferte [1]); 1 Kön. xxii zeigt aber, daß die Vorstellung nicht auf die Jerusalemer Tradition beschränkt war [2]): sie gehört, wie es scheint, allen sedentären Hochkulturen des alten vorderen Orients an.

2. Die Seraphe als Hofstaat des königlichen Jahwe sind wie der *ṣᵉba' hăššamăyim* von 1 Kön. xxii die ersten Adressaten der Frage Jahwes (V. 8a), in der er sich durch den Präpositionalausdruck *lanû* zugleich mit ihnen zusammenschließt. Das hinter Jes. vi 8 stehende uralte szenische Motiv sieht jeweils vor, daß aus dem ratlos-verlegenen Hofstaat ein Mächtiger gesucht wird, der eine schwierige oder gefährliche Aufgabe zu erfüllen hat [3]). So führt uns bereits das sumerische Epos von Gilgamesch und Agga, dessen Text der ersten Hälfte des 2. Jahrtausends entstammt [4]), mit Z. 48 ff. in die Versammlung der Waffen tragenden Männer um Gilgamesch, wo ein mutiger Freiwilliger gesucht wird, der die hoffnungslos belagerte Stadt Uruk verläßt, um vor den feindlichen König, Agga von Kisch, zu treten. Die Verlegenheit der Belagerten ist perfekt: „ In less than five days, in less than ten days / Agga, son of En-me-bara-gi$_4$-e-si, *enveloped the Urukeans.* / Uruk panicked. / Gilgamesh, the Lord of Kullab, / says to its heroes: 'My heroes *frown* . . .' ". — Darauf richtet Gilgamesch an seine Helden eine Frage, die derjenigen von Jes. vi 8a entspricht (Z. 54): „'Who has heart, let him stand up, to Agga I would *have him* go!' " Es folgen zwei Vorgänge, die in Jes. vi 3 und 8b Parallelen haben. Der Antwort auf die Frage des Königs geht eine dem Lobgesang der Seraphen vergleichbare Huldigung an diesen voran (Z. 55 f.): „Birhurturri (?), *his head* . . . *man*, / utters praises to the king". Darauf stellt sich Birhurturri wie Jesaja in unserer Szene für den Auftrag zur Verfügung und macht sich auf den Weg (Z. 57-59): „'I would go to Agga, / verily his judgment will be confounded,

---

[1]) Dazu das Folgende und H. P. Müller, *Ursprünge und Strukturen alttestamentlicher Eschatologie*, 1969, S. 38-49, 86-101, „Zur Funktion des Mythischen in der Prophetie des Jesaja", *Kairos* XIII, 1971, S. 266-281 (Lit!).

[2]) Vgl. W. H. Schmidt, „Jerusalemer El-Traditionen", *ZRGG* XVI, 1964, S. 302-313, bes. 313.

[3]) Vgl. zum Folgenden H. P. Müller, „Die himmlische Ratsversammlung. Motivgeschichtliches zu Apc 5,1-5", *ZNW* LIV 1963, S. 254-267, wozu hier zugleich einige Korrekturen angebracht werden.

[4]) Faksimile, Transkription, Übersetzung und Kommentar von S. N. Kramer-Th. Jacobsen, „Gilgamesh and Agga", *AJA* LIII 1949, S. 1-18; vgl. *ANET*, S. 44 f. Zeilen 48-50 sind von Th. Jacobsen, *ZA* LII 1957, S. 118, übernommen.

verily his counsel will be dissipated.' Birhurturri went out through the city gate". — Das Motiv wird im Verlaufe seiner Geschichte vom menschlichen König auf den göttlichen übertragen und somit aus einem Element des Epos zu einem solchen des Mythos [1]).

Innerhalb von Jes. vi bereiten die Stichworte *ŠLḤ* und *HLK* von V. 8 auf den Wortkomplex *HLK*, *'MR* und *l*^{e} mit Adresse von V. 9 vor: V. 8 f. sucht die größtmögliche Legitimation für einen prophetischen Auftrag, dessen Erfolg und Sinn begründeten Zweifeln unterliegt [2]); zu vergleichen sind die Ankündigungen über Erfolg und Sinn der Sendung in nahestehenden Beauftragungsszenen wie Ex. iii 18a. 19 f. J; 1 Kön. xxii 22b (*w*^{e}*găm-tûkal*); Hes. ii 5; iii 5-7. Vor allem aber hat die Rolle Jesajas als Verstocker seines Volkes (V. 10) ihre Parallele nicht nur in der Betörung Ahabs durch seine Heilspropheten (1 Kön. xxii 20-22), sondern auch in der Irreführung Agamemnons durch Zeus mittels eines täuschenden Traums (οὖλος ὄνειρος) in Ilias ii 1 ff, wonach der griechische König ebenso wie der israelitische durch ein falsches gottgesandtes Omen in einen unglücklich endenden Kampf gelockt wird [3]): diese List hilft Zeus aus der Verlegenheit, die ihm Zwist und Mißtrauen der Olympier, insbesondere der Göttinnen, verursachen. Eine Kontrastparallele hat Jes. vi 8-10 darüber hinaus noch an (ugar.) 2 K V 10-13: während El in der Ratsversammlung seiner Söhne jemand sucht, der die Krankheit KRTs heilen kann, um sich nach sechs vergeblichen Anfragen selbst ans Werk zu machen, wird der Prophet aus der Ratsversammlung Jahwes entsandt, um jede Heilung zu verhindern (*pän* .. *l*^{e}*babô yabîn w*^{e}*šab* [!] *w*^{e}*rapa' lô*) [4]). Der Streit der Götter ist nach Jes. vi

[1]) So im akkad. Mythos vom Raub der Schicksalstafeln durch *Anzû* (II 2ff. der altbab., II 23ff. der assyr. Fassung [ANET S. 111 ff.]), ganz fragmentarisch in Z. 4 f. des assyr. (parodistischen) Kultkommentars KAR 143 (W. von Soden, *ZA* LI, 1956, S. 130-165, bes. 132 f.) und ausführlich in der ugar. Erzählung 2 K V 10-30. — Die von I. Engnell (*The Call of Isaiah*, *UUÅ* 1949:4, S. 42) zitierte Beschwörung Maqlû I 50-60 ist insofern anders gelagert, als der von Anu und Antum gesandte Beschwörer mit seiner an Jes vi 8 erinnernden Frage offenbar einen Dritten gegen *seinen* Zauberer und *seine* Zauberin um göttliche Hilfe aussenden will; Transkription und Übersetzung bei G. Maier, *Die assyrische Beschwörungsserie Maqlû*, *AfO* Beiheft II, 1967^{2}, S. 9.

[2]) Mit Recht setzt sich die Auffassung durch, daß Jesaja in Kap. vi auf seine gescheiterte Verkündigung in der Zeit des syrisch-ephraimitischen Krieges *zurückblickt*; zuletzt O. H. Steck, „Bemerkungen zu Jesaja 6", *BZ* XVI, 1972, S. 188-206 (Lit.).

[3]) Dazu R. Kittel, *Die Bücher der Könige*, *HkAT* I 5, 1900, S. 175.

[4]) Zu Il/El als Heilgott vgl. die ugar. und bibl. Parallelen bei M. Dahood in L. R. Fisher, *Ras Shamra Parallels* I, 1972, S. 342; die Gegensatzparallele widerrät es m.E. *w*^{e}*šab w*^{e}*rapa' lô* mit G. Fohrer, *Das Buch Jesaja* I 1966^{2}, S. 93, zu streichen.

gleichsam als Widerspruch zwischen Vernichtungsbeschluß und Heilungswillen in Jahwe hineinverlegt: könnte sich in der Sendung des Propheten an sich wohl Jahwes Heilungswillen ausdrücken, so siegt doch in ihrem Scheitern sein Vernichtungsbeschluß, zu dessen Verwirklichung sie effektiv beiträgt. Die Spannung, die der Existenz des Propheten damit auferlegt wird, ist freilich nur der Rolle eines Himmlischen adäquat, in die der Prophet ja durch seine Antwort (V. 8b) eintritt. Der Sinn der prophetischen Existenz, nach dem zu fragen dem biblischen Propheten anders als dem Ekstatiker aufgegeben ist, entringt sich somit einem Freiraum, der sich aus dem innergöttlichen Konflikt eröffnet. Die Entsendung des Propheten aus einer göttlichen Ratsversammlung zeigt, wie selbst ein specificum biblicum nur mit mythischen Mitteln ausgesprochen werden kann.

3. Die Antwort Jahwes auf die Frage des Propheten in V. 11a reicht nicht über V. 11 hinaus [1]). Einen Hinweis auf die Funktion von V. 12 f. liefert die Beobachtung, daß in V. 12 f. von Jahwe in 3. Person gesprochen wird. Während wir nämlich in V. 1-11 einen Visionsbericht vor uns haben, an dessen Höhepunkt (9 f. 11b) Jahwes eigene Worte wiedergegeben werden, folgt in V. 12 f. die Deutung, in der Jesaja wie ein Seher von seiner Vollmacht zu freier, wenn auch nicht eigenmächtiger Rede Gebrauch macht; die gleichen beiden Grundformen seherischer Rede finden sich auch im Visionsbericht 1 Kön. xxii 19-22 und seiner Deutung 23, die von Jahwe wieder in 3. Person spricht [2]). V. 12-13bα gehören somit ursprünglich in den vorliegenden Zusammenhang [3]).

---

w^{e}šab ist dabei adverbiell zu *w^{e}rapa'* wie *w^{e}šabā* zu *w^{e}hay^{e}tā* in V. 13, zumal die Wurzel *ŠŪB* in theologischer Bedeutung beim echten Jesaja allenfalls in vii 3 und xxx 15 vorkommt; zu *ŠŪB* im Jes-buch G. Sauer, „Die Umkehrforderung in der Verkündigung Jesajas", *FS W. Eichrodt*, 1970, S. 277-295.

[1]) Das ergibt bereits eine syntaktische Erwägung: das dem Perf. *ša'û* folgende Impf. *tiššā'ā* (*tišša' er?*) ist jenem gegenüber final bzw. konsekutiv; mit der Benennung einer terminierenden Tatsache, der Entvölkerung der Ortschaften, und ihrer Auswirkung, der Verödung des Landes, ist der mit *'ăd '^{a}šär 'im-* beginnende Satz abgeschlossen.

[2]) Zur Unterscheidung von berichtender und deutender Rede als den Grundformen des Seherspruchs vgl. D. Vetter, *Untersuchungen zum Seherspruch im AT*, Diss. theol. Heidelberg (masch.), 1963, S. 210-215; vgl. noch das Nebeneinander von Visionsbericht und Deutung in Jes. ix 1-6a und 6 b, xvii 12-14a und 14b sowie xxx 27 f. und 29-33, woraus sich an den genannten Stellen das Fehlen von Botenformel und Jahwerede sowie die Unbedingtheit der Heilsankündigung in teleästhetischer Antezipation erklären.

[3]) Richtig erkannte E. Jenni („Jesajas Berufung in der neueren Forschung", *ThZ* XV, 1959, S. 321-339, bes. 330), daß Jesaja die V. 12 f. „von vornherein als Ergänzung zum Visionsbericht gedacht" habe; „dadurch wird der Bericht zum

„Jahwe wird die Menschen hinwegführen,
während die Verlassenheit groß ist im Lande.
Und ist noch ein Zehntel darin,
so wird es wieder verbrannt [1])
wie mächtige Bäume [2])
wenn [3]) die Säule [4]) bei ihnen [5]) 'gefällt ist' [6])".

In Israel wird es also zugehen wie bei der Desakralisierung eines heiligen Hains; die gleiche Bildtopik liegt auch der Unheilsankündigung i 29-31 zugrunde, einem von H. WILDBERGER [7]) in Jesajas Frühzeit datiertem Wort.

II

Dem eigentlichen Korpus der Denkschrift vii 2-17; viii 1-15 geht

verkündbaren Wort umgeprägt". — Dagegen wird V. 13bβ von den meisten zu Recht für eine Glosse angesehen; sie gibt einen Hinweis für die allegorische Auslegung.

[1]) An *Bʿ R I* „brennen" wird man vor allem wegen i 31 mit seiner ähnlichen Topik denken.

[2]) *ʾelā* und *ʾällôn* bezeichnen nicht eine botanische species: insbesondere an unserer Stelle will der Doppelausdruck — wie der Plural *ʾêlîm* i 29 und *ʾelā* 30 (vgl. ii 13) — eine numinose Wertigkeit benennen, wie sie mächtigen Bäumen für die Erfahrensweise des Orientalen bis zum heutigen Tage anhaftet; das zeigt die Nachbarschaft der Begriffe zu *mäṣṣäbät* (Anm. 4).

[3]) *ʾašär* entspricht LXX: ὅταν; syntaktisch handelt es sich um einen realen Bedingungssatz wie Lev. iv 22 (//*ʾim* 27); Dtn. xi 27 (//*ʾim* 28); Jos. iv 21 (GESENIUS-KAUTZSCH, *op. cit.*, § 159 cc).

[4]) Zu *mäṣṣäbät* „Stele, Säule" 2 Sam. xviii 18; phön.-pun. Belege *DISO* S. 164, Weiteres bei S. IWRY, „Maṣṣēbāh and Bāmāh in 1Q Is[a] 6,13", *JBL* LXXVI, 1957, S. 225-232. Die Übersetzung „Triebe" nach aram.—syr. *NṢB* „pflanzen" (H. WILDBERGER, *Jesaja*, *BK* X 1965 ff., S. 234) empfiehlt sich m.E. nicht; denn „pflanzen" ≠ „treiben", und die Vorstellung eines Setzlings liegt fern.

[5]) Zur Ortsbestimmung *b[e]* bei *mäṣṣäbät* vgl. die phön. Wendung *mṣbt bḥym* „Gedenkstein (f.e. Toten) unter den Lebenden" (CIS I 58[1], 59[1], 116[1] [*DISO*]); das Pluralsuffix *-am* bezöge sich dann auf *ʾelā* und *ʾällôn*. Aber auch die Lesung *bah* (100 Mss, Seb) käme in Frage, und zwar mit Bezug auf *ʾelā* als Dominante des Doppelausdrucks. 1Q Jes[a] *bmh* kann die „(kultische) Höhe" meinen; doch wäre das Verständnis von *bmh* als *b* + Pron.-Suff. 3. m. pl. wegen der ähnlichen orthographischen Variante *lšwnmh* Jes. xli 17 in 1Q Jes[a] nicht auszuschließen (vgl. W. H. BROWNLEE, „The Text of Is 6,13 in the Light of DSJes[a]", *VT* I, 1951, S. 296-298).

[6]) Mit 1Q Jes[a] wird man *mäšläkät* lesen, was LXX ἐκπέσῃ entspricht (IWRY, *op. cit.*, S. 229); das Part. Ho. f.s. bezieht sich dabei auf das nahestehende *mäṣṣäbät*, nicht auf *ʾelā* und *ʾällôn*, was den Plural *mšlkwt* erwarten ließe und die Konjektur einer Präposition bei *mäṣṣäbät* erforderte. LXX ἀπὸ τῆς θήκης αὐτῆς entspricht einer Vokalisation *miṣṣäbtah* (*min* + mutmaßliches Verbalnomen *ṣäbät* von *NṢB/YṢB*; vgl. G. R. DRIVER, *JSS* XIII, 1968, S. 38), wobei die Worte des MT *mäṣṣäbät bam zärāʿ qodäš* von LXX übergangen werden. Ähnlich scheint *mäṣṣäbät bam* von Targ aufgefaßt zu sein, das לקיימא מינהון übersetzt.

[7]) *Op. cit.*, S. 70.

in vii 1 eine redaktionelle Exposition voraus, die die ursprüngliche Situationsangabe vii 2 [1]) zu dem Komplex vii 2-9(-17) für eine spätere Zeitgenossenschaft erläutert.

1. Das Heilsorakel vii (3)4-9 vollzieht in seinen beiden Teilen 4-9a und 9b einander gegenläufige Bewegungen.

Zwar scheint der Aufbau der beiden Teile zunächst analog zu sein. Der Aufforderung zu Ruhe und Furchtlosigkeit in V. 4 entspricht im zweiten Teil inhaltlich der Bedingungssatz *ʾim loʾ tăʾᵃmînû* 9 bα: ebenso hat die bedingungslose Heilsankündigung 5-9a sachlich in dem bedingten *kî loʾ teʾamenû* 9bβ ihr Pendant.

Zugleich aber zeigt diese Gegenüberstellung auch den Gegensatz der beiden Teile: innerhalb von 4-9a hat die Heilsankündigung 5-9a gegenüber der Forderung 4 begründende Funktion; in 9b dagegen steht das Angekündigte selbst unter der Bedingung der Forderung [2]).

Indikativ und Imperativ sind also in beiden Teilen reziprok aufeinander bezogen. Das Heilsorakel als Ganzes bringt den Angeredeten in eine Schwebeposition zwischen Determination und Freiheit, Geborgenheit und Verantwortung; göttliches und menschliches Handeln sind interdependent. — Eine solche kunstvolle und reflektierte Gestaltung hat dem Wort schwerlich schon bei seiner mündlichen Verkündigung zugrunde gelegen; sie war vielmehr erst bei der Abfassung der Denkschrift möglich.

2. Innerhalb der bedingten Heilsankündigung von V. 9b wiederholt sich die reziproke Struktur des ganzen Wortes (3)4-9 im Wortspiel zwischen *tăʾᵃmînû* und *teʾamenû*.

(a) Das Hiphʿil von (Hi) *ʾMN* wird hier wie bei einer Reihe von sogleich zu besprechenden Belegen profanen und religiösen Inhalts, die den Eindruck einer ursprungsnahen Verwendung machen [3]), ohne Objekt gebraucht.

[1]) Die Botschaft an die Davididen lautet: „Aram hat sich auf (dem Boden) Ephraim(s) niedergelassen". Schwerlich kann *NŪḤ* „sich vertragen/verbünden" bedeuten; die von O. Eissfeldt (*Kleine Schriften* III, 1966, S. 124-128) dafür herangezogene akkadische Form *in-na-ḫu-u* Idri-mi Z. 41, 48 ist entweder Präsens G-Stamm von *anāḫum* I „müde sein, ermüden" oder Präsens N-Stamm von *nâḫum* „ruhen", also jedenfalls nicht mit der Qal-Form *nāḥā* zu vergleichen; das Substantiv *ma-na-ḫa-te* Z. 47, 51, 54 wird von W. von Soden, AHw 601, als „Ermüdung, Arbeit" erklärt und somit zu *anāḫum* gestellt. — Schwierig bleibt die Femininform *nāḥā* insofern, als *ʾᵃram* in V. 5 mit einer Maskulinform verbunden wird.

[2]) Vgl. die Alternative i 19 f., vor allem aber die Reziprozität in Hos. xiv 2-9; dazu H. -P. Müller, „Imperativ und Verheißung im AT", *EvTh* XXVIII, 1968, S. 557-571.

[3]) Dazu H. Wildberger, „Glauben". Erwägungen zu האמין ", *FS W. Baum-*

Das bereits schließt seine deklarativ-ästimative Erklärung im transitiven Sinne von „für fest, zuverlässig erklären, halten" m.E. aus [1]. — Nicht in Frage kommt auch die denominative Ableitung, wonach das Hi das Bestehen oder den Erwerb einer mit dem entsprechenden Nomen bezeichneten Eigenschaft oder die Hervorbringung eines mit dem Nomen bezeichneten Objekts zum Ausdruck brächte; denn hierzu fehlt ein überzeugender nominaler Wurzelbegriff [2], insbesondere wenn *'omen* „Wärter", *'omänät* „Amme" u.ä. mit W. Baumgartner [3] einer anderen homophonen Wurzel zuzurechnen sind. Ebensowening handelt es sich um sog. Pseudohiphʿil, bei dem zu einem als Hi mißverstandenen Imperfekt Qal nach *yaqtil/yaqīl* analoge Hi-formen gebildet worden wären, neben denen etwa ein Qal von gleicher Bedeutung weiterbestände [4]; denn weder ist letzteres der Fall, noch gibt es innerhalb des vorfindlichen Hi neben der für das Imperfekt nach *yaqtil/yaqīl* und seine falschen Analoga anzunehmenden Grundstammbedeutung eine eigentliche, nämlich kausative oder faktitive Hi-bedeutung, so wie wir sonst bei Verben mit Pseudo-Hi eben eine doppelte Hi-bedeutung finden [5].

---

gartner, *SVT* XVI, 1967, S. 372-386, bes. 375-378, „'Glauben' im AT", *ZThK* LXV, 1968, S. 129-159, Art. אמן, *THAT* I, 1971, Sp. 177-209, bes. 187 f.

[1]) So etwa E. Pfeiffer, „Glaube im AT", *ZAW* LXXI, 1959, S. 151-164.

[2]) Gegen G. Bergsträsser, *Hebräische Grammatik*, 1962, II § 19d, H. Bauer - P. Leander, *Historische Grammatik der hebräischen Sprache*, 1962, § 38b ''' d '''.

[3]) *HAL* 62.

[4]) So Wildberger, *FS Baumgartner*, S. 384².

[5]) Beispiele für das Nebeneinander zweier Hi-Bedeutungen — einer zuständlich-passivischen Grundstammbedeutung des Pseudo-Hi und einer kausativen oder faktitiven des eigentlichen Hi — sind: Hi *BŌŠ* in der Form *hôbîš* mit der Grundstammbedeutung „in Schande sein" (anderer Gebrauch von *hôbîš* auf Grund falscher Analogiebildung 2 Sam. xix 6 „beleidigen" und Hos. ii 7 „schändlich handeln" s.u.) neben *hebîš* mit der faktitiven Hi-bedeutung „zuschanden machen" (zu *mebîš* Prov. x 5 s.u.; zu *BŌŠ* zuletzt M. A. Klopfenstein, *Scham und Schande nach dem AT*, 1972, dazu Rez. des Vf. demnächst in *ZA*), Hi *BĪN* etwa Jes. xxviii 19 „erkennen" wie Qal, dessen Impf. nach *yaqīl* gebildet wird, neben „erkennen lassen", Hi *GĪḤ* Ri xx 33 „hervorbrechen" wie Qal nach *yaqīl* neben „h. lassen", Hi *ḤĪŠ* Ri xx 37 „Eile haben" wie Qal nach *yaqīl* (also nicht *ḤRŠ*) neben „beschleunigen", Hi *ḤRŠ* „still sein" neben „zum Schweigen bringen" (wie mh. Pi), Hi *ḤŠH* „schweigen, zaudern" wie Qal neben „schweigen heißen", Hi *YBŠ* Sach x 11 „trocknen" wie Qal neben „vertrocknen lassen" (wie Pi), Hi *YʿL* Jes. xlvii 12; xlviii 17 u.ö. „Nutzen haben" neben „Nutzen bringen", Hi *YPʿ* „erstrahlen" neben „strahlend sichtbar machen", Hi *YSP* „fortfahren" wie Qal, für das die Lexika kein Impf. verzeichnen, neben „vermehren, vergrößern", Hi *MĪR* Ps. xlvi 3 „wanken" neben „tauschen", Hi *ŠQṬ* Jes. vii 4; xxx 15 „Ruhe haben" wie Qal neben "beruhigen" u.a.m. Auffällig ist der Häufigkeitsbefund bei den Verba I *W-/Y-* und II *-Ī-*, bei denen sich die *yaqtil/yaqīl*-Impf. auch sonst erhalten haben. — Als Hi angesetzte Impf.-Bildungen mit häufig kurzem

Vielmehr gehört Hi *ʾMN* zu einer Gruppe von innerlich faktitiven Hi-bildungen, bei denen das innere Objekt die Daseinsverfassung ist, in die das Subjekt durch die bezeichnete Handlung sich selbst versetzt [1]); freilich lassen sich bei vielen dieser Verben daneben andere Hi-bedeutungen belegen. Hierher zu rechnen sind Hi *BʾŠ* Prov. xiii 5 „sich stinkend machen > niedrig handeln" [2]), Hi *BŌŠ* in der Form *mebîš* Prov. x 5 u.ö. und in der falschen Analogiebildung *hobîšā* Hos. ii 7 „sich in Schande begeben > schändlich handeln" [3]), Hi *BLG* Ps. xxxix 14; Hiob ix 27; x 20 „heiter werden" [4]), Hi *ZĪD* „sich erregen", Hi *ḤPR II* Prov. xiii 5; xix 26 „sich in Verlegenheit begeben > beschämend handeln" [5]), Hi *Yʾ L* „sich (zu etwas) bestimmen, (etwas) in Angriff nehmen [6]), sich (darin) als erster erweisen" [7]), Hi *YḤL* „sich wartend verhalten" (neben gleichbedeutendem Pi), Hi *ṬŪB/YṬB* „gut handeln" [8]), Hi *KŪN* Jos. iii 17; 1 Sam. xxiii 22; Jer x 23 „beharrlich sein" [9]), Hi *NGʿ* Hes vii 12 u.ö. „eintreffen, herankommen", Hi *SKL* „töricht handeln", Hi *ʿŪR* Jes. xlii 13; Ps. xxxv 23; lxxiii 20; Hiob viii 6 „sich regen, aufwachen", Hi *ṢNʿ* Mi. vi 8 „sich demütigen", Hi *QRB* Ex xiv 10 u.ö. „sich nähern", Hi *RḤQ* Jos viii 4 u.ö. „sich entfernen", Hi *Rʿʿ* in der Bedeutung„ schlecht handeln", Hi *RŠʿ* in der Bedeutung „sich schuldig machen", Hi

---

Wurzelvokal (Defektivschreibung) wie יַחֲטִא Ri. xx 16 „er verfehlte sein Ziel", יַאֲהִיל Hiob xxv 5 und יָהֵל Hiob xxxi 26 „er leuchtet", יַיְשִׁרוּ Prov. iv 25 „sie blicken geradeaus", תּוֹתַר Gen. xlix 4 „du hast einen Vorrang", neben denen es kein Pseudo-Hi im Perf., Imp. und Inf. gibt, sollte man in den Lexika als Qal verzeichnen, wie es bereits bei *ʿRM* (Qal יַעְרִם neben echtem Hi יַעֲרִימוּ) geschieht. — Die Entdeckung solcher *ĭ*-Impf. Qal hinter scheinbaren Hi-formen geht auf J. Barth („Vergleichende Studien III. Das *ĭ*-Impf. im Nordsemitischen", *ZDMG* XLIII, 1889, S. 177-191) zurück; der Terminus Pseudohiphʿil stammt von Joüon (*op. cit.*, § 54 f.); vgl. Wildberger, *FS Baumgartner*, S. 384².

1) Vgl. C. Brockelmann, *Grundriß der vergleichenden Grammatik der semitischen Sprachen*, 1961, I § 257 Gh εζ (S. 527).

2) B. Gemser, *Sprüche Salomos*, *HAT* I 16, 1963, S. 112.

3) Das Pseudo-Hi *hôbîš* in der zuständlich-passivischen Grundstammbedeutung „in Schande sein" bezeichnet die gleiche Daseinsverfassung als Ergebnis einer Einwirkung von außen, wobei das Einwirkende durch Adverbialbestimmungen mit *min* (Jer. x 14; li 17), *ʿăl* (Jes. xxx 5) oder durch Begründungssätze mit *kî* (Jer. vi 15; viii 12) benannt wird (Klopfenstein, *op. cit.*, S. 30, 51, 80).

4) Zu *măblîg* Am. v. 9 vgl. W. Rudolph, *Joel, Amos . . .*, *KAT* XIII 2, 1971, S. 196/7.

5) Vgl. Klopfenstein, *op. cit.* S. 43, 174 f., aber auch 173.

6) So Gesenius-Buhl, *ad vocem*.

7) So Köhler-Baumgartner, *ad vocem*.

8) Von Interesse ist die Auflösung des innerlichen Faktitivs in der Wendung *mêṭîbîm ʾät-libbam* Ri xix 22 „sich gütlich tuend".

9) Mit der Auflösung Hi *KŪN* + *ʾät-libbô* bzw. *-panâw* o.ä. „seinen Sinn richten auf".

ŠḤT Dtn. iv 16; Ri. ii 19 „verderblich handeln" (vgl. Pi Ex. xxxii 7 u.ö.), Hi *ŚKL* Jes. lii 13 „einsichtig handeln" und Hi *T'B* „abscheulich handeln" [1]).

Die vom Subjekt durch die vom Hi bezeichnete Handlung an sich selbst gezeitigte Daseinsverfassung wird dabei meist durch andere Stämme der gleichen Wurzel benannt. Es geschieht durch das Qal bei *B'Š* „stinken", *BŌŠ* „in Schande sein > (subj.) sich schämen müssen, (obj.) zuschanden werden" [2]), *ZĪD* „vermessen sein", *ḤPR II* „in Verlegenheit sein > beschämt sein" [3]), *ṬŪB* „gut, angenehm, fröhlich sein" [4]), *'ŪR* „wach sein", pt. pass. *ṣanû^a'* „demütig", *RḤQ* „fern sein", *R''* „schlecht sein", *RŠ'* „schuldig ein", *ŚKL* „Erfolg haben". In gleicher Weise aber kann auch das Niph'al (Ni) gebraucht werden, nämlich in Ni *'MN* „fest sein" (!), Ni *B'Š* „stinkend / verhaßt sein", Ni *KŪN* „fest sein", Ni *SKL* „als töricht dastehen", Ni *R''* „übel fahren", Ni *ŠḤT* „verdorben, entartet sein", Ni *T'B* „abscheulich sein"; hier repräsentiert das Ni neben oder anstelle des Qal die Grundbedeutung der Wurzel. — Ist das Hi in der oben bezeichneten Weise innerlich faktitiv, so ist die im Qal oder Ni repräsentierte Grundbedeutung innerlich passiv und dementsprechend zuständlich [5]).

Hi *'MN* bezeichnet somit eine Weise des Einwirkens des Subjekts auf sich selbst; das Subjekt versetzt sich durch das von *hä'ämîn* bezeichnete Handeln in eine Daseinsverfassung, die dem Begriff des Ni *'MN* zugrundeliegt. Insofern haftet dem Satz Jes. vii 9b etwas Tautologisches an.

---

[1]) Das innerliche Faktitiv ist wieder aufgelöst, wenn Zeph. iii 7 bzw. Ps. xiv 1 als Objekt zu Hi *ŠḤT* bzw. *T'B* das Nomen *'^alîlā* „das Handeln", d.h. die Handlungsweise als Ausdruck der Daseinsverfassung, erscheint; vgl. *w^ehêṭîbû mä'äl^elêkäm* Jer. xxxv 15. In der Wendung Hi *R''* + *lä'^aśôt* ist der Akkusativ durch einen Inf. ersetzt.

[2]) Zum Qal *BŌŠ* gibt es nach dem Ausgeführten also (1) ein ursprüngliches, faktitives Hi *hebîš* „zuschanden machen", (2) ein ursprüngliches innerlich faktitives Hi-Part. *mebîš* „schändlich handeln", (3) ein Pseudo-Hi *hôbîš* „in Schande sein" (= Qal) und (4) falsche Analogiebildungen wie *hobăšta* 2 Sam. xix 6 „du hast beleidigt" (zu (1) gehörig, lege *hebăšta?*) und *hobîšā* Hos ii 7 „sie hat schändlich gehandelt" (zu (2) gehörig).

[3]) Klopfenstein, *op. cit.*, S. 175, 206.

[4]) In *wăyyîṭăb libbô* Ri xviii 20 u.ö. „er wurde fröhlich" ist *libbô* als accusativus relationis aufzufassen.

[5]) Das schließt zugleich die Erklärung A. Jepsens aus (Art. אמן *ThWAT* I 3, 1971, Sp. 313-348, bes. 333), der *hä'ämîn* im Sinne von „beständig werden" mit dem Denominativ *hišmîn* „fett werden" zusammenstellt und dabei die kausative und die deklarative Bedeutung des Hi für die einzigen Alternativen ansieht.

Da der Wurzel *ʾMN* der Begriff der Festigkeit anhaftet [1]), meint Hi *ʾMN* als innerliches Faktitiv das Sich-in-Festigkeit-Versetzen, welche Bedeutung vom Profanen leicht ins Religiöse übergreift. So heißt es Hi. xxxix 24 vom Kriegsroß, daß es sich beim Ertönen des Horns nicht indolent oder träge „fest-setzt". Nach Hiobs wehmütigem Rückblick xxix 24 „versetzten sie sich 'wahrhaftig' *in Festigkeit*" [2]), wenn Hiob „ihnen zulächelte". Dagegen heißt es Hab. i 5 in einem Unheilsorakel namens Jahwes: „Ein Werk tue ich [3]) in euren Tagen — *ihr werdet keine Festigkeit finden*, wenn es erzählt wird". Die Inschrift auf dem Grundstein, dessen Niederlegung die mythische Gründung des Zionsheiligtums wiederholt, lautet Jes. xxviii 16: „*Wer sich in Festigkeit versetzt*, hat keine Eile [4])". Entsprechend berichtet Ex. iv 31 von der Wirkung der durch Mose gewirkten Wunder: „Das Volk *versetzte sich in Festigkeit*". Ps. cxvi 10 schließlich sagt im Rückblick auf überstandene Not: „*Ich habe mich in Festigkeit versetzt*, auch wenn ich sprechen mußte: 'Ich bin tief gebeugt' ". — Soweit die Stellen, an denen Hi *ʾMN* wie in Jes. vii 9 ohne Objekt gebraucht wird.

(b) Freilich wäre es ein Mißverständnis, wollte man den durch Hi *ʾMN* bezeichneten Vorgang für ein innersubjektives Geschehen halten. Vielmehr nimmt der Gewinn einer gefestigten Daseinsverfassung seinen Grund aus einem das Subjekt von außen betreffenden Vorgang, etwa dem Lächeln Hiobs oder den Wundern des Mose, wie umgekehrt dem Ertönen des Horns oder dem Unheilswerk Jahwes. Das *häʾämîn*, das Jes. vii 9b zur Bedingung des „Bleibens" macht, hätte seinen Grund in der Aussicht auf das Rettungshandeln Jahwes, die das Heilsorakel V. 4-9a eröffnen will. Syntaktisch kann der außersubjektive Grund des Sich-in-Festigkeit-Versetzens durch Adverbiale mit b^{e} (in der Paraphrase unserer Stelle 2 Chr. xx 20, ferner Gen. xv 6; Ex. xiv 31) und l^{e} (Ex. iv 9) angegeben werden [5]); erst davon abgeleitet kann von einem „Glauben an" Festigkeit begründende Sachverhalte

---

[1]) Zur semitischen Wurzel H. Wildberger, *THAT* I, 178 f. („fest, zuverlässig, sicher sein", mit Hinweis auf die Bedeutungsverwandtschaft der Wurzel *KŪN*; vgl. W. von Soden, *WO* IV, 1967, S. 38-47), zur hebräischen Wurzel Jepsen, *op. cit.*, S. 347 („Beständigkeit, Dauer, Zuverlässigkeit").

[2]) Wie an einigen anderen Stellen (vgl. F. Nötscher, *VT* III, 1953, S. 374 f., F. Ch. Fensham, *The Bible Translator* XVIII, 1967, S. 73) wird man hinter masoretischem לא ein לו zu vermuten haben.

[3]) Nach LXX wird man *ʾ^{a}nî* einsetzen oder *ʾäpʿäl* statt *poʿäl* lesen müssen.

[4]) Vgl. S. 34 Anm. 5.

[5]) Wildberger (*op. cit.*, Sp. 188 f.) will freilich zwischen den Funktionen des b^{e} und des l^{e} unterscheiden.

gesprochen werden, die etwa in Nebensätzen mit *kî* wie Ex. iv 5 erscheinen.

Entsprechend soll sich die gewonnene Festigkeit an außersubjektiver Wirklichkeit bewähren: das Sich-in-Festigkeit-Versetzen ist Bedingung eines Fest-Seins in konkreter, geschichtlicher Not. Das Subjekt nimmt außersubjektive Wirklichkeit in sich auf, um gegenüber anderer außersubjektiver Wirklichkeit Bestand zu behalten [1]. Insofern beschränkt das außersubjektive Implikat des Begriffes *hä'ᵃmîn* die Tautologie des Satzes Jes. vii 9 b.

Die Interdependenz von Subjekt und Objekt, die dem Begriff *'MN* im Hi und Ni inhäriert, wiederholt diejenige von göttlichem und menschlichem Handeln, die die Struktur des Orakels im ganzen bestimmt. Beide bewegen sich in einem ontologisch-hermeneutischen Zirkel, der das Auswägen eines prae gegen ein post verbietet: im Verhältnis von Ich und Wirklichkeit spiegelt sich die Gleichgewichtigkeit, die Gott dem Menschen als seinem Dialogpartner gewährt.

III

1. Für die cruces interpretum des Abschnitts vii 10-17, die Fragen nach der Identität Immanuels und der Bedeutung seines Namens, kann man vielleicht durch eine genauere Analyse der Form von V. 14b-16 noch einige Anhaltspunkte gewinnen; hinter 14b-16 steht nämlich nicht so sehr eine Königsmythologie [2] als die alte Gattung eines Geburtsorakels, wie wir es noch Gen. xvi 11 f. J; xvii 19 P; xxv 23 J; Ri. xiii 5; 1 Kön. xiii 2 f. (dtr) und Luc. i 31 f. finden [3].

Es besteht aus fünf Elementen: (a) Die Worte *hinnē ha'ălmā harā* „Siehe, die junge Frau ist schwanger" [4] diagnostizieren eine Schwangerschaft: in dieser Form redet ursprünglich ein Mantiker, der Verborgenes sieht [5]; auf eine mantische Institution weist ausdrück-

---

[1] Insofern impliziert *hä'ᵃmîn* hier ein Element des Hoffens, wie es ausdrücklicher Ps. xxvii 13 (mit *lᵉ* + Inf.), Hi. ix 16 (mit *kî* + Nebensatz) u.ö. geschieht; vgl. z.Tl. WILDBERGER, *FS Baumgartner*, S. 384.

[2] So etwa E. HAMMERSHAIMB, „The Immanuel Sign", *StTh* III 2, 1951, S. 124-142.

[3] Zum Folgenden P. HUMBERT, „Der biblische Verkündigungsstil und seine vermutliche Herkunft", *AfO* X 1935/6, S. 77-80.

[4] Die Interpretation von *hinnē* als konditionaler Konjunktion wie 1 Sam. ix 7 (G. FOHRER, *Studien zur alttestamentlichen Prophetie*, 1967, S. 168) liegt innerhalb eines Geburtsorakels fern. — Zum stativischen Verständnis des Perf. vgl. jetzt MEYER, *op. cit.*, § 101, 2.

[5] Der Sitz im Leben der Gattung ist nicht speziell die Orakelbefragung seitens einer Unfruchtbaren, und das Motiv eines „übermenschlichen Ursprungs" des

lich das Geburtsorakel Gen. xxv 22 f. [1]. (b) In dem Satz *w^ejolädät ben* „und wird (bald) [2] einen Sohn gebären" liegt der Akzent bei der Aussicht auf einen männlichen Nachkommen, den der Mantiker im voraus erkennt [3]. (c) Bei der folgenden Anweisung in bezug auf den Namen des Kindes fällt MT in die der Gattung eigentümliche Anredeform zurück, wobei die Anrede wie in Gen. xvi 11bα an die Mutter [4] oder wie in Gen. xvii 19aβ an der Vater gerichtet sein kann [5]; eine ähnliche Anweisung erfährt Jes. viii 3b der Prophet selbst. (d) V. 16 nennt den Grund für die Wahl des Namens [6]; die Formulierung läuft dabei der von viii 4 genau parallel. (e) Der sekundäre V. 15 macht zusammen mit V. 21 f. aus der Sicht der Exilszeit [7] eine Vorhersage über das Schicksal des Kindes [8].

Wenn die vom Propheten beabsichtigte Aussage der Struktur eines

---

Kindes gehört nicht zu ihrer Topik (gegen HUMBERT, der S. 80 selbst Berichte von ganz natürlichen Geburten wie Gen. iv 1; xxix 32 ff.; Hos. i 3 ff. vergleicht). Das Geburtsorakel wird vielmehr allgemein beim Ausbleiben der Menstruation o.ä. in Anspruch genommen worden sein.

[1]) Zur zitierten Wendung vgl. speziell Gen. xvi 11; Ri. xiii 5.

[2]) *jolädät* wird wie futurum instans verwendet.

[3]) Zur Wendung Gen. xvi 11; xvii 19; Ri. xiii 5 (ferner Gen. xviii 10; 2 Kön. iv 16). Die ugar. Texte NK 7 *hl ġlmt tld b[n]* und II D II 14 *ḳyld bn ly* beweisen ebenso wie 1 Sam. i 20 und Jes. viii 3 nur, daß die Terminologie für den Vorgang der Geburt seit Jahrhunderten festlag.

[4]) וקראת als 3.f.s. aufzufassen (so zuletzt WILDBERGER, *Jesaja*, S. 267), empfiehlt sich auch wegen καλέσεις LXX^{BA}, α, σ, θ nicht; Hieronymus Comm. iv 110 las *karathi*, also offenbar 2. f.s. (C. Siegfried, *ZAW* IV, 1884, S. 41; B. KEDAR - KOPFSTEIN, *Textus* IV 1964, S. 194).

[5]) L. DEQUEKER, „Isaie vii 14", *VT* XII, 1962, S. 331-335, will entsprechend 2. *masc.* s. lesen, was von 4 MSS des 12. Jahrhunderts bezeugt wird. — Zu וקראת . . . שמו ist außer den genannten Stellen noch 1 Kön. xiii 2 zu vergleichen.

[6]) Vgl. Gen xvi 11.

[7]) V. 15 stört den Zusammenhang zwischen der Anweisung 14 und ihrer Begründung 16, wie er auch zwischen viii 3 und 4 besteht; zu 15 steht 16 in keiner begründenden Funktion. Dazu nimmt die Wendung *YDᶜ ma'ôs baraᶜ ûbaḥôr bäṭṭôb*, die in V. 15b final eingeordnet ist (zu *l^e* als Pendant eines ut finale P. G. DUNCKER, *Sacra Pagina* I, 1959, S. 408-412), den Temporalsatz 16a vorweg; offenbar wollte der Glossator, dessen Interesse bei 15a lag, mittels der Ausdrucksvariante von 15b eine Beziehung zu 16 herstellen : das Kind wird *ḥäm'ā* (nach Prov. xxx 33 ein Milchprodukt) und Honig essen, damit es (alsbald); heranwachse (15b) und das Feindesland (der Weissagung von 16 entsprechend schnell) der Verlassenheit anheimfalle. Was nun aber 15a meint, sagt 21 f. noch deutlicher: zwar hat man (nach 587) nur noch einen geringen Viehbestand (21) aber wegen der reichen Erträge der wenigen Tiere (22aα) wird man *ḥäm'ā* und Honig verzehren (22bα). Der Messias erfährt schon als Kleinkind, wie sich für den „Rest" (22bβ), dessen Prototyp er ist, die volle Segensfülle des Landes erschließt. Vgl. zur Ansetzung WILDBERGER, *op cit.*, S. 295 f. 306 f.

Vgl. Gen. xvi 12; xvii 19; xxv 23; Ri. xiii 7; 1 Kön. xiii 2; Luc. i 32.

Geburtsorakels adäquat ist, ist die *ʿălmā* weder jede beliebige Frau [1]), noch die des Propheten [2]), sondern vielmehr diejenige des angeredeten Königs, der der Vater des Kindes ist [3]). Jes. vii 14 ist alles andere als eine freie Übertragung des Orakelstils „auf einen mehr literarischen und breiteren Plan" [4]): vielmehr fügt sich zur Rolle des Mantikers die des Propheten leichter als etwa die Figur eines Engels (so Gen. xvi 11 f.; Ri. xiii 5; Luc. i 31 f.); der Rahmen einer Orakelerteilung wird auch nicht dadurch gesprengt, daß Geburt und Namensverleihung nur als „Zeichen" bedeutsam wären, soll doch der königlichen Familie das Kind auch wirklich geboren werden [5]).

Der Name „Immanuel" ist ambivalent wie der des *šeʾar yašûb* [6]). Er spricht einerseits das Vertrauen aus, das der König angesichts solcher Heilsankündigungen wie vii 7b nun endlich bewähren soll [7]). Insofern enstpricht er dem Bekenntnis der Zuversicht, mit dem in dem Zionspsalm xlvi 8.12 die Gemeinde auf ein Völkerorakel wie Ps. xlvi 11 antwortet; das pagane *ʿimmanû ʾel* steht dem kanaanäischen Ursprung der Zionsmythologie sogar noch näher als die observantere Formulierung *YHWH ṣebaʾôt ʿimmanû* des in nachexilicher Zeit fi-

---

1) L. Köhlers kollektive Deutung („Zum Verständnis von Jes 7, 14", *ZAW* LXVII 1955, S. 249-258) ist nur zwingend, wenn *hinnē* die Übersetzung „(jedesmal) wenn" o.ä. erforderte; vgl. aber S. 38 Anm. 4.

2) So zuletzt J. J. Stamm, „Die Immanuel-Perikope im Lichte neuerer Veröffentlichungen", *ZDMG* Suppl I, 1969, Teil 1, S. 281-290.

3) Daß die Ankündigung statt an die Mutter wie in Gen. xvii 19; xviii 10 an den Vater ergeht, bedingt die Umsetzung der ersten beiden Elemente aus der Anredeform in die Aussage.

4) Gegen Humbert, *op. cit.*, S. 79.

5) Die Identifikation Immanuels mit dem Königskind wird jetzt vorsichtig wieder von Wildberger (*op. cit.*, S. 289-292) vertreten.

6) Die Mehrdeutigkeit von *šeʾar yašûb* ist offenbar gewollt (U. Stegemann, „Der Restgedanke bei Jesaja", *BZ* XIII 1969, S. 161-186, bes. 173-176). *yašûb* kann „umkehren (zu Jahwe)" (so der nachexilische „Kommentar" x 20-23) oder „wiederkehren (aus der Schlacht)" (so *ŠÛB* 1 Kön. xxii 28 u.ö.; vgl. zur Sache Jes. xxx 17 und *ŠʾR* Am. v 3) im Auge haben; für letzteres spräche, daß *ŠÛB* „umkehren" beim echten Jesaja allenfalls noch xxx 15 vorkommt (vgl. aber auch dazu G. Fohrer, *Das Buch Jesaja* II 1967², S. 101). *šeʾar* kann verheißenden (so in den sekundären Worten iv 3; xi 11, 16; xxviii 5; xxxvii 31 f., aber der Sache nach auch xiv 32) oder Unheil drohenden Klang haben („*nur* ein Rest"; so xvii 3 und in sekundären Worten x 19, 22a; xxi 17); die Heils-Unheils-Ambivalenz der Restvorstellung spiegelt sich in der Verwendung von Ni *YTR* in i 8 gegenüber i 9. Ist *šeʾar yašûb* asyndetischer Relativsatz („Ein/der Rest, der umkehrt"; L. Köhler, *VT* III, 1953, S. 84 f.), so überwiegt wohl der Unheilsaspekt: das anwesende Prophetenkind demonstriert dann durch seine Existenz, wie wenig übrigbleibt; ist es ein Verbalsatz mit voranstehendem Subjekt, bleibt alles offen wie in einem delphischen Orakel.

7) Vergleichbare Vertrauensnamen bei Stamm, *op. cit.*, S. 286 f.

xierten Psalms [1]). Das Mit-Sein Els oder Jahwes besteht dabei — wie das akkadische *alāku(m)* + *idu*, wenn es im Kriegsorakel oder Kriegsbericht von Göttern gebraucht wird [2]), und wie das aramäische *QŪM ʿim* [3]) — im Erweis kriegerischen Beistandes [4]), der in einem allgemeineren Sinne zugleich Ausdruck des Segens sein kann [5]). — Andrerseits aber spricht der Immanuel-Name auch für die Unheils- und Klagesituation, in der die Betroffenen in solchem Vertrauen ihre Zuflucht suchen. Insofern impliziert die entsprechende Anweisung an die königliche Familie eine Unheilsankündigung [6]).

2. Den Heilsaspekt des Vertrauensnamens erhebt die Deutung des V. 16 durch eine bedingungslose Heilsankündigung, die vii 7 b als Kern von vii 5-9a überbietet: nicht nur wird das Vorhaben der Feindstaaten nicht zustande kommen; auch ihr Land wird der Verlassenheit anheimfallen, so wie es Jesaja im abschließenden Rückblick auf seine Verkündigung dem eigenen Staate ansagt (vi 12 f.). Dabei meint die änigmatische Terminierung der Notzeit einen nahen Wendepunkt: in zwei bis drei Jahren, wenn das Kleinkind Verbotenes von Erlaubtem zu unterscheiden weiß, muß es nicht nur für den realpolitischen Blick des verkündigenden Propheten mit den Kontrahenten zuende sein (vgl. viii 4) [7]); die Zionsmythologie sah ja, darüber

---

[1]) Th. Lescow („Das Geburtsmotiv in den messianischen Weissagungen bei Jesaja und Micha", *ZAW* LXXIX 1967, S. 172-207, bes. 179 f.) zieht einen Zusammenhang des Namens mit Ps xlvi wegen dessen nachexilischer Fixierung in Zweifel. Aber Jesaja greift nicht auf Ps. xlvi, sondern auf die später von diesem und den anderen Zionspsalmen verarbeitete Tradition zurück. Vgl. meine S. 29 Anm. 1 genannten Arbeiten.

[2]) Beispiele bei M. Weippert, „'Heiliger Krieg' in Israel und Assyrien", *ZAW* LXXXIV, 1972, S. 460-493, bes. 471[42], 472[47], 473[55], 480.

[3]) KAI 202 A 14 (vgl. im „Jaʾūdischen" KAI 214, 2); H. D. Preuß, „... ich will mit dir sein!", *ZAW* LXXX, 1968, S. 139-173, bes. 162-164 (dort auch sumerisches und weiteres akkadisches Material).

[4]) Da es für den Völkerkampf, in dem El/Jahwe ihren Beistand erweisen, keine außerisraelitischen Parallelen gibt, es sich also um "ein eigenständiges, aus dem israelitischen Raum stammendes Motiv" handelt (G. Wanke, *Die Zionstheologie der Korachiten*, 1966, S. 72, 77), wird man seinen Ursprung (gegen Wanke) im Zusammenhang mit den Traditionen vom Jahwekrieg suchen, die mit der Lade nach Jerusalem kamen; neben der altkanaanäischen Chaoskampfvorstellung erfuhren die einzelnen Jahwekriege eine Totalisierung zum (urzeitlichen) Völkerkampf.

[5]) Vgl. D. Vetter, *Jahwes Mit-Sein ein Ausdruck des Segens*, 1971, S. 24.

[6]) Als Hilferuf hat den Immanuel-Namen zuletzt Lescow, *op. cit.* S. 176, 180, aufgefaßt; zur Ambivalenz seiner Bedeutung vor allem Stamm, zuletzt *op. cit.*, S. 290.

[7]) A. H. J. Gunneweg („Heils- und Unheilsverkündigung in Jes. vii", *VT* XV 1965, S. 27-34, bes. 31 f.) will nach dem Vorgang anderer V. 16 streichen, womit sowohl die Bedeutungsambivalenz des Immanuelnamens als auch des

hinausgehend, vor, daß Jahwe sich seiner Feinde plötzlich, *lipnôt boqär*, entledigt (Ps. xlvi 6).

Das Unheilsimplikat des Immanuel-Namens dagegen wird entfaltet, wenn an die Deutung des Namens als Element des Geburtsorakels mit V. 17 noch eine Unheilsankündigung angehängt wird, die im Sinne des Denkschriftverfassers der anklagenden Frage von V. 13b und dem daran anschließenden drohenden *laken* von V. 14 entspricht. Als Gerichtswort erweist sich V. 17 dabei zunächst durch das dreimalige *'ăl* mit der Nebenbedeutung „gegen": es wird schlimmer kommen, als es seit der Reichsteilung [1]) je gewesen ist [2]). Auch der Glossator, der aus viii 4 *'et mäläk 'ăššûr* ergänzte, hat den Vers im Gegensatz zu viii 4 als Unheilsorakel für Juda verstanden, ebenso der Redaktor, der in V. 18-20 zwei Fragmente von Gerichtsworten anfügte, und die Damaskusschrift in ihrem Zitat vii 10-12 [3]). Der unvermittelte Übergang von V. 16 und 17 in MT, Targ und Vulg beweist nur, daß beide Worte in der mündlichen Verkündigung noch je für sich standen und wohl erst durch den Denkschriftverfasser ohne sonderliches Geschick zusammengefügt wurden.

Das Nebeneinander von Heils- (V. 16) und Unheilsankündigung (V. 17) entspricht der Sequenz einer bedingungslosen Heilsankündigung und eines bedingten Satzes innerhalb von vii 5-9 [4]). Indem Ahaz mit seiner Weigerung in V. 12 der „Glaubens"forderung widersprochen und die Bedingung des „Bleibens" verfehlt hatte, konnte er sich doch der Entscheidungssituation nicht entziehen; das Entweder-Oder von vii 9b kommt in der Dialektik von Heilsangebot (16) und Unheilsdrohung (17) verschärft auf ihn zurück, bis durch eine endgültige Änderung der Lage die Entscheidungsstunde verstrichen ist. So vertreten die beiden Abschnitte vii 2-9 und 10-17 ein gemeinsames

---

ganzen Orakels verkannt wird. Ebenso erscheint uns die Eliminierung des Relativsatzes in 16bβ, durch die V. 16 zur Unheilsankündigung für Juda wird (so G. Fohrer, *Das Buch Jesaja* I, 1966², S. 169), als willkürlich.

[1]) Zur Verbindung von *le* und *min* in *lemiyyôm* „seit den Tagen" ist neben 2 Sam. vii 6 (vgl. Brockelmann, *Syntax*, § 119b) das Phönizische zu vergleichen (J. Friedrich- W. Röllig, *Phönizisch-punische Grammatik*, 1970, § 253). *le* ist hier also nicht emphatisch (gegen A. Schoors bei Fisher, *Ras Shamra Parallels* I, S. 47)

[2]) Hammershaimb, *op. cit.*, S. 137, versteht V. 17 als Heilsankündigung; die die Restauration der davididischen Herrschaft über das Nordreich ansagt; als Verheißung versteht das Wort auch W. Mc. Kane, „The Interpretation of Isaiah vii 14-25", *VT* XVII, 1967, S. 208-219, bes. 215, was u.E. der Vers selbst und sein Zusammenhang widerraten.

[3]) Vgl. auch J. J. Stamm, „Die Immanuel-Weissagung, ein Gespräch mit E. Hammershaimb", *VT* IV, 1954, S. 20-33, bes. S. 32.

[4]) Wildberger, *op. cit.*, S. 298.

Anliegen: was wie eine selbstgefällige In-Anspruch-Nahme göttlicher Hilfe für die eigenen Waffen klingen mag, ist gegenüber der Spitze einer sich eigengesetzlich verfestigenden Gesellschaft in Wirklichkeit die Unruhe des Ursprünglichen, die der resignierten Orientierung an immobilen Gegebenheiten überdrüssig ist (V. 13b). Mit dem vieldiskutierten Rückgriff auf die Tradition vom heiligen Kriege opponiert Jesaja letztlich gegen die hybride Überzeugung, daß die Gottheit immer bei den stärkeren Bataillonen sei [1]): darum gilt die Unheilsankündigung in V. 16 den Aramäern und Nordisraeliten und genauso in V. 17 den Judäern, die sich ohne Notwendigkeit auf die Seite Tiglat-Pilesers III schlagen wollen.

3. Die Anschlußformel *wehayā bǎyyôm hǎhû'* (V. 18.21.23) erweisen 18-20 ebenso wie 21 f. und 23-25 als redaktionelle Zusätze; sie schafft dabei einen stärkeren Einschnitt als *bǎyyôm hǎhû'* (V. 20), das sich syntaktisch einfügt. Tatsächlich scheinen die beiden Fragmente V. 18 f. und 20 nicht nur auf Jesaja selbst zurückzugehen [2]); sie laufen vielmehr auch weitgehend parallel, so daß ihre Zusammenfügung als ein Meisterstück redaktioneller Kunst angesehen werden muß. In beiden Worten ist die von Jahwe herbeigerufene Großmacht durch Metaphern bezeichnet: in V. 18 als Fliege und Biene [3]), in V. 20 als „gedungenes Messer" (lege *betǎ'arā śekîrā*, weil sich das Verb *tispā* am Ende des Verses auf ein fem. Nomen zurückbeziehen muß [4]); beidemal ist auch die Indienstnahme des fernhergeholten Werkzeugs metaphorisch bezeichnet: in V. 18 durch *yiśroq* [5]), in V. 20 durch *śekîrā*, wobei die lokalen Adverbiale *biqṣē ye'orê miṣrayim* und *be'äräṣ 'ǎššûr* (18) sowie *be'äbrê nahar* (20) zugleich der Dechiffrierung der

[1]) Vgl. H. Donner, *Israel unter den Völkern*, 1964, S. 18.

[2]) Wildberger, *op. cit.*, S. 302. Zur Formel *bǎyyôm hǎhu'* als „an editorial connective formula", u.a. auch zur Anfügung echter Worte an vorgegebene Sammlungen vgl. P. A. Munch, *The Expression Bajjôm Hāhû' — It is an Eschatological Terminus Technicus?* 1936, zu Jes vii 18 und 20 S. 21 f.

[3]) Die Doppelung des Bildes in V. 18 zu elimieren und deshalb die Worte *lǎzzebûb . . . miṣrayim* zu streichen (Wildberger, *op. cit.*, S. 303), empfiehlt sich u.E. nicht. Daß Ägypten z.Zt. des syrisch-ephraimitischen Krieges als politisch-militärischer Faktor zu zählen schien, zeigt die Tatsache, daß sich Assur 734 am *wādi el-'arīš* einen Stützpunkt geschaffen hatte (A. Alt, *Kleine Schriften* II, 1959, S. 160, 227 f.). Wahrscheinlich wurde V. 18 f. darum nicht in die Denkschrift aufgenommen, weil die Ägypten betreffende Ankündigung auch nach 732 nicht erfüllt worden war; nach 701 hat man darüber vielleicht anders geurteilt. Zu Ägypten als Fliege vgl. die Metapher xviii 1.

[4]) Auch im Ugar. ist *t'rt* „Scheide des Schwertes" femininum, I D 207; vgl. III D I 18, 29, wo die Bedeutung des Nomens unklar ist.

[5]) Zu *yiśroq . . . biqṣē* ist *weśarăq miqṣē ha'aräṣ* v 26 zu vergleichen.

Metaphern dienen [1]). Die Verben der jeweils zweiten Spruchhälfte haben dann die von Jahwe engagierten Werkzeuge zum Subjekt und gehören allein der Sachhälfte an: 19 *ûba'û w^enaḥû* (vgl. *naḥā* V. 2) und 20 *tispā̆*.

IV

1. Das änigmatische מהר שלל חש בז viii 1,3 besteht wohl doch — wie der akkadische Name für den Unterweltfährmann *Ḫumuṭṭabal* „Nimm eilends hinweg" [2]) und die ägyptische Redensart *ỉs ḥ3ḳ* (wörtlich:) „eile erbeute" [3]) — aus je zwei Imperativen, von denen der jeweils erste gegenüber dem zweiten adverbielle Funktion hat; das entspricht dem Verständnis von LXX zu viii 3: Ταχέως σκύλευσον, ὀξέως προνόμευσον [4]). Die Punktation lautete dann: מַהֵר שְׁלֹל[5]) חֻשׁ בֹּז (חָשׁ); die Umwandlung in einen Nominalsatz ist offenbar eine stilistische Erleichterung. Zum modalen Imperativ *māher* vor einem anderen asyndetisch angefügten Imperativ sind Gen. xix 22; Ri. ix 48; Ps. lxix 18; cii 3; cxliii 7; Est. vi 10 zu vergleichen [6]), zum adverbiellen Gebrauch der Wurzel *ḤĪŠ* vor *l^e* + Hab. Inf. i 8. Wenn in Jo. iv 11 mit BHS *ḥûšû wabo'û* zu lesen ist, hätten wir hier, in der Anrede an „alle Völker ringsum", eine unmittelbare syntaktische und sachliche Entsprechung. Als Adressat des Imperativ kann entweder wie ursprünglich wohl in dem ägyptischen Gegenstück und Jo. iv 11 cj. das Kriegsvolk gelten, hier das der Assyrer, oder Jahwe, wie denn auch der Name des Unterweltfährmanns aus einem Anruf an das Numen entstanden zu denken ist [7]). Freilich mag wie bei beiden

---

[1]) *b^emäläk 'äššûr* ist Glosse wie die Wendung am Ende von V. 17.

[2]) Belegt in Z. 45 der S. 26 Anm. 2 zitierten Unterweltsvision eines assyrischen Kronprinzen.

[3]) Belegt ist die Wendung in der formelhaften Bedeutung „leichte Beute" für die kriegerische Zeit der 18. Dynastie (A. Erman — H. Grapow, *Wörterbuch der ägyptischen Sprache* I, 1926, S. 126, III, 1929, S. 33). — Zum Zusammenhang mit Jes. viii 1,3 S. Morenz, *ThLZ* LXXIV, 1949, Sp. 697-699.

[4]) Der Vorschlag, alle vier Elemente des Wortgebildes als Imp. zu lesen, stammt von W. von Soden, *OLZ* XXXVII, 1934, Sp. 414[1]; vgl. P. Humbert, *ZAW* L, 1932, S. 90-92.

[5]) So entsprechend dem Inf. Qal Jes. x 6; Hes. xxxviii 12 f.

[6]) Vgl. E. Vogt, „ ‚Eilig tun' als adverbielles Verb und der Name des Sohnes Jesajas in Jes 8,1", *Bibl* XLVIII, 1967, S. 63-69, bes. 64[4], wo für die syndetische Verbindung des Imp. *māher* mit einem zweiten Imp. noch auf Gen. xlv 9 und 1 Sam. xxiii 27 hingewiesen wird.

[7]) Vgl. den phönizischen Personennamen *mhrb'l* (Belege bei L. Benz, *Personal Names in the Phoenician and Punic Inscriptions*, 1972, S. 340 f.), dessen Übersetzung als „Diener Ba'als" (KAI zu 64,2) wegen der Umkehrung *ba'alu-miḫir* EA 245, 44; 258,44; 259,2; 260,2 wohl doch Zweifeln unterliegt; vgl. den ugar. P.N. *ilmhr* (Gordon 2029:18). An *mhr* „to hasten" dachte Z. S. Harris, *A Grammar of the*

nichthebräischen Parallelbildungen der imperativische Sinn der Formel halb vergessen sein. Im Deutewort V. 4 entspricht den beiden adverbiellen Imperativen der Temporalsatz 4a, der wie seine Entsprechung vii 16a auf einen nahen Zeitpunkt zielt.

Im Unterschied zum Namen des Prophetensohns viii 3 wird die gleichlautende Inschrift durch *l^e* eingeführt. Da die Präposition vor dem zweiten Teil des Doppelausdrucks fehlt, kann sie sich nur auf das ganze Wortgebilde beziehen. Wenn wir WILDBERGERS Übersetzung von *ḥäräṭ ʾanûš* als „Unheilsschrift" übernehmen dürfen [1]), empfiehlt sich ein Verständnis der Präposition als Lamed explicativum „nämlich" [2]): der aufgegebene Wortlaut deutet an, was den Unheilscharakter der Inschrift ausmacht

Als Hintergrund von viii 1-4 ist ein erstes Scheitern der prophetischen Verkündigung zu vermuten: da Ahaz offenbar nicht daran dachte, seinen Sohn Immanuel zu nennen, bringt Jesaja unter Zeugen [3]) die Inschrift an und bestimmt den Träger eines ominösen Namens in seiner eigenen Familie.

2. Was viii 1-4 von den Davididen nur vermuten läßt, sagt viii 6 von „diesem Volk da" in dürren Worten. Der Giḥon mit dem damals noch oberirdischen Siloahkanal bezeichnet — wie (später) die mythische Übertreibung Ps. xlvi 5 — die Würde Jerusalems als Gottesstadt: diese aber wird von den Judäern mißachtet, wenn sie vor dem „Unwetter" Rezins und Pekaḥs in lauter Angst zerfließen [4]). Ab-

---

Phoenician Language, 1936, S. 116. Läßt sich ein Gebetsanruf „Eile, Baʿal!/Baʿal, eile!" entsprechend den Anrufen an Jahwe Ps. xxii 20; xxxviii 23; xl 14; lxx 2, 6; lxxi 12; cxli 1 vermuten?

[1]) *Op. cit.*, S. 312.

[2]) Zum Begriff F. NÖTSCHER, *VT* III, 1953, S. 378, der dazu u.a. auf Ps. cxxxv 10 f; 2 Chr. ii 12; xxviii 15 verweist. Die Verwendung des *l^e* in den Samaria-Ostraca und auf Krughenkeln ist nicht vergleichbar: der Prophetensohn, von dem erst in V. 3 die Rede ist, soll weder als Besitzer (Y. YADIN, „Recipients or Owners. A Note on the Samaria Ostraca", *IEJ* IX 1959, S. 184-187) noch als Empfänger von Waren (A. F. RAINEY, „Administration in Ugarit and the Samaria Ostraca", *BASOR* CLXIII, 1961, S. 12-14) bezeichnet werden (zum jetzigen Stand der Diskussion vgl. YADIN, *IEJ* XVIII, 1968, S. 50 f., und RAINEY, *PEQ* CII, 1970, S. 45-51); auch ist ihm die Tafel nicht wie ein Siegel zugeeignet. Die von GESENIUS-KAUTZSCH (*op. cit.*, § 119 u) für Jes. viii 1 und Hes. xxxvii 16 in die Diskussion eingeführte Bezeichnung Lamed inscriptionis kann m.E. entfallen; das akustische Kolon ist auch in solchem Falle *leʾmor* (A. E. EHRLICH, *Randglossen zur hebräischen Bibel* IV, 1968, S. 32), zu Hes. xxxvii 16 vgl. W. ZIMMERLI, *Ezechiel*, 1959 ff., S. 904.

[3]) xxx 8 nennt bei ähnlicher Gelegenheit die Inschrift selbst einen „Zeugen" (lege *l^eʿed* BHS).

[4]) Vermutlich liegt in 6b eine Art Haplographie vor: vor את־רצין sind aus ומשוש die Konsonanten משו noch einmal einzusetzen; der Text lautet dann:

weichend von der Aussageabsicht in Ps. xlvi 5 wird dann in V. 7 aα dem sanften Fluß des Siloah die Abundanz des Euphrat gegenübergestellt [1]), die in den entfaltenden Sätzen 7b. 8a Ausmaße einer Chaosflut annimmt. Auch der letztere Topos hat seinen ursprünglichen Platz in der Zionsmythologie: Ps. xlvi 3 f. spricht von einem Meer, das gegen Jerusalem anbraust. Das Motiv begegnet Jes. xvii 12-14 wieder [2]). Die beiden Verben *ŠṬP* und *ʿBR* von 8aα finden sich außerdem Jes. xxviii 15, 18, wozu noch xxviii 17 *măyim yišṭopû* zu vergleichen ist; die Wendung *ʿăd-ṣăwwaʾr yăggiʿac* von 8aβ hat in *ʿăd-ṣăwwaʾr yăḥăṣā* xxx 28 ihre Entsprechung: sie wird dort für einen durch Jahwes Gewittersturm (*rûaḥ*) reißend strömenden Bach (*năḥăl šôṭep*) gebraucht. — Anders als in Ps. xlvi 3 f., aber ebenso wie in Jes. xxx 28 bringt Jahwe nach viii 7.8a die verderbenbringenden Fluten selber über sein Volk, d.h. Tiglat-Pileser III, den die Judäer ungläubig als Helfer herbeirufen, soll zum Werkzeug des Gerichtes Jahwes werden (vgl. vii 18 f. 20).

Das harte Nebeneinander eines bedingungslosen Heilsorakels und einer Unheilsankündigung in vii 16 f. findet in dem Gegenüber von viii 1-4 und 6-8a sein Pendant [3]). Dabei steht neben der Unheilsankündigung 7.8a in V. 6 eine ausführliche Anklage, die dem Spruch

---

ומשוש משואת רצין; ähnlich K. Budde, „Jes 8,6b", *ZAW* XLIV, 1926, S. 65-67, und danach Wildberger, *op. cit.*, S. 321. Das Perf. *maʾăs* vom Anfang des Satzes wird also durch einen inf. abs. aufgenommen (zur Konstruktion Brockelmann, *Syntax*, § 46 c); משוש gehört dabei zur Wurzel מסס/משש „zerfließen" (zu מסס Qal Jes. x 18). שׁוֹאָה „Unwetter" in משואת ist im Zusammenhang mit מסס/משש ein wirksamer Gegensatz zu *mê hăššiloaḥ hăholekîm leʾăṭ*: anders als eine kanalisierte Quelle bringt jedes Unwetter Sturzfluten, vor denen alles zerfließt. Die angegebene Konjektur erklärt zugleich, warum bei *ûbăn-remălyahû* das Pendant zu der scheinbaren nota accusativi vor *reṣîn* fehlt.

[1]) Wieder ist *ʾăt-mäläk ʾăššûr*, diesmal zusammen mit *weʾăt-kål-kebôdô*, zu streichen.

[2]) Die Echtheit von xvii 12-14 wird (ebenso wie die von viii 9 f.) von G. Fohrer und seinen Schülern bestritten; vgl. dagegen H. M. Lutz, *Jahwe, Jerusalem und die Völker*, 1968, S. 40-51, 215, der freilich den Charakter von xvii 12-14 als Seherspruch verkennt (vgl. S. 31 Anm. 2) und darum 14b falsch beurteilt. Aber selbst wenn etwa xvii 12-14 unecht wäre, ließe sich schwerlich bestreiten, daß der Zionsmythologie für die Verkündigung Jesajas eine Modellfunktion zukommt: die betreffende Topik liegt einer ganzen Reihe von Worten zugrunde, deren Echtheit auch Fohrer nicht bestreitet, etwa viii 18, xiv 24-27, 28-32; xxviii 14-22 (bes. 15-18); xxix 1-7(-8); xxx 27-33*; xxxi 4 f., 8 f. J. Vollmer (*Geschichtliche Rückblicke und Motive in der Prophetie des Amos, Hosea und Jesaja*, 1971, S. 194 f.) bezweifelt noch xiv 32 und xxix 6 f., womit sich aber auch nichts Grundsätzliches beweisen läßt.

[3]) Mit drei sich steigernden Redegängen innerhalb von vii 3-viii 8a rechnet auch O. H. Steck, „Bemerkungen zu Jes 6", *BZ* XVI 1972, S. 188-206, bes. 199[29].

6-8a ein Eigengewicht verleiht, wie es vii 17 innerhalb 13-17 nicht besitzt. Darüber hinaus soll viii 1-4 nun im Lichte von viii 6-8a verstanden werden: daß die Judäer die Würde Jerusalems als der Gottesstadt mißachteten, wurde u.a. an ihrer Unempfänglichkeit gegenüber solchen Worten wie viii (1,3) 4 deutlich, die ihm doch nur Heil in Aussicht stellten. Durch den Hinweis auf die damals unter Zeugen erstellte Inschrift und den Namen des Prophetenkindes, der jedermann im Ohr ist, gibt der Denkschriftverfasser zu erkennen, daß Juda, wenn es am Ende der syrisch-ephraimitischen Krise Vasall der Assyrer wird, dabei nicht an Jahwes Abwendung gescheitert ist, sondern vielmehr gerade an seiner Zuwendung, der es nicht entsprochen hat: das ausgeschlagene Heilsangebot droht als versäumte Gelegenheit zur Unheilsursache zu werden [1]).

V

1. Wie vii 4-9a und viii 1-4 ist viii 9 f. eine bedingungslose Heilsankündigung; stärker als andere Sprüche der Denkschrift ist der Text am Modell der Zionsmythologie orientiert.

(a) In einer Gegensatzentsprechung zum Völkerorakel Ps. xlvi 11, das von einem aussichtslosen Kampf gegen den Zion abzusehen mahnt, wird in V. 9, 10a eine irreführende Aufforderung zum Kampf [2]) an die (abwesenden) Feinde gerichtet, und zwar unmittelbar durch die Imperative רעו „erhebt den Kriegsruf!" [3]) und *hitʾăzzᵉrû* „gürtet euch!", mittelbar durch die imperativischen Wendungen *ʿuṣû ʿeṣā* und *dăbbᵉrû dabar*, wobei der betreffende Plan (*ʿeṣā*) zweifellos mit dem

---

[1]) Entsprechendes gilt von den zurückliegenden Heilsankündigungen, die Jes. xxviii 12a und xxx 15a zitiert werden: Juda wollte auf das Angebot von Ruhe und Geborgenheit (xxviii 12a), von *šûbā* (?), Ruhe, Gelassenheit und Sicherheit (xxx 15) nicht eingehen (xxviii 12b; xxx 15b. 16) und trug sich damit die Okkupation (xxviii 11), ja die Zerstörung ein (xxx 17); die Sätze der einstigen Zusage treten so in den Irrealis.

[2]) Vgl. zu dieser Gattung R. Bach, *Die Aufforderung zur Flucht und zum Kampf im alttestamentlichen Prophetenspruch*, 1962, S. 51 ff.

[3]) M. Saebø („Zur Traditionsgeschichte von Jes. 8,9-10", *ZAW* LXXVI, 1964, S. 132-144) leitet die Form mit Recht von *RŪʿ* (besser: *RĪʿ*; H.-P. Müller, *VT* XXI, 1971, S. 559) ab, das sonst freilich nur im (Pseudo-?) Hiphʿil begegnet; vielleicht ist arabisch *RŪʿ* I (II und IV) „erschrecken, in Angst, Furcht setzen" zu vergleichen. Dann ist entweder רֻעוּ zu punktieren, und zwar assonant und in orthographischer Analogie zu folgendem עֻצוּ (Imp. Qal von *ʿŪṢ*, da ein Imp. Qal von *YʿṢ* fehlt), oder MT רֹעוּ ist als unregelmäßiger Imp. Qal nach Analogie der Verben mediae geminatae aufzufassen (Saebo, *op. cit.*, S. 143). Das von LXX vorausgesetzte דְּעוּ ist als Angleichung an Ps. xlvi 11 ein Zeugnis des Bewußtseins vom Zusammenhang unseres Spruches mit den Zionspsalmen.

der syrisch-ephraimitischen Koalition von vii 5a identisch ist [1]). Durch den Ruf des Propheten ist es hier — wie vii 18 f., 20; viii 7.8a — noch einmal Jahwe, der die Feinde, diesmal aber zu ihrem Verderben, nach Jerusalem ruft. Der Plural der Anrede läßt sich dabei nicht zeitgeschichtlich erklären [2]), sondern entspricht wie die pluralischen Imperative *hărpû ûdeʿû* von Ps. xlvi 11 dem zionsmythologischen Rezeptionsmodell: neben dem Anbrausen des Meeres kennt die Zionsmythologie den Sturm von Völkern und Königen gegen die Stadt [3]). Die mythische Totalisierung einer zeitgeschichtlichen Situation ist einerseits ein Versuch, der Dramatik geschichtlicher Entscheidung gerecht zu werden; insofern die Universalität des Dramas andrerseits dessen künftige Korrektur oder Überbietung prinzipiell ausschließt, wird der Lauf der Geschichte, kaum daß man ihn an einem Höhepunkt realisierte, sofort wieder zum Stehen gebracht [4]).

(b) Während die Feinde Zions durch ihren Kriegsruf noch selber Schrecken erregen sollen, verfallen sie auch schon der von Jahwe unter ihnen angerichteten Panik [5]). Die Zionsmythologie verhilft also nicht nur zu einem religiösen Verstehen andringender Katastrophen, sie ermöglicht zugleich eine Vorstellung des zu Erhoffenden [6]). Neben *wetupar* [7]) bezeichnet *welo' yaqûm*, das vii 7b wieder aufnimmt, das Scheitern der feindlichen Pläne.

(c) Der Sequenz von Imperativen (a) und z.Tl. ebenfalls imperativisch formulierten Ankündigungen (b) folgt ebenso wie in vii 4-9a

---

[1]) Hierin liegt m.E. ein wichtiges Argument für die Echtheit des Wortes; zu Vokabular und Stil des Stücks hat Wildberger, *op. cit.*, S. 331, das Nötige gesagt. Vgl. S. 46 Anm. 2, S. 47 Anm. 3.

[2]) Gegen Donner, *op. cit.*, S. 26, und Fohrer, *Das Buch Jesaja* I, S. 128.

[3]) Ps. xlvi 7; xlviii 5.

[4]) Ebenso ist Jes. xiv 26 bei der Vernichtung der Assyrer (V. 25) zugleich die ganze Erde vom Plan Jahwes betroffen, und die Hand Jahwes ist über alle Völker ausgestreckt. xxviii 22 bringt das Gericht über Juda (V. 14) in Verbindung mit einer Vertilgung, die über die ganze Erde kommt. Der Visionsbericht xxx 28 spricht von *gôyim* und *ʿămmîm* als Opfern der gottgewirkten Katastrophe; die Deutung V. 31 dagegen beschränkt sie auf Assur (vgl. S. 31 Anm 2). Die universale Entschränkung des gegenständlichen Heils- bzw. Unheilsgeschehens erhebt dessen Ankündigung ins Eschatologische.

[5]) Zu *ḤTT* im zionsmythologischen Zusammenhang Jes. ix 3; xxx 31; xxxi 4,9; vgl. vii 8b; xx 5; xxxvii 27 als sekundäre Stücke. Zur Sache noch xvii 13; xxix 5 f.

[6]) Zur Panik in den Zionspsalmen xlvi 7; xlviii 6 f.; lxxvi 6 f.

[7]) *wetupăr* wird statt *wekuppăr* nach Targ auch xxviii 18 zu lesen sein, was auch das Objekt *berît* nahelegt; als Parallelglied erscheint dort ähnlich wie in unserem Spruch *welo' taqûm*.

eine Begründung, die in V. 10bβ freilich nur noch fragmentarisch erhalten ist. Ihr voller Wortlaut ist aber aus 8b zu entnehmen, wo er den Zusammenhang sprengt: von der Topik der Chaosflut 7b.8a kann man nicht zum Bild der Raubvogelflügel überwechseln; vollends grotesk wäre die Vorstellung von Flügeln einer Flut. Vielmehr ist die Wendung *muṭṭôt kᵉnapâw mᵉloʾ roḥăb-ʾărṣᵉka* 8b zwischen die Worte *kî* und *ʿimmanû ʾel* 10bβ einzusetzen: „denn seine [1] ausgespannten Flügel füllen die Weite deines Landes [2], Immanuel". Vermutlich ist der Satz einmal irrtümlich auch an das Ende von 8b geraten; dann schien einerseits *kî* wegen der Spannung des Satzes gegenüber dem Vorangehenden unpassend, so daß es durch die Anschlußformel *wᵉhayā* ersetzt wurde; andrerseits wird man in 10bβ, um eine Wiederholung zu vermeiden, den Satz bis auf das Anfangs- und Endglied getilgt haben. Das Bild von den ausgebreiteten Flügeln bezeichnet Jahwes schützende Macht [3]; im Zusammenhang zionsmythologischer Motive verwendet Jesaja das Bild noch xxxi 5 [4]. Begründete vii 8a, 9a die Aussicht auf das Scheitern der feindlichen Pläne negativ mit dem Hinweis auf die Ohnmacht der Feinde, so geschieht es hier positiv im Vertrauen auf Jahwes heilvolle Gegenwart; den Unheilsankündigungen an die Feinde innerhalb von viii 9, 10abα folgt in dem wiederhergestellten V. 10bβ die Heilszusage an Israel.

2. Bei viii (11) 12-15 handelt es sich um ein Diskussionswort, das einem engeren Kreis abrät, in das Verschwörungsgerede der Öffentlichkeit einzustimmen (V. 12), und den entsprechenden positiven Rat (13) in einer Unheilsankündigung entfaltet (14 f.).

Wenn die Hand (Jahwes) den Propheten daran hindert [5], „auf

---

[1] Vielleicht ist statt *kᵉnapâw*: *kănpê YHWH* zu lesen.

[2] Zu *ʾărṣᵉka* vgl. auf Jahwe bezogenes *ʾărṣî* und *harăy* xiv 25.

[3] Ps. xci 4; Ru. ii 12.

[4] Die *ṣippᵒrîm ʿapôt* von xxxi müssen nicht ängstlich flatternde Kleinvögel sein (gegen O. Procksch, *Jesaja* I, 1930, S. 407): nur als Raubvögel bieten sie ein Pendant zu dem Löwen des Parallelvergleichs von V.4; V. 5 zu streichen, besteht keine Handhabe. Daß *ṣippôr* den Raubvogel bezeichnen kann, zeigt neben Hes. xxxix 4 (Zimmerli, *op. cit.*, S. 929) die Tatsache, daß das Wort wie ugar. *ṣpr* (C. H. Gordon, *UT* Glossary Nr. 2186) als männlicher Vorname verwendet wird. *ʿŪP* bezeichnet das majestätische Schweben, wenn es etwa von den Seraphen (Jes. vi 2,6; xiv 29; xxx 6) oder vom Herabfahren Jahwes auf den Cheruben (Ps xviii 11) gebraucht wird. — Zum Bildtopos als ganzem vgl. den Satz der Asarhaddon-Inschrift Nin A I 67 f.: „Wie ein fliegender Aar (?) breitete ich meine 'Schwingen' aus zur Niederwerfung meiner Feinde"; R. Borger, *Die Inschriften Asarhaddons*, 1956, S. 43 f.

[5] Mit 1QJesᵃ, σ und Syr wird man וַיְסִ(י)רֵנִי zu lesen haben; das Impf. hat hier seine ursprüngliche Funktion als präteritaler Punktual bewahrt.

dem Wege dieses Volkes zu gehen" (V. 11), so beanspruchen solche geheimen Erfahrungen um so eher ein esoterisches Eigeninteresse, als sich auch die Adressaten der inspirierten Rede von „diesem Volk" abheben sollen (12); wie der Anfang der öffentlichen Verkündigung wird auch der erste Schritt in ein arcanum durch eine besondere Offenbarung legitimiert, obwohl das argumentierende Reden von 12-15 einer unmittelbaren göttlichen Autorisierung nicht bedurft hätte. V. 12 zeigt darüber hinaus, wie sehr der Prophet bereits Anlaß hat, wenigstens bei einem kleinen Kreis die Legitimität seines Dienstes [1]) außer Frage zu stellen. Die Mahnung, statt des Propheten Jahwe für einen Verschwörer zu halten (13 [2])), soll an die Stelle der Furcht vor einer politischen Bedrohung durch Worte, die das eigene Dilemma aufdecken, die Angst um den Existenzgrund Israels treten lassen: indem der Prophet an den Verleumdungen seiner Adressaten zu scheitern droht, ist es zugleich „dieses Volk" selbst, das seinen Gott in einen Verschwörer verwandelt, worin die Interdependenz von göttlichem und menschlichem Handeln ihren Verhängnisaspekt enthüllt.

Die Unheilsankündigung (V. 14 f.) verkehrt darum eine Reihe von Motiven der älteren Religion, insbesondere der Zionsmythologie, in ihr Gegenteil [3]). Hieß schon einer der Vätergötter *ʾäbän yiśraʾel* Gen. xlix 24 und verehrte man in Bethel einen Stein als Wohnstatt Els, so ist *ṣûr* die Bezeichnung des Jerusalemer Gottesberges (Jes. xxx 29), insbesondere aber Els [4]) bzw. Jahwes [5]) als seines Besitzers. Doch nun wird der göttliche „Stein" zum „Stein des Anstoßes" [6]), der göttliche „Fels" vollends aus einem „Fels der (rettenden) Macht"

---

[1]) Inwiefern gerade Jesaja allseitig in den Verdacht der Verschwörung geraten mußte, hat DONNER, *op. cit.*, S. 29, dargelegt. WILDBERGER, *op. cit.*, S. 337, denkt, unter Absehung von Jesaja, an einen Umsturzversuch bei Hofe; aber Jesaja hätte keinen Anlaß, eine geplante Palastrevolution zugunsten Ben-Tabels vom Vorwurf der Verschwörung reinzuwaschen.

[2]) Statt *tăqdîšû* und *miqdaš* ist in 13, 14a mit den meisten *tăqšîrû* „(ihn) nennt Verschwörer" und *miqšar* „Verschwörung" zu lesen, nicht *măqšîr*, was als Part. eines deklarativ-ästimativen Hi sinnlos wäre (gegen BHS).

[3]) Daß die ungehorsamen Entscheidungen Judas Jahwes Plan verkehren, sprechen spätere Worte wie xxix 14 und xxviii (23-) 29 aus, wobei der Prophet das Hi *PLʾ* variiert, um das Auffallende, Befremdende solchen Wandels zu beschreiben (vgl. *zar* und *nåkriyyā* xxviii 21); eine andere Bedeutungsbestimmung zu *PLʾ* jetzt bei H. J. STOEBE, *ThZ* XXVIII, 1972, S. 13-23.

[4]) Dtn. xxxii 18; Ps. xvii 3; lxxxix 27; vgl. den ugar. P.N. *ilabn* (GORDON 1131:3).

[5]) Neben Jes. xvii 10 noch Ps. xviii 32, 47.

[6]) Die ähnliche „jaʾūdische" Wendung *ʾbn šḥt KAI* 215, 7 bezeichnet offenbar den Anstifter von Thronwirren.

(Jes. xvii 10) [1]) zum „Fels des Strauchelns", das auf das Anstoßen folgt.

So entspricht dem strahlenden Heilswort viii 9 f. in V. 14 f. eine um so düsterere Unheilsankündigung, mit der zugleich das Korpus der Denkschrift abschließt; wenn dabei sowohl das Heil als auch das Unheil nach zionsmythologischem Modell angesagt wird, macht sich der dialektische Systemwille des Denkschriftverfassers nur noch mit um so größerer Kraft geltend [2]).

3. Man mag den Umgang des Propheten mit der Zionsüberlieferung einen entmyth(olog)isierenden nennen: die Historisierung des Mythos in den Heilsankündigungen, vor allem aber die Umkehrung seiner heilschaffenden Funktion in den Unheilsankündigungen scheinen ihn in der Tat am Nerv seines Wesens zu treffen; dazu kommt die Eklektik der prophetischen Traditionsverwendung [3]). Die Historisierung nimmt aber nur ein geschichtskonformes Element auf, das den handelnden und leidenden Gestalten des Mythos in ihrem Verhältnis zueinander und zur nicht-göttlichen Wirklichkeit immer schon inhärierte [4]), und die Umkehrung seiner Heilsfunktion entspricht einer inhaltlichen Ambivalenz des Mythos, insofern er — etwa als Durchgangssituation [5]) — von vornherein ein Stück unheilbannenden Antimythos' [6]) in sich trägt. — Umgekehrt kann man die Verkündigung Jesajas auch auf die durch sie vollzogene Mythisierung

---

[1]) *maʿôz* ist mit *KBL* eher von *ʿZZ* als von *ʿŪZ* abzuleiten, weshalb sich die Übersetzung mit „Zufluchtstätte" (so *KBL*) wenigstens nicht an erster Stelle empfiehlt.

[2]) Wenn es J. Vollmer (*op. cit.*, S. 192) unklar ist, warum ein Redaktor viii 9 f. „gerade hier plaziert haben soll, wenn es ihm um den Zusammenhang mit Jes. vii 1 ff. gegangen sein soll", da der Spruch „völlig der Intention der Worte im Kontext viii 5-8 und viii 11-15" widerspreche, so liegt das daran, daß das Aufbauprinzip von vii 1 - viii 15 verkannt wird, das durch den Wechsel von Heils- und Unheilsankündigungen bestimmt ist.

[3]) Jesaja konnte das Gericht über Juda auch nach dem Modell des Jahwetages (ii 12-17) oder ganz ohne mythisches Vorbild (etwa iii 1-9; iii 25—iv 1; ix 7-20 + v 25-30) ansagen.

[4]) Daß die übliche Diastatik von Mythos und Geschichte das Wesen beider verkennt, zeigt der Verfasser in: *Mythos — Tradition — Revolution. Phänomenologische Untersuchungen zum AT*, 1973, S. 83-94, auf.

[5]) Worte wie i 21-26; xxix 1-7(8) lassen das Gericht als eine solche Durchgangssituation erkennen und entsprechen darin der Zionsmythologie unmittelbarer: Jahwes Strafe ist ein Läuterungsgericht; auf Unheil folgt plötzliche Rettung. Ähnlich ist in die Unheilsankündigung gegen Juda xxviii 14-22 eine Heilsankündigung für den Rest (V. 16, 17a) eingefügt, die faktisch das Heil an einen Zeitpunkt jenseits des Gerichts verlegt.

[6]) Zum Begriff des Antimythos A. Jolles, *Einfache Formen*, 1968[4], S. 124.

der Geschichte hin abhören: wird doch die Zeitgeschichte einem mythischen Modell anverwandelt, um so in ihrer Kontingenz bewältigt zu werden. Die Mythisierung macht Geschichte allererst überschaubar und als Ort des Handelns Jahwes begreiflich; selbst das Ineinander von Heil und schließlichem Unheil prägt sie noch einem Prototyp nach, der dem Katastrophalen eine Art Harmonie verleiht.

VI

1. Die schon in viii 12-15 vollzogene Wendung an einen engeren Kreis wird mit viii 16-18 vorläufig verewigt.

Der Entschluß, den die Infinitivi absoluti *ṣôr* „verschnüren" und *ḥatôm* „versiegeln" [1]) bezeichnen, richtet sich, was immer man sich konkret darunter vorstellen mag, auf ein Bewahren vor Verminderung oder Veränderung. Insbesondere zu *ḤTM* denkt man an die Konservierung verbaler, vorwiegend rechtsverbindlicher Inhalte etwa in Urkunden [2]). Entsprechend benennt *teʿûdā* die Materialisierung einer rechtlichen Bestimmung in einer deklarativen Handlung (Ru. iv 7) oder, an unserer Stelle, in einem Schriftstück, wie es der wurzelverwandte [3]) Begriff *ʿedût* im Auge hat [4]); in Qumran sind

---

[1]) Die von MT vorausgesetzten Imp. widersprechen nicht nur dem Zusammenhang mit dem zweifelhaften *belimmuday* sondern auch dem mit V. 17 f.

[2]) Jer. xxxii 10 f., 14, 44; Neh. x 1 f.; Est. viii 8, 10 (vgl. Hi. xiv 17). Anders wird *ḤTM* in der nachexilischen Prophetie (Jes. xxix 11) und in der Apokalyptik (Dan. xii 4,9 gebraucht, wenn das Versiegeln der Weissagung diese zeitweilig dem gemeinen Verstande entzieht; doch können die genannten u.ä. Stellen auf allegorischer Auslegung von Jes. viii 16 beruhen.

[3]) Sowohl *teʿûdā*, als auch *ʿed* „Zeuge" und — davon abgeleitet (?) — *ʿedût* leiten sich von Qal/Hi *ʿŪD* (Grundbedeutung: „wiederholen") her; auch im Ugar. ist aus dem abstrakten Begriff *tʿdt* „Botschaft" ein Konkretum („Bote") geworden (GORDON, Nr. 1832).

[4]) Die *ʿedût* von 2 Kön. xi 12 ist wohl weniger ein nach Analogie des ägyptischen *nḫb.t* vorzustellendes „Königsprotokoll" mit den königlichen Thronnamen (so G. VON RAD, „Das judäische Königsritual", *Gesammelte Studien zum AT*, 1958, S. 205-213; dagegen B. VOLKWEIN, „Masoretisches *ʿēdût*, *ʿēdwôt*, *ʿēdôt* — 'Zeugnis' oder 'Bundesbestimmungen'?", *BZ* XIII, 1969, S. 18-40, bes. 28-30), sondern eher die „Urkunde", in der die Bestimmungen des Davidbundes festgelegt gewesen sein mögen (so A. R. JOHNSON, *Sacral Kingship in Ancient Israel*, 1967², S. 23-25). Diese wurden dem König übergeben, wie nach späterer Vorstellung die Tafeln mit den Bestimmungen des Sinaibundes (*luḥot haʿedût* Ex. xxxi 18; xxxii 15; xxxiv 29; *haʿedût* Ex. xxv 16, 21; xl 20) Mose übergeben wurden, wie denn seit dem Dtn-Rahmen (iv 45; vi 17, 20) und dem Dtr (1 Kön. ii 3; 2 Kön. xvii 15; xxiii 3; Jer. xliv 23) der Plural *ʿedot* bzw. *ʿedwotâw* zum terminus technicus für das "Gesetz" wird. — Als Wechselbegriff für „Gesetz" scheint *teʿûdā* auch Jes. viii 20 — neben voranstehendem *tôrā* (!) — aufgefaßt, zumal wir es hier mit einer exilischen oder noch späteren Zufügung zu tun haben.

te'ûdā / te'ûdôt termini technici für die „Bestimmungen" des Festkalenders [1]), des heiligen Krieges [2]), des Gesetzes [3]), der urzeitlichen Providenz [4]), der Naturordnung [5]), aber auch der Setzungen aus Gottes heilsgeschichtlichem Handeln [6]). *tôrā* bezeichnet demgegenüber — als Inhalt der *te'ûdā*, aber weniger juridisch — den „(prophetischen Orakel-) Bescheid", was dem Begriffsgebrauch in Jes. xxx 8 f. entspricht, wo die diesen beurkundende Inschrift zwar nicht wie hier *te'ûdā*, wohl aber ein „Zeuge" (*'ed* [7]) genannt wird. Tendiert der Begriff *te'ûdā* somit auf etwas schriftlich Festzulegendes, so umschreibt er zusammen mit *tôrā* wohl nichts anderes als die vorliegende Denkschrift des Propheten, die zunächst wie die Inschriften von viii 1 f. und xxx 8 f. die Funktion hat, bei der Erfüllung des Angekündigten im Sinne von Hes. ii 5 vor Augen zu führen, „daß ein Prophet unter ihnen war". Das textkritisch unsichere *belimmuday* ist dann um so eher mit G. Fohrer als Verschreibung eines nicht mehr rekonstruierbaren Wortes oder als Zusatz zu betrachten [8]); Jesaja hat seine Worte in einer Denkschrift niedergelegt oder niederlegen lassen [9]) und sich nicht auf das Gedächtnis seiner Getreuen verlassen.

V. 18 schließt den Kreis mit vi 1-4; Jahwe ist, wie ihn Jesaja bei seiner Berufung schaut: *hăššoken behăr ṣiyyôn.*

2. Zuletzt aber bleibt die Frage, die mit der Hoffnung auf die Erfüllung des Angekündigten noch nicht beantwortet ist: welchen Sinn hat Jesajas erfolglose Sendung?

Jes. vi 9-11 überbietet das Wort von Jahwe als Verschwörer (viii 13 f.) durch die Rede von der durch den Propheten herbeigeführten Verstockung. Was war das Verstockende an seiner Verkündigung? 1 Kön. xxii 19 ff. als Vorbild zu Jes. vi weist uns auf die Heilsver-

---

[1]) 1QS i 9; iii 10; 1QM xiv 13; 4QMa 11.

[2]) 1QM ii 8; xi 8; xv 1.

[3]) 1QH vi 19.

[4]) 1QS iii 16; 1QH i 19.

[5]) 1QH xii 9.

[6]) 1QM xiv 4.

[7]) Vgl. S. 45 Anm. 3.

[8]) *Studien zur alttestamentlichen Prophetie*, S. 140-146; dagegen scheint mir das Implikat einer schriftlichen Fixierung im Begriff *te'ûdā* verkannt, wenn Fohrer den Gedanken an ein Aufschreiben der Orakel von viii 16 fernhalten will; den bloßen Beschluß einer resignierten Einstellung der Verkündigung bezeichnet V. 16 angesichts von V. 17 keinesfalls, zumal die *'otôt* und *môpetîm* von V. 18 auch als lebendige Zeugen weiterhin des deutenden Wortes bedürfen.

[9]) Auf komplizierte Abfassungsverhältnisse deutet es vielleicht, daß von Jesaja in Kap. vii in 3. Person, in Kap. vi und viii dagegen im Selbstbericht die Rede ist.

kündigung als Inhalt einer eher kasuellen Sendung [1]). Zwar war Jesaja auch in seinen Heilsorakeln kein von Gott Betrogener wie die Nabi-Gruppe zur Zeit des Ahab; Jahwe hatte ja nicht einem Dritten wie Micha ben Jimla, sondern ihm selbst in seine Täuschungsabsicht Einblick gewährt. Und der Fehler der Judäer bestand nicht darin, ihrem Gott leichtfertig geglaubt zu haben. Vielmehr hatten Ahaz und sein Volk der Bedingung des Bleibens von vii 9b nicht entsprochen, und so war es doch eben das ausgeschlagene Heilsangebot, das die Interdependenz von göttlichem und menschlichem Handeln in ihrem Verhängnisaspekt enthüllte. Noch einmal wird darum in vi 9-11 Geschichte mythisiert, hier freilich nicht so sehr die des Volkes in seiner Auseinandersetzung mit den Weltmächten als vielmehr die des Propheten zwischen Gott and seinem Volk; das Motiv von der Täuschung des Menschen durch Jahwe bzw. der Widerspruch von Vernichtungsbeschluß und Retterwillen in der Gottheit deutet selbst noch die düstere Ambivalenz von Heil und Verhängnis innerhalb des Wirklichkeitsganzen als den Ausdruck eines göttlichen Waltens, das den Menschen allerdings „anstoßen" und „straucheln" läßt (viii 14). Jesajas allerletztes Wort zur syrisch-ephraimitischen Krise ist denn auch die schroffe Unheilsankündigung von vi 11-13. Ähnlich ließ er im Jahre 701, als sich eine Reihe neuer Heilsorakel [2]) cum grano salis erfüllt hatte, seine Verkündigung in Klagen über die Verwüstung Jerusalems wie i 4-9; xxii 1-14; xxxii 9-14 enden, wobei dem relativ hoffnungsvollen Ausblick von i 9 das abschließende Urteil von xxii 5a, 14 noch einmal widerspricht.

---

[1]) So M. Buber, *Der Glaube der Propheten*, 1950, S. 188 ff.; vgl. aber auch J. M. Schmidt, „Gedanken zum Verstockungsauftrag Jesajas (Jes. vi)", *VT* XXI, 1971, S. 68-90.

[2]) x 5-15; xiv 24-27; xvii 12-14; xxix 1-7(8); xxx 27-33; xxxi 4 f. 8 f.

A NOTE ON THE ORACLES OF AMOS AGAINST GAZA, TYRE, AND EDOM

BY

KEITH N. SCHOVILLE

University of Wisconsin-Madison

A recent commentary on Amos and Isaiah portrays the oracles of Amos as "powerful words which have fascinated, moved, and perplexed a hundred generations" [1]. That the Book of Amos continues to attract the interest and to motivate the thinking of contemporary scholarship is evident in the number of articles and studies which have appeared in print recently, studies which deal either with particular problems within the work or with the book as a whole [2]. Perhaps no other section in Amos has stimulated as many questions as have the "oracles against the nations" (i 3-ii 3), and it has been the twice-repeated expression *gālût šᵉlēmāh*, 'a whole captivity,' that has fascinated and perplexed us and moved us to seek out a plausible explanation for the phrase.

Our attention is focussed on three of the oracles in particular—those against Gaza, Tyre, and Edom (i 6-12)—because they appear to be closely connected to one another by a combination of conceptual and terminological binders that include the repeated, specific references to Edom in all three oracles [3], its role as the recipient of the *gālût šᵉlēmāh*, and the fact that both Gaza and Tyre are charged with delivering over such a 'whole captivity'. There is a widely-accepted theory that the oracles against Tyre and Edom are secondary, and this view has recently been reasserted by James L. Mays who argues, particularly concerning Edom, that it fits the conduct of that nation at the time of the collapse of Judah so closely "that it must have been formulated in the same period" and that "its formal correspondence to the Judah oracle also indicates that it did not stand in the original series" [4]. In this writer's opinion, however, Shalom M. Paul has shown quite convincingly in a recent article

---

1) James M. Ward, *Amos and Isaiah* (Nashville, 1969), p. 22.

2) In addition to the several articles consulted in the preparation of this note and cited below, compare the list of works given by Shalom M. Paul, *JBL*, 90 (1971), p. 397.

3) Amos i 6, i 9, and i 11.

4) James L. Mays, *Amos* (London, 1969), p. 36; cf. p. 25.

that "the systematic, coherent literary ordering of all the individual nations" [1]) in these oracles links them together "in an indissoluble bond occasioned by the well-known mnemonic device of the concatenation of similar catch words, phrases, or ideas common to *only* the two units contiguous to one another" [2]). There are, then, sufficient reasons based on literary considerations (and after all we are dealing with a written document) for accepting the original correlation of the oracles [3]). Thus we take these oracles to be the authentic expressions of the prophet, arranged most likely by Amos himself, or possibly by a later editor, as a single literary composite connected by a system of overlapping expressions and ideas which includes the "concatenous literary pattern" [4]). These features are discernible in the oracles leveled against Gaza, Tyre, and Edom where we find the repetition of the charge that both Gaza and Tyre were guilty of 'carrying away captive a whole captivity (people) to deliver them over to Edom' [5]).

It appears that the prophetic writer is alluding to an historical event or a series of historical occurrences in these three oracles. It may be assumed that it was an incident with which his audience was familiar and to whom it had an element of personal meaning [6]). The nature

---

1) "Amos 1:3-2:3: A Concatenous Literary Pattern," *JBL*, 90 (1971), p. 399. Note also the relevant remarks of Erling HAMMERSHAIMB, *The Book of Amos* (New York, 1970), p. 35. He responds to the argument that the threats against Tyre and Edom are not authentic because they do not follow exactly the structural pattern of the other oracles by stating that "it is a bad principle to lay down rules for what verse patterns and strophe formations Amos could have used. He varies the verses freely as he wishes to, and not according to the rules of European metre." James MAYS opts for the view that the series comprises a rhetorical unit (*op. cit.*, p. 26).

2) PAUL, *op. cit.*, p. 401. One need not accept the emphasis on exclusivity that marks his view in order to recognize and appreciate the basic validity of his view. In the case of Gaza, Tyre, and Edom, the phrases and ideas are not restricted only to the two units adjacent to one another.

3) See PAUL, p. 400, who notes with approval the view of M. HARAN that those who consider the Tyre oracle a late interpolation because it contains almost literally a repetition of the charges brought against Philistia have failed to realize that this is a natural way in which to express complicity in a similar crime.

4) PAUL, p. 397.

5) A further tie which binds Tyre to Edom is the repetition of the idea of "brotherly relationships," seen in the expressions in Amos i 9 and i 11, *b*ᵉ*rît* ʾ*aḥîm* and ʾ*āḥî*(*y*)*w* respectively.

6) Y. KAUFMANN, *The Religion of Israel*, trans. M. GREENBERG (Chicago, 1960), p. 364, noted that "the prophecies concerning the nations ... contain historical allusions to events before the time of Amos." There can be little doubt that the prophet had in mind an incident involving either Judah or, more likely, Israel.

of the event seems self-evident: an indeterminate number of people, presumably Israelites, had been forcibly taken captive and deported by their ethnic and political neighbors. These captives had then been delivered over to the Edomites for further disposal.

Traffic in human chattel and slavery were integral features of the life and culture of the Ancient Near East from Babylon to Thebes [1]). Isaac MENDELSOHN, whose work on the subject has yet to be superseded, has pointed out that the ranks of the native populations provided an important source of slaves, particularly as a by-product of economic deprivation [2]). Defaulting debtors, unemployed men and women who sold themselves voluntarily into bondage, and minors who were either sold outright by their parents or who were forced into slavery in order to save their very lives made up the bulk of the slave population. Another substantial group was composed of foreign slaves, either captives of war or imported slaves from neighboring countries [3]).

It is with the latter category that the atrocities of Gaza and Tyre are to be connected. Both nations, for the city names are employed metonymically, were guilty of taking captive and deporting the entire populace, or, perhaps better, the peaceful populace [4]), of some undisclosed place. Mays speaks of it as "an isolated border raid of the kind for which there would hardly be any historical attestation" [5]), and no documentary confirmation of the event, or events, which Amos had in mind can, of course, be expected. Yet the charge that Tyre had ignored the *berít 'aḥîm*, 'the brotherly covenant', suggests that we are dealing here with something more than just an isolated border raid. The incident and its attendant circumstances were so dastardly that they stand out in the mind of the prophet above all other potential or real deeds of malevolence with which he might have charged these peoples. So we have no reason to doubt that an actual historical occurrence is referred to here [6]).

---

[1]) See I. MENDELSOHN, "Slavery in the OT," *IDB*, IV (New York, 1962), pp. 383 ff.

[2]) *Slavery in the Ancient Near East* (New York, 1949), p. 5; cf. *ante*, p. 384 f.

[3]) W. W. HALLO and W. K. SIMPSON, *The Ancient Near East* (New York, 1971), p. 49. Cf. MENDELSOHN, *Slavery in the Ancient Near East*, p. 1 f. and p. 5.

[4]) See Erling HAMMERSHAIMB, *The Book of Amos* (New York, 1970), p. 30. The LXX read "the captivity of Solomon." The reference in Joel iii 4-8 to similar events involving Phoenicians and Philistines is later and connected with Judah.

[5]) *Amos*, p. 32.

[6]) While the events in Amos' vision (vii 1-9) may have no connection with actual historical events, J. WARD believes that the events in iv 6-11 actually

The oracle against Tyre, as we have noted, mentions specifically the 'brotherly covenant'. John PRIEST has examined this phrase in the light of the current state of research into the language and structure of covenants in the Ancient Near East [1]). On the basis of the prominent role which the concept 'brotherhood' played in Hittite treaties, in Achaean civilization (in the Iliad), and in Israelite tradition, the specific expression in our text is best understood as the the breach of a covenant between Israel and Tyre [2]). There is little reason to doubt that the initial covenantal relationship was established by David with King Hiram and that the relationship was continued by Solomon and subsequent kings of both Judah and Israel [3]).

The atrocity with which Amos charges Tyre, we suspect, was the result of the dissolution of a covenant treaty. Love, peace, brotherhood, commercial reciprocity, marriage bonds, all these were part and parcel of political treaties throughout the ancient world [4]). The unilateral violation of such relationships constituted a grievous error, worthy of the approaching divine retribution detailed by the prophet [5]).

It is also possible that such a brotherly covenant had existed between Israel and the Philistines, thus providing a similarity of situation that is reflected in the identical charge of delivering over a *galût šᵉlēmāh* which was leveled at Gaza as well as at Tyre. That possibility is

---

occurred in Israels history; the same premise seems valid here. Cf. *Amos and Isaiah*, p. 57.

[1]) "The Covenant of Brothers," *JBL*, 84 (1965), pp. 400-406.

[2]) *Ibid.*, p. 406. Cf. E. GERSTENBERGER, "Covenant and Commandment," *JBL*, 84 (1965), p. 39, where, discussing treaty relationships and treaty terminology, he substantiates that "the concepts of 'brotherhood' (*aḫḫutu*) played a prominent role ... not only among equally high -or low-ranking potentates but also among partners of unequal status."

In both the Egyptian and the Hittite recensions of the treaty between Ramses II and Hattusilis there is a repeated emphasis on brotherhood. Cf. *ANET*, p. 258, e.g., where one reads, "They ate and drank *together*, being of one heart like brothers, without shunning one another, for peace and brotherhood were between them ...". Cf. p. 199f. and the Hittite version, p. 202f.

[3]) See 2 Sam. v 11; 1 Kings v 15ff. Cf. the remarks of PRIEST, *op. cit.*, pp. 403-404. On David's treaty with Hiram, see F. C. FENSHAM, "The Treaty Between Israelites and Tyrians," *Suppl. to VT*, 17 (1968), pp. 71-87, and particularly p. 75. Cf. W. L. MORAN, "The Ancient Near Eastern Background of the Love of God in Deuteronomy," *CBQ*. 25 (1963), p. 81f., as noted by FENSHAW. On the renewal of the treaty by Solomon and Ahab, see Samuel AMSLER, *Amos* in *Commentaire de l'Ancien Testament*, XIa, 1965, pp. 173-174.

[4]) Cf. PRIEST, p. 404.

[5]) Cf. Exodus xxi 16. (The technical term for covenant violation in the Bible is *lᵉhāpēr bᵉrît*.)

suggested by the close relationship that existed between Achish of Gath and David [1]). Hanna E. KASSIS has proposed and argued persuasively that such a treaty did exist [2]). KASSIS is inclined, however, to distinguish the inland cities of the Philistine pentapolis, illustrated by Gath, from the coastal cities, suggesting that the inland cities were actually Canaanite under Philistine political suzerainty while the seacoast cities tended more toward a predominantly Philistine society and culture [3]). It is unnecessary, however, to draw this distinction much beyond the time of David. The height of Philistine power was attained about the middle of the eleventh century [4]), but even at that time the Philistines were beginning to assimilate with the more virulent Canaanite culture [5]). Recent archaeological evidence from sites adjacent to the sea as well as those to the inland increasingly supports this view [6]). It is not surprising, then, to note that Philistines were numbered among King David's bodyguard [7]). A continuation of some sort of formal relationship between a part of the Philistine area and Israel may be inferred in the early stages of Solomon's reign. Gath, still ruled by Achish, is tied to Israel in some sort of a treaty

---

1) Cf. 1 Sam. xxvii-xxix.

2) "Gath and 'Philistine' Society," *JBL*, 84 (1965), pp. 259-271, particularly p. 269.

3) Ibid., and p. 270, KASSIS' view that "Philistines" is more a geographic than an thnic term is intriguing. W. F. ALBRIGHT, in *Yahweh and the Gods of Canaan*, (London, 1968), p. 189f., stressed the restriction of the Canaanites to approximately coastal Phoenicia by the incursions of Philistines, Aramaeans and Israelites in the Early Iron Age. The power of the Phislitines was broken by the alliance between the Tyrian kings, Abibaal and Hiram, and David, king of Israel. From that time on, however, Phoenicia expanded her sea trade aggressively, reestablishing commercial and cultural dominance in the area of Philistia, it would seem. It is also suggestive that while Phoenicia and Philistia are in close proximity along the Mediterranean littoral, they are often cited together in the Bible, e.g., Joel iv 4-8; Jer. xlvii 4; Ezek. xxv 16-17.

4) See T. C. MITCHELL, "Philistia," *Archaeology and Old Testament Study* (Oxford, 1967), p. 414.

5) See Y. AHARONI, *The Land of the Bible* (Philadelphia, 1967), p. 251.

6) See W. G. DEVER *et al.*, *BA*, 34 (1971), p. 129, where it is noted that "Philiststine culture at Gezer was near exhaustion by the middle of the 11th century B.C.; Stratum 4 succeeded Stratum 5 without even a destruction, and the distinctive Philistine pottery merely ceases to be made." Cf. the report of director James SWAUGER on the fifth season at Tell Ashdod, *ASOR Newsletter* 5 (1969-70) where he indicates that "the purely Philistine city ceased to exist in the 10th century." The evidence indicates that "there was a transition period at Ashdod during the 10th century B.C. which began a change resulting in the major Canaanization of the Philistine culture."

7) 2 Sam. viii 18; xx 23. Cf. T. C. MITCHELL, *op. cit.*, p. 414.

relationship that provides for the extradition of runaway slaves [1]).

Edom, too, had a brotherly relationship with Israel [2]). Do the biblical references imply only an ethnic tradition, or was there also in existence a 'brotherly covenant treaty'? In 1 Kings xi 14, mention is made of the opposition of Hadad, heir of the Edomite throne, to King Solomon. Hadad had survived the invasion and conquest of Edom carried out by David's army while he was just a lad, and he had sought refuge and had been reared in the household of an Egyptian Pharaoh whose identity is not certainly known [3]). Upon David's death, he returned to Edom and continued as an adversary throughout Solomon's reign [4]). But by and large his activities were ineffectual, consisting primarily of guerrilla warfare tactics [5]). Israelite control of Edom apparently continued unabated until the reign of Jehoram of Judah [6]).

It appears highly probable that David established some form of suzerainty treaty with Edom as well as with the other states that fell to him in conquest. Michael FISHBANE has argued on the basis of the expression *w^{e}šiḥēt raḥ^{a}mā(y)w*, 'and he cast off his mercy', which he advocates as a technical term expressing a special legal or treaty relation, that such a treaty relationship provides the proper background for Amos i 11 [7]). Thus he renders verse 11b:

> . . . for he pursued his brother by the sword,
> and he utterly destroyed his allies/friends;
> because he nurtured his ire e'er,
> and kept his wrath beyond measure [8]).

The integral relationships that existed between these three adjacent peoples, or geographic areas, we suggest, are bound up in a series of covenant treaties which by and large seem to have been established

---

1) 1 Kings ii 39f. Cf. KASSIS, *op. cit.*, p. 268f.

2) Amos i 11. The employment of brotherly terminology to represent the relationship between Edom and Israel occurs with some frequency, e.g., Num. xx 14; Deut. ii 4; Obad. 10, 12.

3) It hardly seems likely that it could have been Pharaoh Shishak I, ca. 940-919 B.C.; one must assume Psusennes II, the last of the Dynasty XXI monarchs, for his predecessor, Siamun, is thought to have given his daughter to Solomon as a wife, suggesting close diplomatic ties. See HALLO and SIMPSON, *op. cit.*, p. 286.

4) 1 Kings xi 25.

5) Cf. Nelson GLUECK, *The Other Side of the Jordan* (Cambridge, 1970), p. 100.

6) S. COHEN, "Edom," *IDB*, vol. 2, p. 26. Cf. Y. KAUFMANN, *op. cit.*, p. 364, n. 1.

7) "The Treaty Background of Amos 1_{11} and Related Matters," *JBL*, 89 (1970), pp. 313-318.

8) *Ibid.*, p. 316f.

in the time of David and continued for some time thereafter by his successors. The *gālût šᵉlēmāh* charge of Amos against both Tyre and Gaza, and involving Edom, reflects the offense of a broken treaty and the crime of man-stealing, both of which were equally abhorrent to the spiritually sensitive prophet.

When did these atrocities occur in relation to the time of the prophet Amos? Were they committed contemporaneously with his unwelcomed appearance at the king's sanctuary in Bethel, or did they antedate him? And what circumstances would be the most propitious for the dissolution of such binding relationships? Such questions as these naturally arise if the view is accepted that the crimes of Tyre, Gaza, and Edom against which Amos inveighs involve broken treaties.

There is ample evidence that the proclamations of Amos were made in a period of relative stability and prosperity for Israel. If the *gālût šᵉlēmāh* was composed of Israelites, which seems to be the most plausible explanation [1]), then it is highly unlikely that the nations that are named as the perpetrators of the crimes could have succeeded when the power of Jeroboam II precluded such uninhibited and collusive activity [2]). As Professor HALLO has indicated, "Given the internal stability that chanced to prevail in Judah and Israel at the same time [that the Assyrians, Arameans, and Urarteans had fought each other to a standstill], it is no wonder that the divided kingdom briefly regained the economic strength and territorial extent of the Solomonic empire" [3]). The events which Amos calls to mind, then, had transpired in the past, but they were still so vivid in the historical memory of Israel that his audience would have no problem identifying them. We suggest that the events were not contemporaneous with Amos but occurred almost a century before, near 841 B.C.

The relationship between Edom and the remnants of Solomonic sovereignty had always been tenuous; the major break between Edom and Judah came, however, during the reign of Jehoram, son of Jehoshaphat, who reigned c. 852/50-845/43, or, according to another c. 849-842 B.C.[4]). This break should be viewed, though, against the backdrop of the tumultuous international scene which featured the

---

1) Cf. MAYS, *Amos*. p. 32.

2) Cf. HALLO and SIMPSON, *op. cit.*, p. 132.

3) *Ibid.*

4) See M. FISHBANE, *op. cit.*, p. 317. The earlier dates are those employed by Y. KAUFMANN, the latter are those of E. F. CAMPBELL, Jr., *The Bible and the Ancient Near East*, G. E. WRIGHT, ed., (Garden City, 1965), p. 292.

dramatically growing threat of Assyrian aggression. Assyrian interest in the Aramean kingdoms to the west had been evident even in the reign of Ashurnasirpal II (c. 883-859), but under Shalmaneser III (c. 859-828), Assyrian expansionary policies had intensified. He had campaigned against and captured the Syrian kingdom of Bit Adini (857-855), seizing the 'scepter-wielder of Beth-eden' mentioned in Amos i 5 and threatening the surrounding area [1]). In response to the Assyrian monarch's agressive policies, a coalition of kings was formed in order to oppose the continuing western incursions by Assyria. While neither Judah nor Edom are mentioned in the Assyrian annals that list the participants in the coalition, the tenor of the times could not help but have affected their relations. The climate of conflict on the international scene seems to have provided conditions that Edom felt were conducive to the dissolution of its relationships with Judah. Not long before the crucial year 841 the rebellion came, and Judah never again dominated Edom [2]).

The year 841 was destined to be a most extraordinary year in the history of the Ancient Near East. Earlier, the alliance of western states, including King Ahab of Israel, had been formed to oppose the incursions of Shalmaneser III. They had apparently inflicted a telling blow on the Assyrian warlord in the Battle of Qarqar in 853 [3]). After a considerable interval, he returned to Syria in 849, 848, and 845 to face the renewed opposition of essentially the same coalition [4]). But in 841, it now appears, he conquered Damascus and marched westward through Israel to reach the Mediterranean Sea at "Ba'ali-ra'si", probably Mount Carmel [5]). Here King Jehu paid him tribute, thereby submitting to his overlordship as it is so dramatically portrayed on the Black Obelisk.

The year witnessed in rapid succession, then, the conquest of Damascus by Assyria, the fall of the Omride dynasty in Israel, its consequent replacement by the house of Jehu after he had slain King Joram, the death of Ahaziah of Judah (also at the hand of Jehu), the march of Shalmaneser across Israel to the shores of the Mediterranean, and the payment of tribute by Jehu to the Assyrian monarch. These

---

1) Hallo and Simpson, *op. cit.*, p. 127, note that "a hundred years later, Amos was to recall the downfall of perhaps this very "scepter-wielder from Bet-Eden"."

2) Cf. M. Haran, *BIES* [Hebrew], esp. pp. 63ff. (After N. Fishbane).

3) See Hallo and Simpson, *op. cit.*, p. 127f. Cf. Michael C. Astour, "841 B.C.: The First Assyrian Invasion of Israel," *JAOS*, 91 (1971), pp. 383-389.

4) Cf. Astour, p. 384, n. 10.

5) *Ibid.*, p. 384f. and the supporting literature cited therein.

events certainly appear to be interconnected. The action of Jehu in killing Ahaziah and Joram at Jezreel, when coupled with the payment of tribute to the Assyrian ruler, indicates the institution of an abrupt change of policy from that followed previously by the House of Omri. Jehu had submitted to Assyria, and in so doing he had placed Israel on the side of the Assyrian aggressors and in direct opposition to those very countries with which she had formerly been allied. The brotherly covenant relationships had been sundered by Israel, and ideal conditions had now been created for the execution of the vengeful activites with which Amos was to later charge Gaza, Tyre, and Edom [1]).

Approximately a century separated Amos from the events with which, we believe, the oracles against Tyre, Gaza, and Edom are to be associated. No other historical period of which we are aware better fits the setting required by the historical hints in the text. And so awesome had been the effects of the Assyrian invasion of 841 on Israel that Hosea as well as Amos later referred to them [2]).

In sum, then, the *gālût šᵉlēmāh* event that came to the prophet's mind and sparked the fiery invective of his oracles against Gaza, Tyre, and Edom, had occurred almost a century earlier. It had been the violent but natural reaction of these neighbors of Israel to the new international policies of Jehu.

---

1) Note MAYS, *op. cit.*, p. 34, who comments trenchantly, "But these relations had been violently interrupted by Jehu's purge." The actions affected Tyre in two significant respects: politically, in the abnegation of treaty responsibilities, and religiously, with the carried out on the worshippers of the Tyrian Baal.

2) As HALLO and SIMPSON have noted, *op. cit.*, p. 128, "More than a century later, the prophet Hosea recalled the trimphal march across the now prostrate westland by "Shalman," that is, Shalmaneser (Hosea 10:14)."

Supplements to Vetus Testamentum, Vol. XXVI

A REAPPLIED PROPHETIC HOPE ORACLE

BY

JOHN T. WILLIS
Abilene, Texas

In recent years, scholars of the prophetic literature have devoted particular attention to re-evaluating earlier criteria used to date hope oracles, analyzing the function of North Israelite prophetic oracles and theology in prophetic books, establishing the *Gattung* or *genre* or *type* of a complex prophetic pericope, tracing a prophetic oracle by traditio-historical methods, and determining the role which a prophetic oracle plays in its present form and position in a prophetic book. Such concerns have given rise to a number of studies on Mic. vii 7-20 (or on Mic. vi-vii). The purpose of the present study is to attempt to reconstruct the history of the hope oracle in Micah vii 7-20 from a traditio-historical perspective.

Micah vii 7-20 reflects a period of distress and affliction. But the mood is optimistic. Yahweh will forgive the sins of his people (vv. 9, 18-19), deliver them from the oppression of their enemies (vv. 9, 15), overthrow their enemies (vv. 10, 13, 16-17), and restore them to their land from the nations to which they have been carried (vv. 11-12, 14), thus fulfilling the oath which he swore to the patriarchs (v. 20). Therefore, it is hardly likely that this oracle was delivered *originally* on the same occasion or to the same audience as the oracles of doom in vi 1 - vii 6, whose mood is pessimistic, which censure their hearers, and which envision the coming of punishment. However, this is not to deny that vii 7-20 is intimately related to vi 1 - vii 6 in the final form of the book of Micah, or that it was placed in this position because of its affinities with the doom oracles which immediately precede. It is simply to affirm that in order to determine the *original Sitz im Leben* of this hope oracle, it is necessary to examine the internal evidence which it contains separate and apart from vi 1 - vii 6.

The text of Mic. vii 7-20 exhibits a variety of speakers and audiences. In vv. 7, 9-10, an individual speaks to himself: he resolves to trust in Yahweh to save or deliver him, and determines to endure the suffering which he deserves because of his sin, until Yahweh intercedes to save him and to tread down his enemy. In v. 8, an individual addresses his enemy, whom he warns not to gloat over his apparent fall, as Yahweh will raise him up. In vv. 11-13, the speaker addresses a city, and announces that its walls will be built, its boundary (or the boundary of its country) will be extended, and its exiled citizens will be returned. In vv. 14, 16-20, the nation (Israel? Judah?) or a spokesman for the nation speaks to Yahweh, asking him to shepherd his flock and to strike terror in the hearts of her enemies, and praising him for his forgiveness and fidelity to his oath to the fathers. And in v. 15, Yahweh promises Israel that he will do marvelous things in her behalf. This variety has led scholars to find two (vv. 1-13 + 18b-19a; 14-18a + 19b-20)[1]), three (vv. 7-10, 11-13, 14-20) [2]), or four (vv. 7-10, 11-13, 14-17, 18-20) [3]) originally independent oracles in this pericope.

However, an analysis of Mic. vii 7-20 taken as a whole reveals a distinct *abab* pattern. In the first and third pericopes (vv. 7-10 and 14-17), an individual speaks as the nation's representative. The nation is in great distress because of an enemy, apparently referring to nations which have attacked and overpowered God's people. But the nation ("I") resolves to trust in Yahweh to deliver her from her distress (vv. 7-10), and prays to Yahweh with the assurance that he will deliver her (vv. 14-17). The first pericope begins with the personal resolution to trust in Yahweh (v. 7), continues with a warning to the enemy not to gloat over his victory, because Yahweh will raise her up (v. 8), and concludes with a resolution to trust in Yahweh to

[1]) K. Marti, *Das Dodekapropheton. Kurzer Hand-Commentar zum Alten Testament* (Tübingen, 1904), 298; W. Nowack, *Die Kleinen Propheten übersetzt und erklärt. Göttingen Handkommentar zum Alten Testament*, 3. Auflage (Göttingen, 1922), 197, 234; and E. Sellin, *Introduction to the Old Testament*, trans. W. Montgomery (New York, 1923), 179.

[2]) B. Duhm, "Anmerkungen zu den Zwölf Propheten, III. Buch Micha," *ZAW*, XXXI (1911), 92; G. Hylmö, *Kompositionen av Mikas Bok* (Lund, 1919), 282; F. C. Eiselen, *The Prophetic Books of the Old Testament*, II (Cincinnati, 1923), 486; S. Mowinckel, "Mikaboken," *NTT*, XXIX (1928), 25; *Det Gamle Testamente*, (*GTMMM*), III (Oslo, 1944), 671, 692; J. Marty, *L'Ancien Testament*, II (Paris, 1947), 782; R. Meyer, "Michabuch," *RGG*³, IV (1960), col. 931; and D. W. Thomas, "Micah," *Peake's Commentary on the Bible* (New York, 1962), 634.

[3]) G. A. Smith, *The Book of the Twelve Prophets. An Exposition of the Bible*, IV (Hartford, 1904), 548-49; P. Riessler, *Die Kleinen Propheten* (Rottenburg, 1911), 128; C. Steuernagel, *Lehrbuch der Einleitung in das Alte Testament* (Tübingen, 1912), 629; R. H. Pfeiffer, *Introduction to the Old Testament* (New York, 1948), 592; A. George, "Michée (Le Livre de)," *Dictionnaire de la Bible, Supplément*, (*DBS*), V (Paris, 1952), col. 1258; and R. F. von Ungern-Sternberg, *Die Botschaft des Alten Testaments* (Stuttgart, 1958), 163.

deliver him and destroy his enemy (vv. 9-10). Following a similar pattern, the third pericope begins with a prayer that Yahweh would shepherd his flock as he had done formerly (v. 14), continues with Yahweh's reply, promising to intervene in behalf of his people (v. 15), and concludes with the affirmation that the nations who are afflicting God's people will be overthrown (vv. 16-17).

There are also affinities between the second and fourth pericopes (vv. 11-13 and 18-20). The former is a promise of the coming day of Yahweh's deliverance, in which the walls of God's people will be built, the borders of their territory extended (v. 11), dispersed Israelites returned to their homeland (v. 12), and the nations made desolate (v. 13). Similarly, the final pericope praises Yahweh out of the belief that he will soon come and forgive the sins of his people which are responsible for their present affliction (vv. 18-20). In light of this analysis, Mic. vii 7-20 may be outlined in this way:

A. 1. Resolution to Trust in Yahweh while suffering affliction (vv. 7-10)

2. Promise of coming day of Yahweh's deliverance (vv. 113-13).

B. 1. Prayer that Yahweh will deliver his people from their affliction, with trust that he will do so (vv. 14-17).

2. Hymn of praise to Yahweh for his mercy, which he will soon manifest by forgiving his sinful people (vv. 18-20 [1]).

Since essentially the same pattern occurs in several psalms (as xxiv; xcv 1 ff., 6 f.; c 1 ff., 4 f.; etc.), the prayer of king Assurbanipal, and Is. xxxiii, there is no reason to deny that Mic. vii 7-20 is a unit,

[1]) This pattern of Resolution-Promise-Prayer-Hymn is an attempt to define more sharply the pattern of Dirge-Divine Oracle-Dirge-Hymn, suggested by H. Gunkel, "The Close of Micah: A Prophetical Liturgy," *What Remains of the Old Testament and Other Essays* (New York, 1928), 115-149, especially p. 142, and adopted by the present author for the more general purpose of demonstrating the coherence of the book of Micah in "The Structure of the Book of Micah," *SEÅ*, 34 (1969), 5-42, especially pp. 36-37. After more reflection, I have become convinced that "Dirge" does not correctly describe the *Gattung* or *genre* represented by vv. 7-10 and 14-17, since these passage are not really laments or even pessimistic, but rather express great faith and hope in a period of distress. Furthermore, as the present study suggests, it is doubtful that Gunkel is justified in calling vv. 7-10 a "Dirge *of Zion*." To be sure, the statements which allude to the present distress *could* fit the situation of the Fall of Jerusalem in 587 B.C., and this pericope may have been applied in this way in *one stage* of its development, but the surrounding context indicates that originally it had a North Israelite provenance; see below for the pertinent arguments.

and to divide it into smaller original units, although it is certainly likely that the original oracle was modified somewhat in the course of oral and written transmission. Consequently it seems best to examine the entire passage in attempting to determine its *Sitz im Leben* and the historical situation which led to its origin [1]).

THE ORIGINAL SITZ IM LEBEN OF MICAH VII 7-20

In harmony with trends of their times, several scholars in the early decades of the twentieth century assigned Mic. vii 7-20 to the Maccabean Age [2]). But this view justifiably enjoys virtually no support in contemporary critical circles [3]).

Perhaps the most predominant view is that Mic. vii 7-20 is an exilic or postexilic hope oracle originating in Judah or in Judean circles. In essence, this is based on four assumptions, none of which can be demonstrated objectively. First, the calamity reflected in this passage is taken to be the destruction of Jerusalem in 587 B.C. Secondly, the "city" of v. 11, whose walls need to be built or rebuilt, and whose boundary is to be extended, is thought to be Jerusalem [4]),

---

[1]) Among scholars who have insisted on the coherence of Mic. vii 7-20 are K. J. GRIMM, *Euphemistic Liturgical Appendixes in the Old Testament* (Leipzig, 1901), 94-95; B. STADE, "Streiflichter auf die Entstehung der jetzigen Gestalt der alttestamentlichen Prophetenschriften," *ZAW*, 23 (1903), 164-171; GUNKEL, *loc. cit.*; G. W. WADE, *The Books of the Prophets Micah, Obadiah, Joel and Jonah, with Introduction and Notes* (London, 1925), 60; E. SELLIN, *Das Zwölfprophetenbuch übersetzt und erklärt. Kommentar zum Alten Testament*, XIV (Leipzig, 1929), 349; P. F. BLOOMHARDT, *Old Testament Commentary*, edited by H. C. ALLEMAN and E. E. FLACK (Philadelphia, 1948), 850; D. DEDEN, *De Kleine Propheten. De Boeken van het Oude Testament* (Roermond en Maaseik, 1953), 229; G. FOHRER, "Micha," *EKL*, II (1956), col. 1328; R. E. WOLFE, *The Interpreter's Bible* (*IB*), VI (Nashville, 1956), 945; A. WEISER, *Das Buch der zwölf kleinen Propheten. Das Alte Testament Deutsch* (*ATD*), 24, 4 Aufl. (Göttingen, 1963), 288-289; and A. DEISSLER, *Les Petits Prophètes. La Sainte Bible* (*StB*), VIII (Paris, 1964), 359.

[2]) STADE, *op. cit.*, 167; MARTI, *op. cit.*, 264, 298, 300, 301; P. HAUPT, "The Book of Micah," *AJSL*, 27 (1910), 15, note 11; 37-40, 42; NOWACK, *op. cit.*, 198, 234; and T. H. ROBINSON, *Die zwölf kleinen Propheten. Handbuch zum Alten Testament* (*HAT*), XIV/1, 3. Aufl. (Tübingen, 1963; first printed in 1936), 151 (possibly).

[3]) A rare exception is the study of R. TOURNAY, "Quelques relectures bibliques antisamaritaines," *RB*, 71 (1964), 514-524, 531-536, who assigns Mic. vi 9-16 to the Maccabean Period; and yet, even he thinks vii 8-20 is from Jerusalemite scribes of an earlier time, cf. pp. 522-523.

[4]) So J. WELLHAUSEN in F. BLEEK, *Einleitung in das Alte Testament* (Berlin, 1878), 425, note 1; W. R. SMITH, *The Prophets of Israel and their Place in History to the Close of the Eighth Century B. C.* (New York, 1882), 439, note 13; G. H. SKIPWITH, "On the Structure of the Book of Micah and on Isaiah ii 2-5," *JQR*, 6 (1894), 585; J. WELLHAUSEN, *Die Kleinen Propheten übersetzt und erklärt* (Berlin, 1898), 149; STADE, *loc. cit.*; G. A. SMITH, *op. cit.*, 534; R. F. HORTON, *The Minor*

and the "remnant" of v. 18 the Judeans who survived this catastrophe. Thirdly, the enemy responsible for this destruction (vv. 8, 10, 16-17) is assumed to be Babylon [1]). And fourthly, since Micah was a Judean prophet, it seems reasonable to believe that later hope oracles added to his genuine oracles of doom would also be of Judean origin.

However, if attention is given to the objective evidence in this passage, it is clear that the provenance was originally North Israel, and it is likely that the enemy was Assyria, and that the calamity which is reflected is some Assyrian invasion of Israel between 745 and

---

Prophets, I. The New Century Bible, XX (Oxford, 1905), 267; J. M. P. SMITH, *A Critical and Exegetical Commentary on Micah, Zephaniah, Nahum, Habakkuk, Obadiah, and Joel* (*ICC*) (New York, 1911), 15, 148, 149; DUHM, *loc. cit.*; E. STAVE, *Inledning till gamla testamentets kanoniska skrifter* (Stockholm, 1912), 216; STEUERNAGEL, *op. cit.*, 628; H. SCHMIDT, *Die Schriften des Alten Testaments* (*SAT*), II (Göttingen, 1915), 153; HYLMÖ, *loc. cit.*; EISELEN, *loc. cit.*; SELLIN, *Introduction, loc. cit.*; WADE, *op. cit.*, xxiv, 60-62; L. E. BINNS, *A New Commentary on Holy Scripture including the Apocrypha*, edited by C. CORE, H. L. GOUDGE, and A. GUILLAUME (New York, 1928), 589; GUNKEL, *op. cit.*, 130, 144; MOWINCKEL, "Mikaboken," 25; *GTMMM*, 671, 692-694; J. LINDBLOM, *Micha literarisch untersucht* (Åbo, 1929), 131; T. H. ROBINSON, *loc. cit.* (possibly); MARTY, *loc. cit.*; A. BENTZEN, *Introduction to the Old Testament*, II (Copenhagen, 1948), 149; BLOOMHARDT, *loc. cit.*; F. NÖTSCHER, *Zwölfprophetenbuch. Echter-Bibel* (Würzburg, 1948), 106; PFEIFFER, *op. cit.*, 593; A. WEISER, *The Old Testament: Its Formation and Development*, trans. D. M. BARTON (New York, 1948), 255; *ATD*, *op. cit.*, 288; J. RIDDERBOS, *De Kleine Profeten. Korte Verklaring der Heilige Schrift*, II (Kampen, 1949), 101; A. LODS, *Histoire de la Littérature Hébraïque et Juive* (Paris, 1950), 290; GEORGE, *DBS*, *loc. cit.*; *Michée, Sophonie, Nahum. La Sainte Bible* (*StB*) (Paris, 1958), 13; W. K. L. CLARKE, *Concise Bible Commentary* (New York, 1953), 608; DEDEN, *op. cit.*, 229, 231; WOLFE, *IB*, *op. cit.*, 946; J. FICHTNER, *Obadja, Jona, Micha. Stuttgartes Bibelhefte* (Stuttgart, 1957), 34, 59; T. HENSHAW, *The Latter Prophets* (London, 1958), 109; UNGERN-STERNBERG, *op. cit.*, 170; N. GOTTWALD, *A Light to the Nations* (New York, 1959), 307; J. MARSH, *Amos and Micah. Torch Bible Commentaries* (London, 1959), 124-125; H. W. ROBINSON, "Micah," *Encyclopedia Britannica*, XV (1960), 407; J. H. GAILEY, *The Layman's Bible Commentary*, XV (Richmond, Va., 1962), 36; HANON in J. STEINMANN et A. HANON, *Michée, Sophonie, Joël, Nahoum, Habaqqouq. Connaître la Bible* (Bruges, 1962), 31; O. SCHILLING, "Micha," *LTK*, 7 (1962), col. 391; THOMAS, *loc. cit.*; H. BRANDENBURG, *Die Kleinen Propheten* (Giessen, 1963), 115; DEISSLER, *op. cit.*, 355, 356, 359; B. RENAUD, *Structure et Attaches littéraires de Michée IV-V* (Paris, 1964), 101; and E. G. KRAELING, *Commentary on the Prophets*, II (Camden, N.J., 1966), 226. Most of the scholars listed here date Mic. vii 7-20 between the time that the walls of Jerusalem were razed to the ground in 587 B.C. and the time that they were rebuilt by Nehemiah in 445 B.C.

[1]) WELLHAUSEN, *Kleinen Propheten*, *loc. cit.*; W. W. G. BAUDISSIN, *Einleitung in die Bücher des Alten Testaments* (Leipzig, 1901), 531, 532, note 2; MOWINCKEL, "Mikaboken," 25; LINDBLOM, *op. cit.*, 130; WEISER, *ATD*, 289; and DEDEN, *op. cit.*, 231.

721 B.C. Three arguments support the North Israelite provenance of this oracle [1]). First, all the places which are specifically mentioned are located in North Israel. These include Carmel, Bashan, and Gilead (v. 14) [2]). In light of this, it is more likely that the unnamed city of v. 11 is Samaria than Jerusalem [3]). V. 12 names *Assyria* as the place from which the scattered peoples of God will return to Palestine, which makes it likely that the "enemy" of vv. 8 and 10 is Assyria [4]).

Secondly, the traditions mentioned in this passage are almost

---

[1]) Among the scholars who have attributed Mic. vii 7-20 to a North Israelite origin are G. G. Findlay, *The Books of the Prophets in their Historical Succession*, I (London, 1900), 248; G. A. Smith, *op. cit.*, 534; A. van Hoonacker, *Les douze petits prophètes* (Paris, 1908), 352, 394, 409; "Micheas," *The Catholic Encyclopedia*, X (1911), 278; F. C. Burkitt, "Micah 6 and 7 a Northern Prophecy," *JBL*, 45 (1926), 159-160; Binns, *op. cit.*, 583; A. Clamer, "Michée," *Dictionnaire de Théologie Catholique*, X (1929), cols. 1658-1659; B. Reicke, "Mik. 7 såsom 'messiansk' text, med särskild hänsyn till Matt. 10:35 f. och Luk. 12:53," *SEÅ*, 12 (1947), 280, 282 = "Liturgical Traditions in Mic. 7," *HTR*, 60 (1967), 349-367; A. Goldman, *The Twelve Prophets* (Bournemouth, Hants, 1948), 188; J. Coppens, *Les douze petits prophètes: bréviaire du prophetisme* (Bruges-Paris, 1950), 31; J. Chaine, *God's Heralds* (New York, 1955), 64; A. S. Kapelrud, "Eschatology in the Book of Micah," *VT*, 11 (1961), 405; "Mikas Bok," *Svenskt Bibliskt Uppslagsverk*, 2nd ed., II, col. 107; G. W. Anderson, *A Critical Introduction to the Old Testament* (London, 1962), 157, 158; O. Eissfeldt, "Ein Psalm aus Nord-Israel, Micha 7, 7-20": *ZDMG*, 102 (1965), 259-268; *The Old Testament: An Introduction*, trans. P. R. Ackroyd (New York, 1965), 412; J. Dus, "Weiteres zum nordisraelitischen Psalm Micha 7:7-20," *ZDMG*, 115 (1965), 14-22; J. Scharbert, *Die Propheten Israels bis 700 v. Chr.* (Köln, 1965), 325-326; A. S. van der Woude, "Deutero-Micha: Ein Prophet aus Nord-Israel?" *NedThT*, 25 (1971), 365-378; and H. L. Ginsberg in a personal correspondence to the author dated July 20, 1972.

The reader will note that by limiting the arguments to three, I am deliberately registering my hesitation to adopt other suggestions favoring this view, which are not convincing. Eissfeldt, "Ein Psalm aus Nord-Israel," 262-264; and Dus, *op. cit.*, 21-22, argue that שֹׁכְנִי לְבָדָד יַעַר בְּתוֹךְ כַּרְמֶל in v. 14 is an address to Yahweh and refers to him as "the One who dwells solitarily in a forest in the midst of Carmel." However, the context and syntax indicate that this clause refers to Israel, Yahweh's "flock," as van der Woude, *op. cit.*, 372-373, has recently reaffirmed. Van der Woude, *op. cit.*, 371-372, 374-376, points out linguistic similarities between Mic. vi-vii and other North Israelite texts in the Old Testament such as Hosea and Deuteronomy, but while this sort of argument shows that it is *possible* that Mic. vi-vii are of North Israelite origin, it cannot be said to be conclusive.

[2]) All of the scholars mentioned in the preceding note have pointed this out, with the exception of Findlay, Coppens, and Anderson.

[3]) Burkitt, *op. cit.*, 159; Binns, *loc. cit.*; and Eissfeldt, "Ein Psalm aus Nord-Israel," 265.

[4]) Burkitt, *loc. cit.*; Chaine, *loc. cit.*; Kapelrud, "Eschatology," 405; "Mikas Bok," col. 107; and Scharbert, *op. cit.*, 325.

exclusively North Israelite [1]). They include the Exodus (v. 15), the incomparability of Yahweh (v. 18; cf. Ex. xv 11; Deut. xxxii 12; xxxiii 26; 1 Sam. ii 2), and the oath which Yahweh made with the fathers (v. 20, where "Jacob" is specifically mentioned).

Thirdly, there is good reason to believe that Mic. vi 1-vii 6 or a portion thereof had its origin in North Israel. Then, it would be natural for vii 7-20 to be attached to this material, since it was of the same provenance.

(a) vi 16 censures its hearers for keeping the statutes of Omri and all the works of the house of Ahab. As Omri and Ahab are North Israelite kings, these words originally would have had more significance for a North Israelite audience [2]) than for one in Judah [3]). "Es muss . . . zugegeben werden, dass der Ausdruck 'die Satzungen Omris und alle Taten des Hauses Achabs bewahren' viel besser von einer Stadt passt, wo Omri und Achab wirklich gelebt und das moralische Leben gepragt hatten als von Jerusalem, das mit Omri und Achab gar nichts zu tun gehabt hatte" [4]).

(b) The condemnation of unjust weights and measures, and of the rich who mistreat the poor in vi 10-12 recalls similar reproaches by Amos (cf. ii 6-7; iv 1; v 11-15; viii 4-6), who preached in North Israel. And the description of widespread intrigue in vii 1-6 suggests the period of rapid-fire murders in North Israel from Zechariah to Hoshea, which is mentioned several times in the oracles of the North Israelite prophet Hosea (cf. iv 2; vi 7-10; vii 3-7; x 7-10; xiii 10-11).

(c) The traditions of the exodus, of Moses, Aaron, and Miriam,

---

[1]) Burkitt, *op. cit.*, 160; Eissfeldt, "Ein Psalm aus Nord-Israel," 264; and van der Woude, *op. cit.*, 369.

[2]) Among those critics who believe that vi 9-16 (or at least vi 16) originated in North Israel are J. T. Beck, *Erklärung der Propheten Micha und Joel* (Gutersloh, 1898), 61; van Hoonacker, *Les douze petits prophètes*, 351, 395; "Micheas," 278; L. W. Batten, *The Old Testament* (Sewanee, Tenn., 1917), 230; Burkitt, *loc. cit.*; Clamer, *op. cit.*, 118, 136, note 1; L. M. Pákozdy, "Michabuch," *BHHW*, II (1962), col. 1211; Kapelrud, *SBU*², col. 107; Brandenburg, *op. cit.*, 108; Scharbert, *op. cit.*, 318; Eissfeldt, *Introduction*, 411; Kraeling, *op. cit.*, 223; and van der Woude, *op. cit.*, 368.

[3]) Sellin, *Zwölfprophetenbuch*, 345; J. Lippl, *Die Heilige Schrift des Alten Testamentes*, VIII (Bonn, 1937), 216; Ridderbos, *op. cit.*, 109; Deden, *op. cit.*, 199, 200; Fichtner, *op. cit.*, 47; and Scharbert, *op. cit.*, 313, 315, 318, acknowledge the reference to North Israel in vi 16, but contend that Micah himself or some other Judean prophet was using the sins of North Israel as an example to Judah in this oracle.

[4]) Lindblom, *op. cit.*, 118.

of Balak and Balaam, and of the crossing of the Jordan at the beginning of the conquest in vi 4-5 are North Israelite, and thus complement the North Israelite traditions in vii 7-20.

(d) In light of this evidence, the "city" in vi 9 is probably Samaria [1]), and not Jerusalem [2]).

Three historical settings for the original utterance of Mic. vii 7-20 have been proposed by critics who accept the North Israelite origin of this oracle. (1) Dus finds the key to the historical background in the question of the enemy in v. 10: "Where is Yahweh your God?" The answer is: He sits enthroned on the ark. Thus, this oracle reflects the situation connected with the battle of Aphek in 1 Sam. iv (ca. 1100 B.C.), and the enemy mentioned in vv. 8 and 10 is the Philistines [3]). (2) Ginsberg thinks the key is to be found in v. 14, which describes Cisjordan as only "scrub surrounded by farm land." The assumption seems to be that Israel has regained its original territory West of Jordan, perhaps under Jehoash (2 Kgs. xiii 24-25), but it cannot compare with Bashan and Gilead. Thus, this oracle must come from the early part of the reign of Jeroboam II, before "he restored the border of Israel from the entrance of (Lebo of) Hamath as far as the Sea of the Arabah" (2 Kgs. xiv 25) [4]). (3) The

---

[1]) Van Hoonacker, *Les douze petits prophètes*, 350, 351, 394, 398, 400-405; *The Catholic Encyclopedia*, 278; Sellin, *Introduction*, 178; Lindblom, *op. cit.*, 118-120, 136, 138; Ridderbos, *op. cit.*, 107; Brandenburg, *loc. cit.*; Scharbert, *op. cit.*, 318; Kraeling, *loc. cit.*, and van der Woude, *op. cit.*, 369.

[2]) C. von Orelli, *The Twelve Minor Prophets*, trans. J. S. Banks (Edinburgh, 1893), 215; Skipwith, *loc. cit.*; Wellhausen, *Kleinen Propheten*, 147; G. A. Smith, *op. cit.*, 533; M. L. Margolis, *Micah* (Philadelphia, 1908), 65; J. M. P. Smith, *op. cit.*, 131; E. Stave, *Israels Profeter*, III (Stockholm, 1919), 46; Eiselen, *op. cit.*, 485; Wade, *op. cit.*, 53; Sellin, *Zwölfprophetenbuch*, 344; J. E. McFadyen, *The Abingdon Bible Commentary* (Nashville, 1929), 796; T. H. Robinson, *op. cit.*, 149; E. A. Leslie, *The Prophets Tell Their Own Story* (Chicago, 1939), 132, 267, note 7; Mowinckel, *GTMMM*, 690; Marty, *op. cit.*, 780; Bentzen, *op. cit.*, 148-149; Bloomhardt, *op. cit.*, 848; Goldman, *op. cit.*, 182, 183; Nötscher, *op. cit.*, 103; P. M. Schumpp, *Herders Bibelkommentar*, X (Freiburg, 1950), 217; Weiser, *ATD*, 283; Deden, *op. cit.*, 226, 227; Wolfe, *op. cit.*, 941; Marsh, *op. cit.*, 123; Thomas, *op. cit.*, 633; and Deissler, *op. cit.*, 347-349.

This is not the place to discuss in detail the various implications of the view that all or part of Mic. vi l-vii 6 is of North Israelite origin. For the point being made in the present paper, it is sufficient to suggest the possibilities that Micah himself may have preached in North Israel like Amos, or that Micah sent one or more of his disciples to North Israel to deliver these oracles, or that a prophet before or contemporary with Micah originally delivered these oracles in North Israel, and later Micah adapted them to a similar situation in Judah.

[3]) Dus, *op. cit.*, 15, 22.

[4]) Ginsberg, *loc. cit.*

present writer is more inclined to think that the catastrophe assumed here is the Assyrian invasion against Pekah in 734-732 B.C., or against Hoshea in 724-721 B.C., and that the oracle itself was uttered as an encouragement to the Israelites who survived this catastrophe [1]). VAN DER WOUDE thinks that vi 1-vii 6 belongs to the period just before the fall of Samaria in 721, and that vii 8-20 was composed just after this event. The author of Mic. vi-vii was a North Israelite contemporary of Micah, who may have had the same name [2]). However, v. 14 seems to indicate that Israel had been reduced to a territory around Carmel, and that the author is praying that Yahweh would restore the territory of Bashan and Gilead which had been lost (apparently recently) to an enemy. This seems to reflect the circumstances surrounding the aftermath of the Syro-Ephraimitic War, after the Assyrians had conquered Israel's territory in the North (Galilee) and to the East of Jordan (Gilead) (cf. 2 Kgs. xv 29; Is. viii 21-23 [Eng. viii 21-ix 1]; and perhaps Hos. v 11, 13-14). Thus, with cautious reserve, the present writer suggests that the most likely original setting for Mic. vii 7-20 (or its nucleus) was shortly after 732 B.C. [3]).

THE ADAPTATION OF MICAH VII 7-20 TO A JUDEAN SETTING

The basic reason that scholars cannot agree on the historical situation assumed in Mic. vii 7-20 is that this passage is filled with ambiguities. Of course, it could be argued that these ambiguities are viable only to modern man, and that if we could have been present when this hope oracle was first delivered, the identity of the enemy, the city, the catastrophe, and the territory would have been clear. But another explanation suggests itself. This oracle originally may have been delivered to one audience in one historical situation, but later adapted to another audience in another historical situation, at which time some of the precise information connected with the original setting of the oracle was omitted so that the oracle could be made more appropriate for the new circumstance.

And as a matter of fact, there are two items in Mic. vii 7-20 which seem to indicate that it was adapted to a Judean milieu. First, there is a striking similarity between the terminology in this passage and

---

[1]) EISSFELDT, *op. cit.*, 264-265, thinks that either catastrophe could be the historical background of this passage.
[2]) VAN DER WOUDE, *op. cit.*, 377-378.
[3]) So similarly GOLDMAN, *op. cit.*, 188.

Isaiah's Woe against the self-confidence of Assyria in Is. x 5 ff. Isaiah speaks of Assyria treading Israel down like the mire of the streets (Is. x 6), and Mic. vii 10 announces that Israel's enemy will be trodden down like the mire of the streets. Is. x 13 describes the king of Assyria as boasting because he had removed the boundaries of peoples, and Mic. vii 11 affirms that a day will come when the boundaries of God's people will be far extended. According to Is. x 10-11, the king of Assyria boasts of his ability to overthrow the idols and images of Samaria and Jerusalem, and Mic. vii 10 quotes the proud cry of the enemy: "Where is Yahweh your God?" In Is. x 18-19, Yahweh announces that he will destroy the forest and fruitful land of Assyria, so that only a "remnant" of her trees will be left, and Mic. vii 14 describes God's people as a flock of sheep dwelling alone in a forest. Further, the transition from darkness to light in Mic. vii 8-9 recalls Is. viii 21-ix 1 (Eng. viii 21-ix 2). Secondly, the middle line of Mic. vii 20 refers to Yahweh's "steadfast love to *Abraham*," which indicates a Judean tradition.

Several scholars believe that Is. ix 7-x 4 (Eng. ix 8-x 4) is composed of three oracles originally delivered to North Israel (viz., ix 7-11, 12-16, 17-20 [Eng. ix 8-12, 13-17, 18-21]) by Isaiah himself or some other prophet, which Isaiah later adapted for a Judean audience, at which time he added x 1-4. Isaiah saw parallels between sin and punishment which North Israel had already experienced and the present situation in Judah [1]). Similarly, the present text of Mic. i 2-7 specifically mentions Jerusalem along with Samaria as the object of prophetic censure, and yet the announcement of punishment is directed against Samaria alone (vv. 6-7). Therefore, it seems probable that this is an oracle which originally was uttered against North Israel and later applied to Judah [2]). Indeed, the same may be the case with Mic. vi 9-16.

[1]) Cf. e.g., R. B. Y. Scott, *The Interpreter's Bible*, V (Nashville, 1956), 234-235, 238; J. Bright, *Peake's Commentary on the Bible* (London, 1962), 497; and F. L. Moriarty, *The Jerome Biblical Commentary* (Englewood Cliffs, N.J., 1968), 272. Other scholars, like G. B. Gray, *A Critical and Exegetical Commentary on the Book of Isaiah I-XXXIX (ICC)* (New York, 1912), 189-191, insist that if x 1-4 originally belonged with ix 7 ff. (Engl ix 8 ff.), it referred to North Israel. Still others, like G. Fohrer, *Das Buch Jesaja. 1. Band. Zürcher Bibelkommentare*, 2. Aufl. (Zürich-Stuttgart, 1966), 90-91; and O. Kaiser, *Isaiah 1-12. The Old Testament Library*, trans. R. A. Wilson (London, 1972), 70, move Is. x 1-4 immediately after v 8-24, where they think it originally belonged.

[2]) Cf. Stave, *Israels profeter*, 8-9; George, *StB*, 21; Scharbert, *op. cit.*, 315 (possibly); and J. T. Willis, "Some Suggestions on the Interpretation of Micah I 2," *VT*, 18 (1968), 374.

Now while all of these are doom oracles, there is no reason why hope oracles also could not have been adapted to new situations. Undoubtedly, the aftermath of Sennacherib's conquest of the cities of Judah and siege of Jerusalem in 701 B.C. was similar to that of Tiglath-pileser III's overthrow of Galilee and Gilead in 732 B.C., or to that of the fall of Samaria in 721 B.C. The prophet Micah would have seen the relevance of its encouragements in face of this catastrophe. Under the influence of Isaiah, he may be responsible for some of the terminology in Mic. vii 7-20 which parallels Is. x 5-19, and for the allusion to the Abraham tradition in v. 20. Now that Samaria and North Israel no longer exist, Judah is the only "Israel" that remains [1]). Like Samaria three decades earlier (732), the walls of Jerusalem now stand in need of repair, and the borders of Judah now need to be extended (v. 11). With divine help, some day her territory once again will include the territory East of Jordan (v.14).

Micah VII 7-20 in the Present Form of the Book of Micah

The book of Micah exhibits a striking coherence which follows an A (I-II) - B (III-V) - A (VI-VII) pattern. Each section begins with oracles of doom and ends with oracles of hope. The "horizontal" affinities between the hope of sections (ii 12-13; iv-v; and vii 7-20), and the "vertical" affinities between the doom oracles in vi 1-vii 6 and the hope oracle in vii 7-20, are many and striking [2]). This little prophetic work was probably put in its final form in the exilic period by a circle of Micah's disciples or some member of that group [3]). Mic. vii 7-20 in particular would have had a fresh

---

[1]) This is not to imply that "Israel" was used with reference to Judah *only* after the fall of Samaria in 721 B.C. In my dissertation, "The Structure, Setting, and Interrelationships of the Pericopes in the Book of Micah" (Nashville, 1966), 178 ff., I have tried to show that "Israel" was used for all twelve tribes in connection with their association with the ark and its traditions from a very early time.

[2]) For a lengthy defence of these affirmations, cf. my essay, "The Structure of the Book of Micah," *SEÅ*, 34 (1969), 5-42, esp. pp. 23-31, 34-38. I regret that van der Woude apparently did not have access to this article when he denied any real affinities between Mic. i-v and vi-vii in his essay, "Deutero-Micha," because then perhaps he would have been more guarded in his statements on pp. 366-368, or at least would have shown reasons for rejecting my arguments.

[3]) In "The Structure of the Book of Micah," 41-42, I have given evidence to support the view that this was done in Palestine by members of a Mican school which may have included Jeremiah and some of his disciples. For other opinions on the date of the final form of the book of Micah, see my dissertation, 302-303, and most recently T. Lescow, "Redaktionsgeschichtliche Analyse von Micha

relevance for this new situation. Now, the unnamed enemy could be interpreted as Babylon; the catastrophe, as the fall of Jerusalem in 587 B.C.; the walls which needed to be built, as the levelled walls of Jerusalem; the territory that should be expanded, as the land which Judah had lost; and the returning exiles, as the Jews who had been carried to Babylon.

As the book of Micah now stands, vii 7-20 is the climax to other hope oracles in ii 12-13 and chapters iv-v. These oracles describe or announce a transition from the present situation of distress to a glorious future, in which present conditions will be reversed, but they make no attempt to explain the reason for this transition. vii 7-20 supplies this missing link. It affirms that the catastrophe and its existing results are Yahweh's punishment for the sins of his people (v. 9). With all her objects of trust now gone, God's people realize that they must trust in Yahweh, who alone can deliver them from their enemy (vv. 8, 10, 14-17), and restore her to her former status (vv. 11, 14).

The speaker acts out a dialogue in which he is sometimes the voice of the nation, sometimes a prophetic voice to the nation, and sometimes the voice of Yahweh to the nation. His words are not the words of the people, dejected because of their plight, but serve as a dramatic enactment of the optimistic fervor which a people who serve Yahweh should possess. The prophetic tone of this passage would suggest that he was a prophet (rather than a priest or the king or a member of the royal court representing the king). Reicke thinks that he functions here as the official representative of the king in the cultic drama [1]). However, it seems more likely that he is imitating the form of speech used by the king's representative in such a drama (which would have been quite familiar to the people) as a means of achieving the purposes which he has in mind. He places himself in the position of the people, and seeks to stimulate them to imitate his attitudes and actions. His plight is miserable. An enemy has soundly defeated him, and he sits in darkness (vv. 8, 10). He is completely alone and helpless, unable to defend himself (v. 14). This forces him to reflect on the *explanation* for the catastrophe which has fallen upon him, and he concludes that Yahweh is punishing

---

1-5," *ZAW*, 84 (1972), 46-84, especially 82-84, who dates it in the beginning of the fourth century B.C., particularly because i 6-7 betrays an anti-Samaritan polemic.

[1]) Reicke, *op. cit.*, 267.

him for his sins (v. 9). He resolves to bear the divine indignation, to acknowledge the impotence of human and material aid in which he had formerly trusted, and to trust in Yahweh alone (vv. 7, 9, 15-17), fully expecting him to forgive him and to deliver him from his distress (vv. 18-20). The structure, tone, and presentation evident in this text seem to indicate that the prophet intends to enact his drama so skillfully that it will cause the people to *empathize* with him, and inspire them to make his thinking their thinking and his actions their actions.

Recently, J. JEREMIAS has argued at length that certain doom oracles of Micah were reapplied to new situations in the exilic period by the addition of verses of phrases or short pericopes (i 5, 7, 13; ii 3-4, 10; iii 4; v 9-13 [Eng. v 10-14]; vi 14, 16) [1]). In a similar way, the present paper suggests that the nucleus of Mic. vii 7-20 originated in the aftermath of the overthrow of Galilee and Gilead in 732 B.C. by Tiglath-pileser III, and that it was reapplied to the situation immediately following Sennacherib's invasion of Jerusalem in 701 (perhaps by Micah himself), and later to the situation which existed in Judah shortly after the fall of Jerusalem in 587 B.C.

The structure, terminology, and intention of Mic. vii 7-20 would suggest that it originated in the cult. These factors, coupled with its present position at the end of the book, point to the liturgical nature of this oracle, which has long been recognized [2]). This would explain how it was preserved (first in North Israel and, after the fall of Samaria, in Judah), and why it would have been well known, and therefore accessible for a prophet to use in a new situation which was similar to the situation out of which it originally emerged.

---

[1]) J. JEREMIAS, "Die Deutung der Gerichtsworte Michas in der Exilszeit," *ZAW*, 83 (1971), 330-354. I have not attempted to delineate what words, phrases, and verses in vii 7-20 are additions made shortly after 701 or 587 (as JEREMIAS has tried to do with the doom oracles), because it seems to me that the interplay between tradition and traditionist is far too subtle and intricate to allow the modern scholar to be so exact in differentiating between the two.

[2]) Cf. GRIMM, *loc. cit.*; STADE, *loc. cit.*; REICKE, *op. cit.*, 263-286; GEORGE, "Michée (Le Livre de)," col. 1259; DEDEN, *op. cit.*, 229; UNGERN-STERNBERG, *op. cit.*, 163; MEYER, *op. cit.*, cols. 929-930; Hanon, *op. cit.*, 31; WEISER, *ATD*, 232, 288; RENAUD, *op. cit.*, 102, 115; and EISSFELDT, "Ein Psalm aus Nord-Israel," 259-268; *Introduction*, 411.

THE ELIMINATION OF A *CRUX*? *

A Syntactic and Semantic Study of Isaiah xl 18-20

BY

TRYGGVE N. D. METTINGER

Lund

It is not without reason that ELLIGER, when commenting upon Isa xl 18-26, leaves v. 20a untranslated [1]). The words *hămsukkan tᵉrûmā* are a classic *crux interpretum*. In spite of an almost embarrassing richness of contributions to the discussion, it seems to the present writer that there are still one or two things in vv. 18-20 that have so far escaped notice, and among these a possible clue to the understanding of the enigmatic words in v. 20a.

In the following paper I shall discuss vv. 18-20 on the basis of the assumption that they form an integrated part of the context. The attempt to excise vv. 19-20 as a later addition has been rightly criticized by PREUSS [2]). These verses make sense as the "rhetoric" answers to the rhetoric questions in v. 18. I shall first offer my own translation and then present the basis for this interpretation of the text. In my analysis, I shall argue on two levels and pose the questions of (a) the syntactic texture of the passage, and (b) the semantic content of some highly problematic lexical items.

---

*) I here record my gratitude to my friends Mr Erik Bernhoff, who read the typescript most carefully and made a number of valuable criticisms, and Mrs Margaret Greenwood-Peterson, who corrected my English.

1) K. ELLIGER, *Jesaja II* (*BK XI*, 1, Neukirchen 1970) p. 59. Apart from ELLIGER's comprehensive discussion the most recent treatments are found in P. TRUDINGER, "'To Whom Then Will You Liken God' (A Note on the Interpretation of Isaiah xl 18-20)", *VT* XVII, 1967, pp. 220-225, G. JOHANNES, *Unvergleichlichkeitsformulierungen im Alten Testament* (Diss. Ev.-Theol. Fak. Mainz 1968) pp. 99-102, H. D. PREUSS, *Verspottung fremder Religionen im Alten Testament* (*BWANT* V, 12, Stuttgart 1971) pp. 193 ff., A. SCHOORS, "Two Notes on Isaiah xl — lv", *VT* XXI, 1971, pp. 501-503.

2) For the excision see C. WESTERMANN, *Das Buch Jesaja. Kapitel 40-66* (*ATD* vol. 19 Göttingen 1966) pp. 46 f. (English edition *Isaiah 40-66*, London 1969, p. 53) and K. ELLIGER, *op. cit*,. p. 65 f. — For the criticism see H. D. PREUSS, *op. cit.*, pp. 193 ff. Note also the same author's reluctance against moving xli vv. 6-7 from their present context and connect them with xl 19-20, *op. cit.*, pp. 201 f.

18 וְאֶל־מִי תְּדַמְּיוּן אֵל וּמַה־דְּמוּת תַּעַרְכוּ־לוֹ׃

19 הַפֶּסֶל נָסַךְ חָרָשׁ וְצֹרֵף בַּזָּהָב יְרַקְּעֶנּוּ
וּרְתֻקוֹת כֶּסֶף צוֹרֵף׃

20 הַמְסֻכָּן תְּרוּמָה עֵץ לֹא־יִרְקַב יִבְחָר
חָרָשׁ חָכָם יְבַקֶּשׁ־לוֹ לְהָכִין פֶּסֶל לֹא יִמּוֹט׃

18. With whom then will you compare God,
or what counterpart will you put forward to match him?
19. Maybe an idol —
the craftsman casts it,
whether the goldsmith plates it with gold
or the silversmith with silverplates?
20. Maybe an image, which is a prescribed offering —
a tree that will not rot one chooses,
seeking out a skilful craftsman
to sep up an image that will not fall?

The interpretation of these verses must build on a general observation on their inner structure. V. 18 consists of two questions. These two questions are taken up by vv. 19-20, which contain two imagined answers and thus form a corollary to v. 18. According to this interpretation of the structure, the word *m^{e}sukkan* in v. 20a. must in some way correspond to the word *pæsæl* in v. 19a. These verses both contain descriptions of how an idol is made. In both verses this description consists of three parts.

V. 18. ELLIGER's interpretation of the expression *'arăk d^{e}mût* as meaning "einen Vergleich anstellen" [1]) leans too heavily on the unwarranted excision of vv. 19-20 and seems to be a somewhat anaemic rendering of the Hebrew. The only other instance of the word *'arăk* in Isa xl — lv is in chap. xliv 7 in the context of a trial speech, where the word should best be taken to mean "arrange one's arguments for 'battle' in a lawsuit". We also find the expression *'arăk mišpaṭ* twice in Job (xiii 18 and xxiii 4) with a similar reference. LIEDKE includes these instances in Job among his examples of *mišpaṭ* meaning "Urteilsvorschlag", a suggestion for arbitration put forward by the judge or by one of the parties in the lawsuit, and is thereby enabled to take *'arăk* in its pregnant sense "zum Kampf aufstellen" [2]). - Now, the literary genre of Isa xl 18 ff. is that of a disputation, a

---

[1]) ELLIGER, *op. cit.*, pp. 65 and 73.

[2]) G. LIEDKE, *Gestalt und Bezeichnung alttestamentlicher Rechtssätze* (*WMANT* vol. 39, Neukirchen-Vluyn 1971) p. 91.

Gattung which is closely allied to the trial speech or *rîb* [1]). It therefore seems natural to presume that the expression *ʿarăk dᵉmût* implies something more than a mere comparison: a challenge to the listeners to advance a counterpart to God, that could claim to be his equal, that could match him in a competition [2]). The use of the preposition *lᵉ* in the sense "against" present no difficulty, since the verb *ʿarăk* is found with the same construction in Jer l 9. As for *dᵉmût*, the linguistic distinction between sense and reference is quite helpful. The word may have an abstract sense, but vv. 19-20 make it evident that the reference is to patently concrete idols [3]). In my opinion, v. 18 contains an allusion to the creation of man "in the image of God" (Gn i 26 ff.).

V. 19. The questions in v. 18 are followed by two imagined answers in vv. 19-20. The first words of these two verses, *hăppæsæl* and *hămsukkan*, can best be taken as being direct objects of the verb *ʿarăk* in v. 18. Although the Massoretes seem to have taken the *hă-* to be the article [4]), it seems better to follow the Septuagint, the Vulgate, and the Targum, and take it to be the interrogative particle.

The word order in *hăppæsæl nasăk ḥaraš* represents the type *x qatăl*. The discussion is still unsettled as to whether this type is to be understood as being a verbal sentence [5]) or a composite nominal sentence [6]). The above translation represents the latter alternative. It should be noted that when a composite nominal clause occurs in poetry, the verb can stand without a suffix [7]), that is, our *nasăk* corresponds to a *nᵉsakô* in prose.

The remaining parts of v. 19 (b-c) are closely connected. I suggest the following interpretation. If one takes it that the verb in 19b *yᵉrăqqᵉʿænnû* also governs v. 19c, the participle *ṣorep*/*ṣôrep* in both clauses readily offers itself as the subject of this verb and is therefore

---

[1]) See above all J. BEGRICH, *Studien zu Deuterojesaja* (*BWANT* IV, 25, Stuttgart 1938) pp. 42-47, and C. WESTERMANN, *Forschung am Alten Testament* (*Theologische Bücherei* vol. 24, München 1964) pp. 124 ff.

[2]) As a translation of the word in Ps xl 6; lxxxix 7; Job xxviii 17. 19, I would like to suggest the English word "match", which has a range of meaning which is very similar to that in *ʿarăk*.

[3]) Contra ELLIGER, *op. cit.*, pp. 65 ff. and 71 ff.

[4]) Note the gemination in the first word and see BAUER-LEANDER § 80 h.

[5]) See above all W. RICHTER, *Traditionsgeschichtliche Untersuchungen zum Richterbuch* (*BBB* vol. 18, Bonn 1963) pp. 354 ff.

[6]) So H. S. NYBERG, *Hebreisk Grammatik* (Uppsala 1952) pp. 259 f., and D. MICHEL, *Tempora und Satzstellung in den Psalmen* (*Abhandlungen zur evangelischen Theologie* vol. 1, Bonn 1960) pp. 177 ff.

[7]) H. S. NYBERG, *op. cit.*, § 94m Anm. (p. 309).

best understood as being an agent noun, "smith". The *plene* writing in 19c could probably be explained as being due to the *pausa*. With this interpretation 19b-c forms a beautiful chiasmus. If the words *băzzahab* (19b) and *r^e tuqôt kæsæp* (19c) correspond, which seems to be a natural conclusion to come to, both expressions should denote the material. An objection to this interpretation of the latter expression would be that it stands without the preposition *b^e*. The answer to this is that *b^e* in 19 b also governs the designation of the material in 19c, just as the verb in 19b belongs to both members of the parallellism. This use of a prepostion, to govern both members of a parallellism, although it occurs in the first member only, is clearly attested in other cases in Biblical Hebrew, even if it is not a device that is frequently used [1]).

The repeated *w^e* to introduce the two clauses 19b and 19c can be interpreted in two different ways. (a) If it means "and . . . and", 19b-c refers to two subsequent stages in the process of making the idol in 19a. (b) An interesting alternative, which I should like to draw attention to, is to consider the *w^e* as being another example of the use of an iterative *w^e* to denote two altenatives (see e.g. Ex xxi 16; Deut xxiv 7): "whether . . . or". It seems to be virtually impossible to definitely rule out either of these two possibilities.

The Qal passive participle *r^e tuqôt* is a notorius obstacle in the path of the translator [2]). Could it perhaps be derived from a verb that is attested in Mhe. with the sense "to knock"? [3]). In that case, the passive participle could refer to something beaten out, "plates". The sense "plates" would seem to fit neatly into our context: "or the silversmith (overlays it) with silverplates". I think that this interpretation applies to the derivative *răttiqôt* (*zahab*) in 1 Kings vi 21, which I would translate as "goldplates", since the context speaks of plating (*ṣippā*).

V. 20. The most crucial words in the whole passage are found in v. 20a, where the Massoretic Text has *hămsukkan t^e rûmā*. The Peshitta and the Vulgate have no traces of these words. The Septuagint has

---

1) GES-K (1902[27]) § 119 hh. For an interesting attempt to explain Ex vi 3 as an example of this use see J. A. MOTYER, *The Revelation of the Divine Name* (London 1969, The Tyndale Press) pp. 13 ff.

2) See the survey of interpretations in ELLIGER, *op. cit.*, p. 76.

3) M. JASTROW, *A Dictionary of the Targumim* . . . (New York 1926) p. 1504. For a Syriac *r^e tăq* with the same sense see the Peshitta of Luke xii 36 and Matth vii 7 and cf. BROCKELMANN, *LS*, p. 748.

ἢ [1]) ὁμοίωμα κατεσκεύασεν αὐτόν. The Targum has *'wrn bry*, an exegesis which is probably influenced by the enumeration of trees in Isa xliv 14, where *'oræn* occurs in the M.T. [2]).

Since the various interpretations of this *crux* have recently been surveyed and criticized by ELLIGER in his commentary [3]), there is no need to append a new list here. One cannot but agree with ELLIGER in his final statement: "Zutrauen erweckt keiner der mannigfaltigen Heilungs- und Deutungsversuche" [4]). — Any serious attempt at an interpretation must stand up to three requirements. (a) It must fit into the structural framework of the passage (see above). That is to say that *hămsukkan* has its counterpart in *hăppæsæl* in v. 19a. This observation indicates the general direction in which we must look to find a solution. (b) It has to make sense of *t^erûmā*. (c) It has to account for the vocalization of *m^esukkan*. As far as I can see, all the interpretations suggested come into conflict with one or more of these requirements. There is therefore room for still one more attempt to come to grips with these enigmatic words.

John GRAY has drawn attention to the existence of a Ugaritic root *skn*, which he found in a noun denoting a stele [5]). Connecting *hămsukkan* with this Ugaritic root, he suggested two possibilities: (a) to assume a Piel participle from the same root and emend the M.T. to *hamsăkken t^emûnā*, "he who would set up an image" or (b) to assume a *ma-nomen* from this same root and emend to *hămiskan y^erômen*, "would one set up an image" [6]). In spite of the fact that these suggestions come into conflict with more than one of the above-mentioned requirements, I think that GRAY has made a contribution which could form the point of departure for some further reflexions on the passage.

Starting from GRAY's suggestion that *hămsukkan* is to be connected with the Ugaritic root *skn*, I should like to draw attention to the Ugaritic verb *skn*, which is probably a denominative from *skn*,

---

1) So S^ca, see J. ZIEGLER, *Septuaginta. XIV Isaias* (Göttingen 1939).

2) In the same direction did H. ZIMMERN move, when he connected *m^esukkan* with Akk. *musukkannu*, *ZA* IX, 1894, pp. 111-112. On this word see now W. VON SODEN, *AHw*, p. 678: "Makan-Baum, Dalbergia Sissoo".

3) ELLIGER, *op. cit.*, pp. 60 ff.

4) ELLIGER, *op. cit.*, p. 62.

5) See now AISTLEITNER, *WB*, no. 1908.

6) J. GRAY, *The Legacy of Canaan* (*VTSuppl* XV, Leiden 1957) p. 192. I have not had access to the second edition of this work.

"stele", with the sense "to make a statue or an image", "to form" [1]), and to suggest taking the word *hămsukkan* as a Pual participle of an otherwise not attested Hebrew counterpart of this verb. A Pual participle of this word would have the sense "a thing formed", "an image". We would then appear to be on the same track as the Septuagint with its ὁμοίωμα.

Connecting this with JENNI's theories on the Piel, I think there is double reason for using a passive from the D-stem and not a Qal passive participle. First, while the Qal denotes direct action, the Piel is used where the subject is not personally involved in the action, that is indirect action (the type *Caesar pontem fecit*, where Caesar certainly was not one of the workers) [2]). In Isa xl 20 we are faced with an indirect action, since someone chooses a craftsman, *ḥaraš*, to make the idol for him. JENNI further points out that there is a group of verbs "die im Qal eine allgemeinere, im Piʿel dagegen eine technische Bedeutung auf dem Gebiet des Bau- oder Kunsthandwerkes besitzen" (e.g. *ṣph*, *rqʿ*, *ḥbr*). [3]). From this point of view as well, the the use of the D-stem of *skn* would seem to be justified.

As for the word *tᵉrûmā*, it is difficult to escape coming to the conclusion that the word is even here used in its normal sense "contribution for sacred uses". If ELLIGER is right the word refers in particular to "die von der Gottheit selbst zugeordnete, für die verschiedensten Zwecke des Kultus in wechselnder Form 'erhobene' Abgabe", [4]), not to something a person dedicates of his free will. If this is so we must probably see an ironic hint in the following words of the prophet: "a tree that will not rot one chooses". The most natural thing would have been to deliver the most precious image, of the kind described in v. 19, to the temple, but says the prophet, this is precisely what is not done. Instead one chooses the less expensive way of making an idol of wood. For the idol which is to be dedicated as a sacred contribution one is content with the minimum requirement that it will not fall, *pæsæl loʾ yimmôṭ* (v. 20c). The listeneres are not good practicers of

---

[1]) See AISTLEITNER, *WB*, no. 1908, and see further A. SCHOORS, *op. cit.* (above p. 77, note 1), who discusses the occurrences of this Ugaritic verb. SCHOORS accepts GRAY's suggestion to emend *mᵉsukkan* into a Piel participle. An interesting translation of Isa xl 20a is that of P. A. H. DE BOER, "the image of offering (?)", in *id.*, *Second Isaiah's Message* (= *OTS* XI, 1956) p. 5, but DE BOER does not comment upon this translation in his notes on the passage p. 42.

[2]) E. JENNI, *Das hebräische Piʿel* (Zürich 1968) pp. 140 ff.

[3]) JENNI, *op. cit.*, p. 163.

[4]) ELLIGER, *op. cit.*, p. 77.

their religion, says the prophet. Their own actions testify to the nothingness of their gods.

How are we to interpret the syntactic construction in *hămsukkan tᵉrûmā*? — The fact that the Pual participle has a *qamaeṣ* in the last syllable makes it difficult to take the phrase as being a construct relation. The word *tᵉrûmā* can be interpreted in two ways. (a) It may stand in apposition to the participle: "maybe an image, a sacred contribution". (b) The more probable alternative is to see it as an asyndetic attributive clause: "maybe an image which is a sacred contribution".

The great advantage of this interpretation of v. 20a is that it makes it wholly unnecessary to have recourse to the guesswork of emending the Massoretic text. Even the vocalization appears to make good sense. And, last but not least, it is based on a principle that should be basic to any approach to a textual *crux*, the principle that the word thus explained should make sense as an integral part of the contextual structure.

MY SERVANT JACOB, IS. XLII 1

A SUGGESTION

BY

N. L. TIDWELL

Johannesburg

Of primary importance for the question of the identity of the Servant in the so-called "Servant Songs" of Isaiah xl - lv are naturally those passages in which the equation Servant = Israel is explicit. In MT the only such case is xlix 3 and so long as this stands alone in its witness it will be rightly regarded with suspicion. Textual grounds for the deletion of *yiśrā'ēl* from this text are not weighty [1]) and metrical arguments have proved inconclusive [2]). Moreover, in view of the highly individualised portrait of the Servant presented in the "Songs" and the predominant application of the term *'ebed* to individual figures in the Old Testament outside Is. xl — lv, together with the difficulty of explaining how the Servant — Israel can have a mission to Israel (xlix 5,6), it is not surprising that commentators should feel uncertain of the genuineness of *yiśrā'ēl* in xlix 3. There is, of course, another witness to the Servant = Israel equation, namely, the LXX text at xlii 1ab, but this reading is readily and commonly dismissed on the grounds that "it would give a 4 : 4 line in a 3 : 3 context, and is clearly a gloss from passages like xli 8." [3]). One wonders, however, whether the clarity with which such glosses may be perceived is not very much in the eye of the beholder [4]). H. M. ORLINSKY, while discarding *yiśrā'ēl* at xlix 3 and rejecting the LXX text of xlii 1 as

---

[1]) Only Kenn. 96 omits the word. MUILENBURG considers this an "inferior" MS. For a full discussion of the question cf. J. A. BEWER's article, "The Text-Critical Value of the Hebrews MS Kenn. 96 for Israel, 49, 3" in S. W. BARON and A. MARKS (ed), *Jewish Studies in Memory of G. A. Kohut*, New York, 1935, pp. 86-88. *Yiśrā'ēl* is present in IsQA.

[2]) Cf. C. R. NORTH, *The Suffering Servant in Deutero-Isaiah*, 2nd edition, Oxford, 1963, pp. 118-119; H. M. ORLINSKY, "The So-Called 'Servant of the Lord' and 'Suffering Servant' in Second Isaiah" in H. M. ORLINSKY and N. H. SNAITH, "Studies in the Second Part of the Book of Isaiah", *SVT*, XIV, 1967, pp. 83ff.

[3]) C. R. NORTH, *op. cit.*, p. 119.

[4]) The same kind of "obvious" gloss from xliv 23 is claimed for *yiśrā'ēl* in xlix 3.

"secondary" nonetheless believes that the "gloss" entered the text before the Greek translation at the stage of the Hebrew *Vorlage* of the LXX [1]). He also opines that, though the textual question in xlix 3 has been very throughly researched, the problem of xlii 1 "merits closer study" [2]). In fact one notable trend in recent comment on Deutero-Isaiah invites such a closer examination of this verse and it is our suggestion that a clue provided by a "new approach" to Hebrew prosody put forward a decade ago by H. KOSMALA indicates one direction along which such an investigation might be conducted [3]).

Apart from the difficulties presented by the one explicit reference to the Servant as Israel (xlix 3, MT) the whole question of the identity of the Servant depends chiefly upon the extent to which and the manner in which the "Songs" are seen to be related to their present context. In recent work on Deutero-Isaiah there is a notable tendency to stress the importance of studying the "Songs" in their context—this, of course, is to be expected in any tradition-history study of these texts—and an increasing demand to see the "Songs" as an integral part of Is. xl-lv [4]). The significance of this trend for the "closer study" of xlii 1 is that nowhere else in the "Servant Songs" are the links between the Songs and the wider context of II Isaiah so many or so obvious. Thus *ʿaḇdî* and *beḥîrî* (xlii 1ab) are descriptive of Jacob/Israel at xli 8-10, xlii 10, and xliv 1; *t-m-k* (xlii 1a) is used of Israel at xli 10 and, though the correspondence here is less striking, the spirit given to the Servant (xlii 1c) is promised to the community in xliv 3. The especially remarkable relationship between xli 8-10 and xlii 1 is, of course, the basis for the view that it was xli 8-10 which inspired the "glossator" to add Jacob/Israel at xlii 1. This explanation of the LXX text, however, has little to commend it when

---

1) *Op. cit.*, p. 83ff.

2) *Op. cit.*, p. 85.

3) H. KOSMALA, "Form and Structure in Ancient Hebrew Poetry", *VT*, XIV, 1964, pp. 423-445 and XVI, 1966, pp. 152-180.

4) This particular emphasis is notable, for example, in: C. WESTERMANN, *Isaiah* 40-66, SCM OT Library, London, 1969; J. MUILENBURG, "Isaiah 40-66", *IB* V, New York, 1956; J. D. SMART, *History and Theology in Second Isaiah*, Philadelphia, 1965; U. SIMON, *A Theology of Salvation*, London 1961; H. M. ORLINSKY, *op. cit.*; W. A. M. BEUKEN, "*Mišpaṭ*. The First Servant Song and its Context", *V.T.* XXII, 1972, pp. 1-30; J. JEREMIAS, "*Mišpaṭ* im ersten Gottesknechtslied," *VT*, XXII, 1972, pp. 31-42. Cf. also, J. LINDBLOM, *Prophecy in Ancient Israel*, Oxford, 1962, p. 269. See P. A. H. DE BOER, *Second Isaiah's Message*, O.T.S. XI, Leiden 1956, pp. 110 f., where more authors are quoted who do not dissolve the connection of the songs and their context.

xlii 1-4 is seen to be so integrally and climactically related to its present context as it is in, for example, MUILENBURG's highly impressive analysis of the poems of II Isaiah [1]). For MUILENBURG this first "Servant Song" is not in any respect an independent composition but belongs to a longer poem made up of nine strophes, extending from xli 1 to xlii 4 [2]). xlii 1-4 is in fact the last strophe of this longer poem, the climax of the whole composition. Further, the nine strophes of the poem are arranged in triads in such a way that the third member of each triad is itself a subsidiary climax. The third member of the first triad is xli 8-10 and of the last triad, xlii 1-4. MUILENBURG also remarks of xlii 1-4 that "the style here is essentially the same as in xli 8-10" [3]). There could be no more convincing demonstration of the original and integral relationship of xlii 1-4 to its context and to xli 8-10 in particular, but even this is not all that can be said of this relationship. The central, controlling position of *mišpāṭ* in this "Song" is noted by every commentator and this concept, so vital to the structure and meaning of the poem, requires elucidation from the wider context, especially from the use of *mišpāṭ* in the preceding two chapters of II Isaiah [4]). This increasing recognition that this Servant Song in particular must not be separated from its context is not in itself proof that the LXX text of xlii 1 is genuine and original. MUILENBURG himself continues to reject the LXX text as a later, correct but unnecessary gloss—for him the identity of the Servant in the total context of xli 1 - xlii 4 is sufficiently clearly established by xli 8-10. This means, however, that the whole case for the rejection or retention of Jacob/Israel in xlii 1 hangs on the question of metre—the "gloss" is so "inspired" and shows such true appreciation of the lines connecting xli 8-10 and xlii 1 that the added words might equally well reflect the inspiration of the original poet as much as that of a later "glossator".

The decision then has to be made *metri causa*, and judging a textual question on the grounds of alleged materical schema in Hebrew poetry is an extremely hazardous undertaking [5]). Typical of what

---

1) *Op. cit., ad loc.*

2) *Op. cit., in loc.* S. SMITH, *Isaiah chapters XL-LV*, Schweich Lectures 1940, Oxford, 1944, pp. 183-4, for quite different reasons also sees xlii 1 - xlii 9 as a unity.

3) *Op. cit., in loc.* U. SIMON, *op cit.*, p. 82, looks upon xli 8-10 as properly the first Servant Song.

4) Cf., especially W. A. M. BEUKEN, *art. cit.*; P. A. H. DE BOER, *op. cit.*, pp. 90-91.

5) On the difficulties and uncertainties involved, cf. S. GEVIRTZ, *Patterns in the Early poetry of Israel*, Studies in Ancient Oriental Civilisation, No. 32, Chicago,

results when a textual problem is approached in this way is the bewildering variety of opinions—even among supporters of the same basic theory—which one can find concerning the authenticity of *yiśrāʾēl* in MT xlix 3 [1]). But, despite our uncertainty about the principles of metre or rhythm of sound in Hebrew poetry, at least there is no doubt that Hebrew poetry had a definite form [2]) and that parallelism, a rhythm of thought, is the basis and most distinctive feature of that form. H. KOSMALA [3]) draws attention also to the fact that there is "parallelism" not only within individual "lines" of a poem but also between line and line so that the whole form of a poem expresses its contents. This kind of overall symmetry he discovers especially in Is. xlii 1-4 [4]) and from this point of view his understanding of the poem is not very different from that of MUILENBURG who describes this "strophe" as a "model of literary form and style" and instances, especially, the sevenfold *lōʾ* and the threefold *mišpāṭ*. Similarly BEUKEN [5]), without reference to any metrical schema, finds the clue to the structure—and therefore meaning—of the poem in the thrice repeated *mišpāṭ*. Here, if anywhere, is a Hebrew poem in which we may justifiably look for symmetry, perhaps perfect symmetry. Here, if anywhere, we may expect that the "sound should seem an echo of the sense", the thought-rhythm should be reflected in sound-rhythm or metrical structure.

In common with many, MORGENSTERN [6]) construes this poem as a uniformly 3-unit pattern throughout [7]) (whether 3 : 3 or 3 : 3 : 3) but since in the first stanza this pattern is disturbed by the longer text

---

1963, pp. 2, 12-14. Also T. H. ROBINSON, "Hebrew Poetic Form: The English Tradition", *SVT* I, Leiden, 1953, p. 129.

[1]) E.g. J. MORGENSTERN, "The Suffering Servant—a New Solution", *VT*, XI, 1961, p. 306, writes "The V. is manifestly a 4/3, just as are the two distichs of V. 2, immediately preceding, and the first distich of V. 4 which follows." While H. M. ORLINSKY, *op. cit.*, p. 85, equally categorically asserts that "both the verse that precedes and the verse that follows it end in 3 : 2 metre ..... exactly the metre that our V. 3 exhibits with the deletion of *yiśrāʾēl*. KÖHLER deletes *yiśrāʾēl* and construes the verse as 2 : 2 : 2."

[2]) Cf. T. H. ROBINSON, *art. cit.*, p. 139; also G. B. GRAY, *The Forms of Hebrew Poetry*, London, 1915. This has been recognised ever since Bishop LOWTH's Lectures were published in 1753.

[3]) *Art. cit.*, p. 427.

[4]) *Art. cit.*, p. 157ff.

[5]) *Art. cit.*, p. 3.

[6]) *Art. cit.*, p. 293.

[7]) It is not clear whether C. R. NORTH's "3 : 3 context", *op. cit.*, p. 119, embraces the whole poem or only verse 1.

of the LXX the added words Jacob/Israel are considered unoriginal. Such an analysis is based upon the commonly accepted system of counting "beats" or significant-word-units in which such unstressed or dependent words as monosyllabic prepositions and negatives are not "counted", unless, as occasionally in the case of negatives, they are of more than normal importance in the context [1]). Now in xlii 1-4 it may be true that the negatives are not in as emphatic a position as, for example, in Is. i 3 [2]) but they are certainly not unimportant or entirely without emphasis. In fact in this poem BH employs *makkeph* to bind the negative to its verb in only one instance, verse 2b (*wᵉlōʾ—yašmîaʿ*). To produce 3-unit cola throughout the poem MORGENSTERN introduces *makkeph* also at 2a (*wᵉlōʾ—yiśśāʾ*), 3a (*lōʾ—yišbōr*), 3b (*lōʾ—yᵉḵabbennāh*) and 4a (*wᵉlōʾ—yārûṣ*) [3]). BH thus permits analysis into 4-unit cola in 2a, 3ab and 4a and since we "need not accept every use of *makkeph* in M.T. as corresponding to the original intention of the writers" [4]) even 2b may be construed as 4 units. This is how S. SMITH sees the poem [5]) The M.T. thus yields the pattern:

1 abcd	3 : 3 : 3 : 3
2 ab	4 : 4
3 abc	4 : 4 : 3
4 abc	4 : 3 : 3

The longer text of the LXX at 1ab makes the 4 unit colon predominant and it is then not difficult to see that this textform points not to a uniformly 3 unit pattern but to the following form:

1 abcd	4 : 4 : 3 : 3
2 ab	4 : 4
3 abc	4 : 4 : 3
4 abc	4 : 3 : 3

With this pattern before us what seems more obvious than that 1d should stand at 2c, that in 4b the *makkeph* should be disregarded and *ʿaḏ* given full value as a "unit", thus yielding a uniformly 4 : 4 : 3 structure throughout?

---

[1]) T. H. ROBINSON, *art. cit.*, p. 143; G. B. GRAY, *op. cit.*, pp. 139, 158.
[2]) On this verse cf. G. B. GRAY, *op. cit.*, pp. 139, 158.
[3]) *Art. cit.*, p. 293.
[4]) G. B. GRAY, *op. cit.*, p. 138. The effect of *makkeph* on accentuation is in any case disputed, cf. A. SPERBER, *A Historical Grammar of Biblical Hebrew*, Leiden, 1966, p. 473.
[5]) *Op. cit.*, p. 54.

The clue to this structure was provided by H. KOSMALA's "new approach" to the question of form and structure in Hebrew verse, but there is one significant difference between his reconstruction of the original form of the poem and mine. KOSMALA, by defining a "unit" in Hebrew poetry as "everything that can be expressed by one essential word" and by applying this definition in such a way that *lō'* (but not *'al*) would form such a unit [1]), concludes that the original structure of Is. xlii 1-4 was:

1 abc	3 : 3 : 3	Introduction
2 abc (=1d)	4 : 4 : 3	Stanza 1
3 abc	4 : 4 : 3	,, 2
4 abc	4 : 4 : 3	,, 3

He arrives at this pattern by noting the significant position of the *mišpāṭ*-clause in stanzas 2 and 3 and observing that the 3-unit *mišpāṭ*-clause which clearly should complete stanza 1 is in our present text wrongly placed at 1d. He finds some hint of the misplacement of the original 2c colon in the IsQA reading of *ûmišpāṭô* in this clause [2]).

Thus he restores *mišpāṭ laggôyīm yôṣî'* to 2c and is left with an introductory 3: 3 : 3 stanza which he regards as the "headline ...... not only of the first song but also of the whole cycle" [3]). KOSMALA unfortunately makes no reference to the LXX text of xlii 1. Had he done so he would have rediscovered a poem with the perfectly symmetrical structure of four stanzas of three lines each, each stanza having the identical 4 : 4 : 3 pattern. This brings vividly to mind the statement of T. H. ROBINSON that "while there may be strong objection to conjectural emendation *metri causa*, we can feel justified in accepting *the Egyptian tradition* where it gives us *regularity*" (our italics) [4]). There is a further point worth considering also. The LXX of xlii 1 not only provides metrical regularity and perfect symmetry of stanza structure after the restoration of 1d to 2c but the resulting poem displays a theological and conceptual pattern closely related to Is. xi 1-5. That the portrait of the Servant in xlii 1-4 owes something to the figure of the king in Israelite thought is generally acknowledged [5])

---

[1]) *Art. cit.*, p. 426.

[2]) *Art. cit.*, p. 159 n. 2.

[3]) *Art. cit.*, p. 157.

[4]) *Art. cit.*, p. 148 n. 2.

[5]) As e.g., by MORGENSTERN, *art. cit.*; S. H. BLANK, *Prophetic Faith in Isaiah*, London, 1958, p. 77; C. R. NORTH, *op. cit.*, p. 139; I. ENGNELL, "The 'Ebed Yahweh Songs and the Suffering Messiah in 'Deutero Isaiah' ", *BJRL*, XXXI, 1948, p. 65.

and commentators commonly point out the theological relationship between *wᵉnāḥāh ʿālāw rûaḥ yhwh* (xi 2) and *nāṯattî rûḥî ʿālāw* (xlii 1c). In xi 1-5, also, the endowment with the spirit equips the royal child to dispense true *mišpāṭ* (xi 3,4), just as in xlii 1 the servant is designated and endowed with the spirit for a mission that is concerned with the establishing of *mišpāṭ*. Not only from the parallelism between stanzas three and four of xlii 1-4 but also on the analogy of Is. xi 1-5 one would expect to find *mišpāṭ laggôyīm yôṣîʾ* in the second and not in the first stanza, i.e. at 2c not 1d. The designation (xlii 1ab, cf. xi 1) and the endowment with the spirit (xlii 1c, cf. xi 2) are followed by a definition in negative terms of the designated one's method (xlii 2ab, cf. xi 3bc) [1]) and then, as the climax, a positive statement of his achievement (xlii 2c = 1d, cf. xi 4). The case for regarding 1d as misplaced seems very plausible indeed and once that step is taken the way is open to accept the metrical soundness of the LXX reading in 1ab.

If, however, the longer 4 : 4 text in 1ab is admitted as genuine and original—with all its implications for the question of the identity of the Servant—then our present MT requires explanation. On our view we must explain both the misplacement of the *mišpāṭ*-clause and the omission of Jacob/Israel. KOSMALA is obliged to explain only the former which he does by seeing it as the work of an "editor" more interested in religious "instruction" than poetic structure [2]). This editor moved the *mišpāṭ*-clause to its present position in order to make clear at the outset the purpose of the Servant's vocation. This theory may find some support from other instances of editorial disruption of Hebrew poetic forms, although, as KOSMALA admits, elsewhere this is usually the result of the insertion of extra-metrical marginal comments and not a deliberate displacement of a colon of the poem. KOSMALA does not suggest that the misplacement may be the result of a simple scribal error in the transmission of the text at an early stage, yet this idea has something to commend it.

The possibility and likelihood of scribal error is apparent in the text itself from a number of angles. Firstly, a scribe who either knew the text well to begin with or who was wont to read through and ponder a complete unit of the text—i.e. a complete oracle, poem or strophe—before copying it might well have received so vivid an

[1]) Is. xi 3a appears to be unoriginal. Cf. O. KAISER, *Isaiah 1-12*, SCM OT Library, London, 1972, p. 156 n.d.
[2]) *Art. cit.*, p. 159.

impression of the controlling position in the thought-rhythm of the threefold *mišpāṭ*-clause that he inadvertently introduced it before its proper time at 1d instead of 2c. We can imagine that "that expectation which is the psychological basis of all poetic form" [1]) would operate strongly upon the mind of the reader or hearer of a poem of such symmetry as Is. xlii 1-4. The regular 4 : 4 : 3 stanzas with *mišpāṭ* in or near the 3-unit cola in stanzas 2, 3 and 4 could easily create a state of mind and memory in which the expectations of *mišpāṭ* in stanza 1 was psychologically almost inevitable. The wish is then the father to the thought and act. At the same time *rûḥî ʿālāw* and *baḥûṣ qôlô* are not so far removed from one another in sound, sight and position as to rule out the possibility of confusion by a tired, inattentive or, as above, psychologically motivated scribe [2]). By these means a text emerges, such as must have been the text of the LXX *Vorlage*, in which, by the misplacement of 2c, the 4 : 4 : 3 structure of the poem is upset leaving an asymmetrical 4 : 4 : 3 : 3/ 4 : 4 / 4 : 4 : 3/4 : 4 : 3.

The next stage in the corruption of the original may have been theologically motivated—i.e. the removal of Jacob/Israel from verse 1 because of objections to such an equation as Servant = Israel—or may have resulted from the simple recognition that verse 1 is now overloaded by two units and should be a "3 : 3 context". Beyond this is required only the massoretic *makkeph* (*weloʾ—yašmîaʿ* and *ʿaḏ—yāśîm*) to create 3-unit cola at 2b and 4b and soon the "obvious" solution is that the whole poem is made up of 3-unit cola, the opinion of many commentators and the only acceptable grounds for the rejection of the LXX text at xlii 1, *aḇdî yaʿaḵōḇ beḥîrî yiśrāʾēl.*

---

[1]) T. H. Robinson, *art. cit.*, p. 145.

[2]) Both phrases consist of two short words having a total of eight letters. Both phrases share *w* and *ḥ* in common in the middle of the first word although in reverse order in the second phrase and the second words of each phrase have *l* and *w* in common. Of the remaining letters *b* and *r* are at times confused even in the MT square script (cf. A. Sperber, *op. cit.*, p. 482) and were readily confusable in the old "Phoenician" script. The same is true of *y* and *ṣ* (A. Sperber, p. 487) as also, in the square script of *ṣ* and ʿ (cf. E. Würthwein, *The Text of the Old Testament*, Oxford, 1957, p. 72). The *q* and ʿ too were probably interchangeable and, both being glottals, probably confusable in sound—cf. H. J. Dreyer, "The roots *qr*, *ġr*, *ṭr* and *ṣ*/*ṭr* = stone, wall, city, etc." p. 21 and note 9, in *De Fructu Oris Sui*, ed. I. H. Eybers *et al.* Leiden, 1971.

DIE BILDMOTIVE IN DEN VISIONEN DES PROPHETEN SACHARJA*

VON

KLAUS SEYBOLD

Kiel

Das Buch Sacharja enthält bekanntlich in den Kapiteln i - vi, versetzt mit verschiedenen andersartigen Prophetenworten, einen Zyklus von acht, ursprünglich aber wohl nur sieben Visionsdarstellungen [1]). Dieser Zyklus, der in i 7 unter das Datum des Jahres 2 des Perserkönigs Darius (d.i. das Jahr 519) gestellt ist, bildet, vielleicht mit dem abschließenden Bericht von einer prophetischen Symbolhandlung, nämlich der Anfertigung einer Krone aus einer Goldspende [2]), nach allgemeiner Meinung eine in sich einheitliche, selbständige literarische Größe [3]). Die sieben Berichte geben sieben visionär erlebte Szenen wieder — dadurch zusammengehalten, daß ein Begleiter, der als der "Bote, der mit mir redete", vorgestellt wird, den Propheten führt und das Geschaute erklärt, dann und wann auch —

---

* Vortrag, gehalten in verschiedener Form als Antrittsvorlesung an der Universität Kiel am 25.1.1973 und als Gastvorlesung an der Augustana Hochschule Neuendettelsau am 25.5.1973.

[1]) Außer den Kommentaren vgl. J. W. ROTHSTEIN, *Die Nachtgesichte des Sacharja*, BWAT 8, 1910; P. HAUPT, "The Visions of Zechariah", JBL 32, 1913, 107-122; L. G. RIGNELL, *Die Nachtgesichte des Sacharja*, Lund 1950; B. UFFENHEIMER, *The Visions of Zechariah: from Prophecy to Apocalyptic* (hebr., engl. summary), Jerusalem 1961; M. BIČ, *Die Nachtgesichte des Sacharja*, BSt 42, 1964; W. A. M. BEUKEN, *Haggai — Sacharja* 1 - 8. *Studien zur Überlieferungsgeschichte der frühnachexilischen Prophetie*, StSN 10, 1967; H. GESE, "Anfang und Ende der Apokalyptik, dargestellt am Sacharjabuch," ZThK 70, 1973, 20-41 (49).

[2]) Dazu vgl. G. WALLIS, "Erwägungen zu Sacharja VI 9-15", in: Congress Volume Uppsala 1971, SVT 22, 1972, 232 ff.

[3]) Zur literarischen Frage vgl. A. JEPSEN, "Kleine Beiträge zum Zwölfprophetenbuch III", ZAW 61, 1945/48, 95 ff., dann K. GALLING, "Die Exilswende in der Sicht des Propheten Sacharja", VT 2, 1952, 18 ff. (*Studien zur Geschichte Israels im persischen Zeitalter*, Tübingen 1964, 109 ff.), W. A. BEUKEN, a.a.O. 230 ff. und S. AMSLER, "Zacharie et l'origine de l'apocalyptic", in: Congress Volume Uppsala 1971, SVT 22, 1972, 227 ff., auch R. NORTH, "Prophecy to Apocalyptic via Zechariah", ebda. 47 ff.

wie der Prophet — in das Geschehen eingreift. Jede Szene aber ist durch ihre *Bildsymbolik* bestimmt:

Er sah einen Reiter auf rotbraunem Pferd, der mit Reitern auf andersfarbigen Pferden "zwischen den Myrten" hielt; er sah vier Hörner, dazu vier Schmiede; dann einen Landvermesser auf dem Wege zur Stadt Jerusalem — ein Bote eilt ihm nach, ihn zurückzuholen; einen kelchförmigen Goldständer mit sieben Lampenschalen, von zwei Olivenbäumen flankiert (mit verbindenden Röhren); er sah eine riesengroße fliegende Schriftrolle; sodann eine Tonne mit einer darin eingesperrten Frauengestalt, weggetragen von zwei geflügelten Wesen "zwischen Erde und Himmel" ins Babylonische; er sah schließlich vier Gespanne mit verschiedenfarbigen Rossen zwischen metallenen Bergen herauskommen und auf ein Startzeichen hin in alle Winde davonfahren.

Es scheint, als ob Bildmotive in einem Textzusammenhang etwas zustande brächten, was in der Exegese sonst nur widerstrebend und mühsam geschieht: Fasziniert verläßt der Ausleger seinen angestammten Platz und findet sich unversehens auf fremdem Boden unter fremden Leuten wieder. Sind es Bilder aus der Welt des alten Orients — wie bei den Visionen des Propheten Sacharja —, betritt er ein Gebiet, für das sich auch die *Archäologie* und die *Ikonographie* interessiert. So war etwa die gemeinsame Suche nach dem Vor-Bild des Leuchters aus dem 4. Nachtgesicht von Erfolg gekrönt, was man jedoch von den Reitern zwischen den Myrten im ersten und den Wagen zwischen den Bergen im letzten Gesicht nicht in gleichem Maße sagen kann. Enthalten die Bilder Motive und Figuren aus der "Welt von Mythus und Märchen" — wie man annehmen kann, steht der Ausleger im Zauberwald der *Mythologie* und läßt sich suggerieren, die Farben der Pferde im 1. und 7. Gesicht hätten mit den astralmythologischen Farbsymbolen der Planeten, die zwei ehernen Berge mit den Sonnenbergen auf akkadischen Siegelzylindern zu tun und überhaupt sei die Symbolwelt des babylonischen Neujahrsfestes das Milieu, aus dem der sacharjanische Bilderbogen stamme. Sind vollends die Bildmotive Ergebnis visionären Schauens, zieht es den Ausleger in den Bannkreis der *Psychologie*, die ihrerseits in solchen Bildsymbolen Signale aus den Tiefenschichten der prophetischen Psyche erkennen will, "Dramatisierungen unbewußter Vorgänge", so daß beispielsweise die 6. Vision von dem Behälter, in welchem die personifizierte Bosheit abtransportiert wird, aus der "Verdrängung" eines Schuldgefühls zu erklären wäre. Die Bildmotive als Zeichen und Chiffren schließlich eines in sich geschlossenen Systems könnten den Exegeten auf das Terrain des *Strukturalismus* führen, um von dessen linguistischen Theorien und Methoden zu profitieren. Die vier Hörner des 2. Gesichts etwa bieten sich als "Ideogramm", bzw. als semantisches Kernelement der Visionsdarstellung einer Analyse geradezu an. Aber gerade auf diesem Gebiet sind bisher nur wenige Schritte getan worden. Doch beginnt auch hier die Exegese sich neu zu orientieren.

Angesichts der Möglichkeiten, die sich hier nach verschiedenen Richtungen hin auftun, empfiehlt es sich, den Ertrag des bisher Geleisteten einmal zu prüfen, zu sichten und zu ordnen, je nachdem zu ergänzen, vor allem aber für ein Gesamtverständnis der Visionen nutzbar zu machen. Dabei sollen die psychologischen, ikonographischen und mythologischen sowie linguistischen Gesichtspunkte eingebracht und in den Dienst der Texinterpretation gestellt werden. Dies soll so geschehen, daß in *vier Anläufen* die Bildmotive der Visionen

(1) nach ihrer psychischen Motivation,
(2) nach ihren altorientalischen Analogien,
(3) nach ihrem Verhältnis zum Wort der Audition und
(4) nach ihrer Bedeutung innerhalb der Gesamtkomposition des Zyklus befragt werden.

I

Die Frage nach der psychischen Disposition des Propheten beim Empfang von Visionen hat immer etwas Mißliches, weil die zur Verfügung stehenden Textzeugnisse sich zu dieser Seite der Sache meist nicht äußern. Wenn sie es aber einmal tun, wie im vorliegenden Zusammenhang, dann so allgemein, daß man nur zögernd Schlüsse daraus zu ziehen wagt.

Zu Beginn der *Leuchter*-Vision findet sich eine weiter ausholende Einführung, welche den einleitenden Satz der ersten Vision: "Ich habe des Nachts gesehen" (i 8) variiert: "Der Bote, der mit mir redete, kam wieder und weckte mich wie einen, den man vom Schlafe weckt" (iv 1). Wie die Vergleichspartikel anzeigt, ist nicht von einem alltäglichen Wachwerden, wohl aber von einem dem Wachzustand vergleichbaren Befinden die Rede, das dadurch charakterisiert ist, daß der Prophet offenbar im Vollbesitz seines Bewußtseins nichtalltägliche, aber erkenn- und benennbare Dinge sieht, deren Funktion ihm allerdings zunächst unbekannt ist. Meint er ein Erwachen *zum*

Traumgesicht, ein Träumen? Das lösende Wort fällt nicht. So wird man im Anschluß an jene Formulierung eben nur von einem besonderen Wachzustand sprechen können [1]). Kann hier die Frage nach der Erscheinungsweise der visionär erlebten Vorstellungen weiterführen?

Die letzte mir bekannt gewordene Äußerung zu dieser Frage — von R. NORTH [2]) — deutet jene Bemerkung von iv 1 und die Visionen insgesamt vom Traum her und dies deshalb, weil "für den Traum die Kombination von Bildern charakteristisch ist, die im wirklichen Leben niemals zusammen wahrgenommen werden: fliegende Rolle v 1; Mädchen in der Flasche v 7; Hörner ohne Kopf, . . . grüne Pferde" [3]). Sollte diese Begründung genügen können und dieses Urteil zutreffen, daß die Gesichte als echte Träume zu deuten oder doch in Analogie zu Träumen zu verstehen sind [4]), hätte das weitreichende Konsequenzen. Dann könnte man sich nämlich des ganzen Instrumentariums psychoanalytischer Traumdeutung etwa in der klassischen Freudschen Ausprägung [5]) bedienen. Man muß sich jedoch darüber im klaren sein, daß man ohne die Textintention näher geprüft zu haben von der Prämisse ausgeht, es lägen hier in der Tat Berichte von Traumerlebnissen vor. Insofern wird man die Erfolgsaussichten eines entsprechenden Versuchs nicht allzu hoch einschätzen können. Dies auch angesichts einer psychoanalytischen Untersuchung auf der Basis der Jungschen Tiefenpsychologie von F. HAEUSSERMANN[6]), die mit ihrer Interpretation der Visionen als "psychischer Dramatisierungen" weit hinter den Erwartungen zurückbleibt. Kann man also auf den Traum als Bezugsgröße nicht mit Sicherheit rekurrieren, so bleibt im Blick auf die Genese und Formation der Gesichte nur das weite Feld der "revelatorischen Phan-

---

[1]) Vgl. hierzu J. LINDBLOM, "Die Gesichte der Propheten. Versuch einer Klassifizierung", StTh 1, 1935, 26 f.; I. P. SEIERSTAD, *Die Offenbarungserlebnisse der Propheten Amos, Jesaja und Jeremia*, Oslo ²1965, passim.

[2]) R. NORTH, a.a.O. (Anm. 3).

[3]) A.a.O. 48 (v. Vf. üb.).

[4]) Nahe zueinander rückt B. O. LONG, "Prophetic Call Traditions and Reports of Visions", ZAW 84, 1972, 494 ff., Traum und Vision: "In short, dreams — sometimes 'vision of night' — and the genre for reporting such experiences, ought to be seen in the context of visions in general" (496).

[5]) S. FREUD, *Die Traumdeutung*, ¹1900 (*Studienausgabe* Bd. II, Frankfurt ⁸1972).

[6]) *Wortempfang und Symbol in der alttestamentlichen Prophetie. Eine Untersuchung zur Psychologie des prophetischen Erlebnisses*, BZAW 58, 1932, etwa 93 ff. u.a. Eine Auseinandersetzung mit dieser Arbeit findet sich bei I. P. SEIERSTAD, a.a.O. 25 ff.

tasiegebilde" (J. LINDBLOM) [1]) oder der "eidetisch-akustischen Anschauungsbilder imaginärer Art" (I. P. SEIERSTAD) [2]).

A. L. OPPENHEIM hat in einer Studie mit dem Titel "The Eyes of the Lord" [3]) den interessanten Versuch gemacht, von den hinter diesem im alten Orient verbreiteten Ausdrucksschema stehenden Vorstellungen auf die Erfahrungsbasis zu schließen, und in diesem Zusammenhang auch die Visionsbilder Sacharjas herangezogen. Ausgehend von den dabei gewonnenen Erkenntnissen spricht er im Anbetracht der Sacharjavisionen, speziell der hier auffallend im Vordergrund stehenden himmlischen Vollzugsorgane (Reiter, Wagen, "Satan" iii), die Vermutung aus, ob sich denn nicht auch bei Sacharja der traumatische Effekt bemerkbar mache, den der im alten Orient berüchtigte und gefürchtete königlich-persische Geheimdienst — genannt die "Augen des Königs" (vgl. iv 10) — allgemein hervorgerufen hat; ob er nicht aus indirekten oder gar direkten Erfahrungen mit jener Institution dazu bewogen worden sei, die geheimen Aktionen seines Gottes auf analoge Weise zu schildern. Die Überlegung überrascht und fasziniert — nicht zuletzt aus methodischen Gründen. Denn hier wird an einem Detail ein Ansatz sichtbar, der die in Ekstasen- bzw. Traumhypothesen festgefahrene Diskussion wieder flottmachen könnte. Drei Punkte scheinen mir weiterzuführen:

1. Der Ausgangspunkt ist bei der sprachlichen Manifestation, nicht bei einer Hypothese über (die) Visionen als psychisches Phänomen genommen.
2. Die Frage nach der Motivation der Wort- und Bildwahl erweist sich als fruchtbarer als die Frage nach der psychischen Disposition des Schauenden.
3. Der psychologische Aspekt kann nur auf der Basis und im Rahmen der Selbst- und Welterfahrung des antiken Menschen zur Geltung kommen — d.h. bei den Bildmotiven: im Kontext der antiken Bildsymbolik überhaupt, im besonderen der sacharjanischen Bildwelt und ihrer Herkunft.

---

[1]) A.a.O. 22 ff. LINDBLOM rechnet die Nachtgesichte zu den "revelatorischen Phantasiegebilden", genauer zur Gruppe der "revelatorischen Allegorien", deren besonderes Characteristicum es ist, daß es sich nicht um ekstatisch-visionäre Erlebnisse, vielmehr um "Gleichnisse in der Form von Visionen" handelt, die aus Bildern bestehen, welche "vom Propheten ausgedacht sind und beabsichtigen, eine irdische Wirklichkeit zu symbolisieren" (25 ff.). Vgl. auch *Prophecy in Ancient Israel*, Oxford [2]1965, 143 ff.

[2]) A.a.O. 58.

[3]) JAOS 88, 1968, 173 ff. S.u. IV 1.

Insgesamt gesehen muß man feststellen, daß die Anwendung psychologischer Gesichtspunkte bei der Interpretation der Visionen die notwendige methodische Sicherheit noch nicht gewonnen hat, wenn auch im einzelnen da und dort Fortschritte erzielt worden sind.

II

Verliert sich der Weg zu den Quellen der Bildmotive in den dunklen Tiefen der Psyche, eröffnet sich ein neuer Zugang zu den Visionen, wenn man sich der Welt der altorientalischen Bildsymbolik zuwendet, um nach Vergleichbarem zu suchen. Diese Suche ist bisher nur zum Teil erfolgreich gewesen, hat aber Ergebnisse erbracht, die sich für das Verständnis als grundlegend erweisen können. Auszugehen ist von der Figur, die am besten aufgehellt ist: von dem Leuchter des 4. Nachtgesichts.

Das in iv 2 minutiös beschriebene Aussehen des geschauten Leuchters ist durch die philologischen und archäologischen Untersuchungen von K. Möhlenbrink, K. Galling [1]) und neuerdings R. North [2]) weitgehend geklärt. Die von Galling versuchte Rekonstruktion eines kelchförmigen, blumenverzierten, mit Blattüberfallornamenten versehenen goldenen Ständers, auf dessen breitem Rand sieben Lampenschalen mit je sieben Dochtstellen stehen, wurde von North aufgrund erneuter Durchsicht des zudem vermehrten Vergleichsmaterials im ganzen bestätigt, in Teilen aber auch korrigiert. Er setzt den Kelch auf einen zweiteiligen, hohen säulenartigen Ständer, verzichtet auf Ornamente, läßt aber die sieben (eindochtigen?) Lampen fest mit dem Kelchrand und einem dem Ölzufluß dienenden Röhrenring verbunden sein. Die wichtige Erkenntnis Möhlenbrinks wird dadurch von neuem bestätigt, daß nämlich das Vorbild des visionär Geschauten nicht in dem siebenarmigen Leuchter von Ex xxv, abgebildet auf dem Titusbogen in Rom, sondern in den (dem) 2 Reg vii 49f. beschriebenen goldenen Leuchter(n) zu sehen ist, die (der) im Hauptraum des salomonischen Tempels (hêkal) vor dem Schrein des Allerheiligsten aufgestellt war(en) [3]).

Da man nicht annehmen kann, die goldenen (bzw. der goldene) Leuchter des salomonischen Tempels hätten die Katastrophe von

---

[1]) K. Möhlenbrink, "Der Leuchter im fünften Nachtgesicht des Sacharja. Eine archäologische Untersuchung", ZDPV 52, 1929, 257-286; K. Galling, BRL 347 ff.

[2]) R. North, "Zechariah's Seven-Spout Lampstand", Bibl 51, 1970, 183-206, Abb. 201.

[3]) Vgl. M. Noth, *Könige* I, BK IX/1, 1968, 141 ff.

587 überstanden [1]) und seien dem 70 Jahre später in jungen Jahren auftretenden Sacharja in Jerusalem oder Babylon zu Gesicht gekommen, ist die auffällige Abhängigkeit nur so zu erklären, daß dem dem Priestertum nahestehenden Propheten diese Bildidee auf dem Wege einer *Tradition* zugetragen wurde, die die Erinnerung an den vorexilischen Tempel und die daran gebundenen Glaubensvorstellungen wach hielt. Wenn es sich aber so verhält in diesem Fall, legt sich die Frage nahe, ob nicht auch andere Figuren und Motive diesem Quellbereich entstammen könnten.

Letztlich noch nicht geklärt sind die Bildmotive der ersten und letzten Vision (*Reiter* und *Wagen*). Rätselhaft bleiben die doch wohl sinntragenden Angaben zur Szenerie: Was ist mit den "Myrten an der Tiefe" gemeint, zwischen denen der Reiter verhält; was mit den beiden Erzbergen, zwischen denen die Wagen herauskommen? Trotz der Fülle des hierzu z.B. von F. Horst [2]) bereitgestellten Vergleichsmaterials kann nicht verborgen bleiben, daß die mythologisch-kosmologischen Vorstellungen der Sumerer und Babylonier von einem Götterhain in der Urtiefe des Meeres und Sitz des Götterkönigs, von den Himmelsbergen, zwischen denen die göttliche Sonne aufgeht, die Visionen kaum weiter aufzuhellen vermögen, vor allem dann nicht, wenn dabei nur herauskommt, daß solcherart eben "der Eingang zum Himmel" symbolisch dargestellt sei. Geht man an jene Motive aber heran mit der Frage nach den Beziehungen zur *Tempeltradition* und ihren Symbolformen, öffnen sich überraschende Einblicke.

Es erübrigt sich zunächst der Rekurs auf ferne mythologische Assoziationen in der angedeuteten Weise [3]). Es erübrigt sich beim ersten Gesicht die topographische Deutung, welche die Myrten in einer Taltiefe bei Jerusalem sucht [4]), oder die Deutung, welche statt *m*^{e}*ṣulā* 'Tiefe' *m*^{e}*ṣillā* liest und darunter einen bautechnischen Terminus etwa 'Schattendach, Überdachung', auch 'Audienzzelt, Baldachin', gar 'Apadana' versteht [5]); oder beim 7. Gesicht die Erinnerung an die

[1]) Dies wird bestätigt durch die Existenz des *siebenarmigen* Leuchters im zweiten Tempel sowie durch das Fehlen in entsprechenden Urkunden, etwa Esr i 8 ff. (vgl. aber auch 2 Reg xxv 13 ff.).

[2]) HAT I 14, [3]1964, 217 ff.

[3]) Vgl. die Kommentare. Konsequent durchgeführt etwa von M. Brč, a.a.O.

[4]) So die verbreitete Verlegenheitsübersetzung "Talgrund", speziell die Auslegungen, welche die Szene in einer Schlucht o.ä. am Fuße des Tempelbergs lokalisieren wollen, vgl. dazu L. G. Rignell, a.a.O. 24 ff.

[5]) In dieser Richtung suchte der Vf. zunächst die Lösung dieses Rätsels. Die Anhaltspunkte waren: LXX, die Etymologie (akk. u. aram. Äquivalente), der

Zinnerzmauer von Am vii 7 (vgl. Jer i 18) [1]) oder der Hinweis auf die Pferderennen am babylonischen Neujahrsfest [2]): Denn alle diese Teilaspekte kommen zu einem relativen Recht, wenn man — homolog zum *Leuchter*gesicht — an die alten Symbole des ehernen Meeres [3]) und der beiden ehernen Säulen [4]) denkt, welche zum salomonischen Tempelheiligtum gehört hatten. Daß diese Annahme berechtigt ist, wird dadurch bestätigt, daß verschiedene Visionssymbole ohne vordergründige Analogie wie die Olivenbäume der Gesalbten beim Leuchter [5]), die vier Hörner im 2. Gesicht [6]), die *kabôd*-Feuer-Symbolik des 3. Gesichts [7]), aber auch neben den Salbungsriten der Vogelritus [8]) im Gesicht *Epha* und der Fluchritus [9]) möglicherweise dieselbe Herkunft aufweisen. So gesehen steht Sacharja in der Tradition eines

Sachbezug zu hebr. *bîtan*, akk. *bītānu* (Est i 5; vii 7 f.), etwa 'Königsgartenhalle, Audienzhalle', vgl. ʾăppaedaen* (Dan xi 45) 'Königszelt', dazu: A. L. Oppenheim, "On Royal Gardens in Mesopotamia", JNES 24, 1965, 328 ff.; W. Andrae, "Der kultische Garten", WO 1, 1947-52, 485 ff., bes. 488 ff. und K. Galling, "Apadana", BRL 30.

1) Vgl. G. Brunet, "La vision de l'étain", VT 16, 1966, 387 ff. und W. L. Holladay, "Once more 'ANAK = 'TIN', Amos VII 7-8, VT 20, 1970, 492 ff.

2) Im Anschluß an A. Jeremias, ATO [4]1930, 740 f., H. G. May, "A Key to the Interpretation of Zechariah's Visions", JBL 47, 1938, 173 ff.

3) Für eine solche Beziehung sprechen folgende Gründe: (1) Das semantische Paradigma von m[e]ṣulā ist nach allen atl. Belegen eindeutig und ohne Ausnahme: Meer — Urmeer — Ozean — Meerestiefe — Abgrund — und weist auf einen fernen Unterweltsort, den eigentlich extreme Jahweferne auszeichnet. (2) Die Symbolbedeutung des "Ehernen Meeres" ist in jeden Falle auch eine kosmische, vgl. etwa W. F. Albright, *Die Religion Israels im Lichte der archäologischen Ausgrabungen*, München 1956, 166 ff.; E. L. Ehrlich, *Die Kultsymbolik im Alten Testament und im nachbiblischen Judentum*, in: *Symbolik der Religionen* III, Stuttgart 1959, 24 ff., auch E. Burrows, "Some Cosmological Patterns in Babylonian Religion", in: *The Labyrinth*, 1935, 45 ff. (3) Im Visionskontext besteht nur so die Möglichkeit, das kosmische Mythologumenon als Ortsbezeichnung im Bereich der Jahwenähe unterzubringen. — Vgl. Th. A. Busink, *Der Tempel von Jerusalem*, 1970.

4) Eine kosmische Bedeutung der ehernen Tempelsäulen ist sehr wahrscheinlich, wobei andere Assoziationen keineswegs ausgeschlossen sind, vgl. W. F. Albright, a.a.O. 161 ff.; E. L. Ehrlich, a.a.O. 25 f.; W. Kornfeld, "Der Symbolismus der Tempelsäulen", ZAW 74, 1962, 50 ff., bes. 52 f. (Anm. 35).

5) Vgl. L. Rost, "Bemerkungen zu Sacharja 4", ZAW 63, 1951, 216 ff. (*Das kleine Credo*, 1965, 64 ff.); v.Vf., "Die Königserwartung bei den Propheten Haggai und Sacharja", Jud 28, 1972, 69 ff.

6) Vgl. S. Amsler, a.a.O. 228 u.s.u. III 2.

7) Zum Hintergrund der *kabôd*-Vorstellung vgl. etwa C. Westermann, "Die Herrlichkeit Gottes in der Priesterschrift", in: *Wort — Gebot — Glaube*, Eichrodt-FS, AThANT 59, 1970, 227 ff.

8) Vgl. L. Rost, "Erwägungen zu Sacharjas 7. Nachtgesicht", ZAW 58, 1940/41, 223 ff. (*Das kleine Credo*, 1965, 70 ff.).

9) Vgl. F. Horst, "Der Diebstahl im Alten Testament", in: Kahle-FS, 1935, 19 ff. (*Gottes Recht*, ThB 12, 1961, 167 ff.).

Jesaja, wohl auch Amos, vor allem aber Hesekiel, die die Symbolsprache ihrer Visionsdarstellungen dem gleichen paradigmatischen System entlehnt haben [1]).

Was aber ist Sacharjas eigener Anteil? Die Antwort muß lauten: Die Figurenausstattung der Szenen. Einige wenige Beispiele:

1. Der *angelus interpres*, der "Bote, der mit mir redete", erinnnert auffallend an den "Einführer" der altorientalischen, insbesondere des persischen Königshofs (Persepolisreliefs) [2]), dessen Funktion bei Audienzen als Sprecher, Vertreter, auch Zeremonienmeister des Großkönigs von besonderer Bedeutung war.

2. Die Myrten, zwischen denen der Meldereiter hält, entziehen sich der klaren Ausdeutung. Das im Alten Testament erst spät bezeugte Wort für den immergrünen Zierstrauch, der Israel vielleicht im Exil bekanntgeworden ist [3]), könnte am ehesten als Symbol für die stilisierte Wiedergabe einer Parkanlage am Königspalast genommen werden [4]).

3. Die Farben der Pferde — unterschiedlich in Kap. i und vi: rot (-braun), fahlgrau (grün) [5]), weiß, bzw. rot(-braun), schwarz, weiß, scheckig, gefleckt [6]) — entsprechen offensichtlich natürlichen Pferdefarben [7]). Ein solcher Reichtum an Pferden ist im alten Orient nur

---

1) Ich hoffe, in anderem Zusammenhang auf den hier nur angedeuteten Traditionskomplex zurückkommen zu können, insbesondere auch auf die von R. G. Hamerton-Kelly, "The Temple and the Origins of Jewish Apocalyptic", VT 20, 1970, 1 ff., angeregte Frage nach der Haltung Sacharjas gegenüber dem ersten *und* zweiten Tempel.

2) Dazu etwa G. Walser, *Audienz beim persischen Großkönig, Lebendige Antike* 24, 1965, bes. 19 ff.

3) Tg. überträgt: "Myrten in Babel".

4) Vgl. BHHW II 1264, BL 1189f., dann CAD I 2 342ff. u.s.u. p. 107 Anm. 4.

5) Hierzu vgl. H. -W. Hertzberg, " 'Grüne' Pferde", ZDPV 69, 1953, 177 ff.

6) Nach W. D. McHardy, "The Horses in Zechariah", in: *In Memoriam* P. Kahle, BZAW 103, 1968, 174 ff., bezeichnet *b^eruddîm* vi 3.6 keine Farbe sondern ein "pattern" ('gefleckt, scheckig', nach Gen xxxi 10.12, vgl. HAL), während *ʾ^amuṣṣîm* vi 3.7 'fleischfarben, grüngelb' bedeuten soll. Vgl. auch R. Gradwohl, *Die Farben im Alten Testament. Eine terminologische Studie*, BZAW 83, 1963, 8, 21 f., 55 f. u.a.

7) So schon A. Wünsche, *Die Bildersprache des Alten Testaments*, Leipzig 1906, 47 (frdl. Hinweis von W. H. Schmidt). — Selbst noch in dem von McHardy rekonstruierten Viererschema: rot, gelb, schwarz, weiß, das er im vorliegenden Text durch Abschreibeversehen aus den Farbabkürzungen: ʾ, ʾ, ś, l entstellt sieht, schimmern noch die natürlichen Pferdefarben durch. Auch F. Horst gibt zu, daß es sich hier nurmehr um eine "starke Abblassung" des von ihm zugrundegelegten "mythologischen Kolorits" planetarischer Symbolfarben handeln könne, gegen die von L. G. Rignell vertretene allegorische Auslegung. — H. Gese, a.a.O. 33 ff., sucht jetzt die Pferdefarben der beiden Visionen von der "antiken Farbsymbolik" her, d.i. auf dem Hintergrund einer "regelrechten Wissenschaft":

an den Höfen der (Groß-)Könige zu vermuten und in der Tat finden sich unter den Wandmalereien der assyrischen Provinzresidenz *Til Barsip* (*Tell Achmar*) am oberen Euphrat im Thronsaal "weiße", "schwarze", "braune" und "rosenfarbene" Pferde abgebildet, die teils als Reit-, teils als Gespannpferde fungieren [1]). Von den Perserkönigen ist sodann bekannt, daß sie sich besondere Gestüte hielten [2]). Schimmel vollends waren im alten Orient offenbar allein Göttern und Königen vorbehalten[3]).

4. Auf die Herkunft des Topos "die Augen des Königs" aus der altorientalisch-persischen Königsinstitution geheimer Dienste ist in anderem Zusammenhang schon zu verweisen gewesen [4]).

Die Schlußfolgerung ist gewiß nicht mehr zu gewagt: Diese Motivgruppe entstammt der Welt des Hofes, und zwar speziell des zeitgenössischen persischen Großkönigs, und gehört insofern zu der Hofstilsymbolik, deren sich auch andere Visionsdarstellungen wie 1 Reg xxii, Jes vi, Hes i in theologischer Übertragung auf je eigene Weise bedient hatten [5]).

Und so läßt sich zu diesem zweiten Angang zusammenfassend sagen, daß Tempelsymbolik und Imperialstil die Motivbildung bei Sacharja bestimmen; daß das Individuell-Charakteristische der Szenerie und Figuration gerade in der Anordnung dieser Motivgruppen besteht; daß die Mythologie nur am Rande direkt, etwa bei den Sphingen oder Genien, über die Tempelsymbole Urmeer, Säulenberge aber mehr indirekt von Einfluß war, wobei es im 6. Gesicht — Verfrachtung der Bosheit und Aufstellung auf einem eigens dafür angefertigten Podest in Babylon — geradezu zu einer Parodie auf

---

einer "Windlehre" und einer "Kontinentenlehre" zu deuten. Ob aber das Beweismaterial für die Behauptung zureicht, hinter der Bezeichnung der Winde mit Farben im 7. Gesicht stecke "einfach eine Meteorologie des westlichen Mittelmeergebietes" (33) wie hinter den drei Farben des 1. Gesichts die geographische Dreiteilung der Erde: "Braun, Hellrot, Weiß für Asien, Europa und Afrika" (35), muß dahingestellt bleiben. Die Feststellung allerdings, daß Sacharja "die Wissenschaft seiner Zeit" — aber auch die bildende Kunst (s.u. IV) — auf seine Weise in den Visionszyklus eingearbeitet hat, erscheint mir wichtig wie auch die wiederholten Bemerkungen zum Einfluß des persischen Kolorits (z.B. 26, 35).

[1]) A. Parrot, *Assur, Universum der Kunst*, 1961, 100 ff. (350) Abb. Nr. 118 ff.

[2]) Vgl. Herodot VIII 98, III 126, dazu Est viii 10.14.

[3]) E. Weidner, "Weiße Pferde", BO 9, 1952, 157 ff.

[4]) S.o. I.

[5]) F. Horst, "Die Visionsschilderungen der alttestamentlichen Propheten", EvTh 20, 1960, 198, zählt die Visionen 1 *Reiter* und 7 *Wagen*, wie auch die Vision in Kap. iii, zu den "Anwesenheits-" bzw. Gottespräsenz-Visionen; vgl. dazu W. A. M. Beuken, der noch 3 *Meßschnur* hinzunimmt.

mythische Denkformen kommt; endlich, daß damit erst die Herkunft [1]), das Motivparadigma, noch nicht die Funktion der Bildelemente im Visionenkontext bestimmt ist, der wir uns nunmehr zuwenden wollen.

III

Die nach ihrer Herkunft bestimmten Bildmotive der Sacharjavisionen bleiben nicht ungedeutet. In den Gesprächen mit dem begleitenden Gottesboten erfolgt eine Klärung des Geschauten bis ins Detail. Dies geschieht auf verschiedene Weise. So verweist der *angelus interpres*, der göttliche Hermeneut den Propheten auf die vor ihm sich abspielenden Vorgänge selbst: Die Reiter zwischen den Myrten erstatten Rapport über die Weltlage und erweisen sich dadurch als ein Spähtrupp des göttlichen Informationsdienstes (1); die Wagen zwischen den Erzbergen starten auf ein Zeichen hin in alle Winde und geben sich als eine Wagenkolonne zur besonderen Verwendung, wohl zu Repräsentationszwecken, zu erkennen (7). Auch gibt der Führer Erklärungen: Die vier Hörner bedeuten die Weltmächte, die durch vier göttliche Schmiede zerschlagen werden (2); der Leuchter mit den brennenden Lampen symbolisiert Jahwes die ganze Welt erhellenden Augen — zu beiden Seiten die ölgesalbten hohen Beamten, der Davidide in persischen Diensten, Serubbabel, und der Hohepriester Josua (4); die fliegende Schriftrolle versinnbildlicht den Fluch gegen Diebe und Meineidige (5), der Behälter mit der personifizierten Bosheit des Landes die Säuberung von Volk und Land (6). Schließlich zieht der Seher selbst seine Erkundigungen ein: Von dem Mann mit der Meßschnur erhält er die Antwort, er sei dabei, Jerusalems Stadtanlage auszumessen (3). Insofern lösen sich die Bilderrätsel vor den Augen des Propheten.

Aus der Gegenüberstellung der in den Gesichten den Bildmotiven beigegebenen Deutung zu dem Symbolfeld, dem sie offenbar entnommen sind, ergeben sich nun interessante Aufschlüsse über die

[1]) Der Hinweis auf die beiden Herkunftsbereiche soll nicht bedeuten, daß andere Einflüsse ausgeschaltet wären. So ist z.B. zu vergleichen: zum Stadtvermesser — Hes xl 3; zum *'epā* — BRL 322 f., BHHW 1163, dazu die gleicherweise merkwürdige wie instruktive Darstellung ANEP Nr. 332 (Szene links); zu den geflügelten Wesen — AOB Nr. 391 (199), BRL 113, auch ANEP Nr. 787. Rost sieht den "personifizierten Schuldspruch" in der Gestalt in dem "den Mißwuchs charakterisierenden leeren Epha" ("Erwägungen zu Sacharjas 7. Nachtgesicht", 227, bzw. 74), Galling erkennt darin "letztlich die Ištar von Babylon" (a.a.O. 119 f.).

eigentliche Bedeutung dieser Bildsymbolik, und es kann die Frage gestellt werden, was denn der besondere Beitrag der bildhaften Elemente für das Sinngefüge der Visionen sei, was das Geschaute für das Gehörte, die Vision für die Audition zu bedeuten habe — kurz: welche Funktion den Bildmotiven in diesen Gesichten zukomme.

1. Eine erste Antwort ergibt sich aus der Erkenntnis, daß das Visuelle jeweils den *Raum* einer Szene absteckt, sozusagen Bühne und Kulisse bildet, aber auch die agierenden Personen vorstellt und damit eine Art Exposition abgibt. Dieser Szenenhintergrund fungiert als Resonanzraum für das entscheidende Wort [1]). In gewissem Sinne stellt er eine "ideale Szene" [2]) für die Audition und knüpft so einen sinntragenden Zusammenhang. Die *Reiter-Myrten*-Vision hinge ohne die räumliche Szenerie und die bunten Requisiten als reines Hörspiel in der Luft und wäre erst ähnlich mühevoll einem Sitz im Leben zuzuordnen wie etwa die Berufungsszene bei Deuterojesaja (xl 1ff.). Denn es würden die ganze, hier in persischem Kolorit gehaltene Großkönigsvorstellung wie auch die Tempel-Gottespräsenz-Symbolik fehlen, welche erst dem Vorgang die sinnhaften Züge und Bezüge einer Prophetenbeauftragung verleihen.

2. Das Verhältnis von Bild und Wort in Sacharjas Visionen — und dies führt zu einer zweiten Antwort — ist dadurch charakterisiert, daß Bild- und Sachhälfte fast völlig ausgeglichen sind. Der Gedanke, daß es sich um eine speziell sacharjanische Verbildlichung, Veranschaulichung abstrakter, wie immer empfangener, Einsichten handelt, erhält darum neue Nahrung durch eine Beobachtung, die man an dieser Stelle machen kann: Immer dann, wenn die Engeldeutung in dem expliziten Zitat eines Jahwewortes besteht, scheint der Kristallisationskern der Vision ein Element dieses Wortes zu sein. Z.B. gehört zu dem Zitat: "Ich selbst will ihm (Jerusalem) — ist der

---

[1]) W. A. M. Beuken verwendet den Begriff "Situation" (237 ff.). Bei 1 *Reiter* geht er z.B. von der "Situation der Klage" aus (nach i 12), was m.E. zwar für die Thematik des Redegangs wesentlich ist, die Szenerie von i 8 jedoch nicht konkretisiert. Der 2. Typ der von Horst so genannten "Wortsymbol- (und -assonanz-) visionen" — nach Beuken 2, 4, 5, 6 (in Abweichung von Horsts Zuordnung bei 3) — bildet aber doch auch Bildszenen bzw. Situationen: die Schmiede "kommen" (ii 4); der Leuchter steht im Raum (iv 2 f.); die Fluchrolle fliegt dahin (v 1.3); die Ephaszene ist belebt! (vgl. *jṣ'*, die geflügelten Gestalten, die Deckelepisode). So vermag ich in dieser Beziehung einen Unterschied zwischen den Visionen nicht zu erkennen, s. auch Beukens abschließendes Urteil (255).

[2]) Vgl. hierzu in weiterem Sinne die Erwägungen von R. G. Hamerton-Kelly, a.a.O.

Spruch Jahwes — eine Mauer aus Feuer sein ringsum und Lichtherrlichkeit in seiner Mitte" (ii 9) das Gesicht von der geplanten Vermessung des Stadtareals. Dem Wort: "Ich lasse ihn (den Fluch) ausgehen — ist der Spruch Jahwe Zebaots — und er soll kommen zum Hause des Diebs und zum Hause des, der falsch schwört bei meinem Namen, sich im Innern seines Hauses einnisten und es samt Holzbalken und Steinen aufzehren" (v 4) ist das Gesicht von der fliegenden Fluchrolle zugeordnet. Gleiches gilt für die *Reiter*- (Völkerruhe i 15) und *Wagen*-Vision (Geistversendung vi 8). Ähnliches auch für die restlichen Gesichte: Ein bildhafter Vorstellungskern verdichtet sich zur plastischen Szenerie (Ölleuchter und Salbung, Mülltransport nach Sinear).

Um das Beispiel der Vision *Hörner* und *Schmiede* herauszugreifen, weil da die Dinge am klarsten liegen: Kernelement der Visionsdarstellung ist das Bildwort 'Horn', in seiner Bedeutung so etwas wie ein Ideogramm, vergleichbar dem Herrschersymbol der Hörnerkrone im sumerisch-babylonischen Raum. Zu diesem Bildkern tritt mit der Vierzahl ein weiteres Symbol, das eine Beziehung zur Vorstellung der Hörner eines Altars, dann allgemeiner zum Begriff der universalen Macht, der Weltmächte herstellt (akk. Weltherrscherprädikat). Zugleich ergibt sich aus der Vorstellung 'Horn' eine Assoziationskette zu den Redewendungen 'das Horn erheben', 'das Haupt erheben' (ii 4, wohl sekundärer Zuwachs) sowie zu der Vorstellung des 'In-die-Luft-Werfens, Worfelns' (*zrh* ii 2.4) [1]) normalerweise mithilfe hornartiger Worfgabeln [2]) und auch zur Vorstellung des Gegenteils, des 'Niederschlagens' (*wdh* ii 4) mit dem Hammer o.ä., wodurch die Brücke zu den Experten des Schlagens, den Handwerkern, Waffenschmieden [3]) geschlagen ist.

Träfe diese Analyse zu, wäre die Darstellung des visionär Geschauten ein sich aus einzelnen Teilelementen um das Bildwort und sein Bild-Wort-Feld herum aufbauendes Sinngefüge eigener und eigentümlicher Prägung, dessen Aussagegehalt sich aus seiner besonderen Konstellation ergibt.

In dieser Bildverdichtung, in der räumlich-plastischen Projektion von Bildelementen der im Offenbarungswort empfangenen Sinngehalte erweist sich Sacharja als ein Schüler Hesekiels, dem in gleicher

---

[1]) Zu *zrh* vgl. Hes v 10.12 (xii 14 f.); xx 23; xxii 15; xxix 12 (xxx 23.26).

[2]) AOB Nr. 166; A. Erman, *Ägypten und ägyptisches Leben im Altertum*, ²1923, Abb. 220 (532, vgl. 519).

[3]) Ähnliche Vorstellungen Jes liv 16 f.; Hes xxi 36.

Weise, wie etwa Kap. xxxvii zeigt, das aufgegriffene Bildwort von den verdorrten Gebeinen (Vers 11) zur visionären Schau, zur "dramatischen Realität" wird [1]).

3. Aus dem Bezugscharakter dieser Bilddarstellungen ergibt sich eine dritte Antwort. Mit diesen Bildsymbolen soll nämlich signalisiert werden, daß sie sich auf mit eigenen Augen gesehene, darum bezeugbar-wirkliche Vorgänge beziehen [2]), deren Realität nun eben damit dokumentiert wird, daß die realitätsbezogenen Zeichen und Figuren der Welt der traditionellen Tempeltheologie entlehnt sind und folglich an die Glaubensvorstellungen seiner Adressaten anknüpft. Dabei verhält es sich nun offenbar nicht so, daß die im Rahmen der geglaubten Welt geschauten Daten und Vorgänge gleichsam mit zeitlicher Verschiebung weit im voraus geschaut und als letztzukünftig gedacht sind; vielmehr — und hier erweist sich Sacharja als Prophet im klassischen Sinn — nimmt er teil an gleichzeitig, simultan — sozusagen live — anlaufenden, der träge dahindämmernden Welt noch nicht sichtbaren, doch bereits in Gang gesetzten Aktionen [3]). Und in der Tat befassen sich ja die Visionen mit sehr aktuellen Problemen der Exilswende: Heimkehr und Wiederaufbau, Besitzansprüche und Bodenrecht, Organisation der Führungsspitze, religiöse Fremdeinflüsse und Säuberung, und natürlich mit der weltpolitischen Lage [4]). Sollten auf diese Weise die Bildgehalte der Beschreibung der bestehenden Lage dienen, in die hinein Jahwe zu wirken begonnen hat — Bildsymbole als Zeichen und Kürzel einer bereits bekannten, geglaubten Welt, mußten jedoch Sacharjas Gesichte — wie es im Wesen des Bildhaften liegt — in der Folgezeit, aus diesem Zusammenhang gerissen und neu fixiert, zum apokalyptisch gedeuteten Repertoire messianischer Zukunftserwartungen werden.

IV

Sucht man unter einem vierten und letzten Aspekt die gemeinsamen Züge aller Bildmotive in ihrer Bedeutung für die Komposition des

---

[1]) W. Zimmerli, *Ezechiel*, BK XIII, 1969, 24* ff., 40* ff.

[2]) Vgl. F. Horst, Die Visionsschilderungen, 198.

[3]) Anders G. von Rad, *Theologie des Alten Testaments*, II, [4]1965, 296 ff., z.B. in dem Satz: "neu ist die Betonung des urbildlichen Vorhandenseins der endzeitlichen Dinge im Himmel" (298).

[4]) Vgl. die verschiedenen Organe und ihre Funktion: Informationsdienst (als Entscheidungsgrundlage), Waffenschmiede — Rüstung, Bauwesen, Verwaltungs- und zugleich Kontrollapparat (persischer Provenienz?), Strafvollzug, Säuberung, Repräsentation.

Gesamtzyklus herauszustellen, geschieht dies in der Erwartung, hierbei der Eigenart dieser Verkündigung, speziell ihres Redens von Gott, ansichtig zu werden und zugleich aus den Beobachtungen einige Folgerungen für das Verständnis dieser Art von Prophetie ableiten zu können.

1. Zuerst ist zu nennen die an den Bildmotiven der Visionen sichtbar gemachte *Bewegung*. Eine Unruhe zieht sich durch die Einzelszenen. Zwar zeigt das erste Bild Reiter, die verhalten, und die hin- und hergehende Rede der fast unbeweglichen Akteure vermittelt die starre Ruhe, die über der Völkerwelt liegt. Doch ist dies gleichsam nur ein Moment des Atemholens: Die Reiter harren nach dem Streifzug neuer Aufträge. Ein Impuls ergeht — er setzt den prophetischen Boten in Gang [1]). Dann bricht die Bewegung los: [2]) Schmiede erscheinen auf der Weltbühne, der Landvermesser geht ans Werk, wird aber über eine dreigliedrige Befehlskette zurückbeordert; wie eine Unheilswolke kommt die Fluchrolle über das Land; dienstbare Geister tragen den Bosheit-Kübel weg; die Gespanne warten auf das Startzeichen und stürzen los, gespannt verfolgt von dem Propheten und dem erregt aufschreienden Begleiter: Ein Wagen ist zum Ziel gekommen. Der Geist Gottes ist zur Ruhe gelangt (so MT; oder: niedergelegt) [3]). Und inmitten dieser Geschäftigkeit, Symbol souveräner Ruhe, der Leuchter mit seinen Lampen: "die Augen Jahwes sind es, die über die ganze Erde hinschweifen" (iv 10).

Es mag sein, daß OPPENHEIM recht hat mit seiner Vermutung, daß sowohl der letztgenannte Ausdruck wie die dargestellten Figuren als auch die Beschreibung der Unruhe in der himmlischen Welt unter dem Eindruck eines weit verbreiteten Traumas gestaltet wurden [4]). Die

---

[1]) Kunstvoll ist die Art und Weise der Darstellung, wie im *Reiter*-Gesicht das Wort zwischen den unbewegten Figuren hin und her geht, sich vom Meldereiter zum Boten, dann vom Spähtrupp zum Boten, alsbald zum göttlichen Hintergrund hin bewegt, sich dort für den Beobachter einen Augenblick verliert, um dann wieder von höchster Stelle über den Jahweboten auf den Propheten zuzukommen und sich in einem Verkündigungsauftrag zu artikulieren.

[2]) Vgl. das auf einen Ausgangspunkt bezogene, häufig wiederkehrende Verbum *jṣ*ʾ (ii 7 Subjekt: Boten ((2mal)); v 3.4 Fluch; v 5 Bote, Epha ((2mal)); v 9 Flügelwesen; vi 1.5.6 ((3mal)) 7.8 Wagen ((mit *min* vi 5)) = 14mal, davon 9mal Part.); dem entspricht: ʿ*md* (i 8.10.11; iv 14), *šlḥ* (i 10), *b*ʾ (ii 4 ((2mal))).

[3]) Z.St. vgl. die Kommentare.

[4]) "Their (sc. der Visionen) variety and especially their intensity lead one to suspect that they are the expression of some specific personal experience of the prophet, perhaps a clash with the Persian 'secret service' since Zechariah was in fact a contemporary of Darius I Hystaspes" (a.a.O.175). "This primary religious experience of being under immediate divine surveillance and protection was

psychologische Frageweise hat ihr Recht und hier wohl auch einmal Erfolg, indem sie die Mittel der Darstellung theologischer Sachverhalte motivieren kann. Jedenfalls macht sie darauf aufmerksam, daß die Gotteserkenntnis dieses Propheten, Erfahrungen des *Deus omnisciens et omnipraesens*, Tiefenschichten der menschlichen Psyche aufrühren und besetzen kann. Nicht umsonst weiß auch Sacharja seine eigene Tätigkeit den auf allen Ebenen beginnenden göttlichen Aktionen zugeordnet.

2. Ein gemeinsamer Zug aller Bildszenen ist weiter das Stilprinzip der *Symmetrie*. Bekannt ist die eigenartig symmetrische Anordnung der sieben Visionen. Zwischen den beiden in Figuration und Kolorit sich entsprechenden Visionen 1 und 7 (*Reiter* und *Wagen*) legen sich in zwei inneren Zuordnungen die paarweise zusammengehörigen zweiteiligen Visionen 2 (*Hörner — Schmiede*) und 6 (*Epha — Genien*) und 3 (*Meßschnur*) und 5 (*Schriftrolle*), wobei jeweils 2 und 3, bzw. 5 und 6 wieder sachliche Entsprechungen zeigen, um das zentrale Visionsbild des *Leuchters* (4) und bilden auf solche Weise ein kunstvoll gebautes symmetrisches Gefüge [1]).

Nicht so deutlich jedoch ist dieses Gesetz bisher in den Einzelvisionen selbst erkannt worden — ausgenommen die Vision *Leuchter* und *Ölbäume* [2]). Sieht man aber näher zu, ist man überrascht, wie konsequent das Prinzip der Gegenständigkeit in allen Visionsdarstellungen durchgeführt ist: Vier Gespanne kommen zwischen [3]) zwei Bergen hervor; zwei geflügelte Wesen tragen beidseitig einen Müllbehälter "zwischen Erde und Himmel" davon; eine Schriftrolle beherrscht als Rechteck von ca. 10 auf 5 Meter den ganzen visionären Bildausschnitt; der Mann mit der Meßschnur geht seines Weges, während von rechts und links zwei aufeinander zutretende Engelboten ins Bild kommen; vier (eiserne oder steinerne) Hörner für vier Schmiedehämmer; endlich die Reiter "zwischen den Myrten am Meer" [4]).

---

rather crudely 'mythologized' by Zechariah in a number of passages found in the collection of his visionary experiences" (ebda).

[1]) Vgl. A. Jepsen, a.a.O. 95 ff., auch H. Gese, a.a.O. 36.

[2]) S. L. Rost, "Bemerkungen zu Sacharja 4", 217 f. (65 f.).

[3]) *bên* 'zwischen' (i 8 ((10.11)) ((iii 7)); v 9; vi 1, sodann "rechts und links", die Zweizahl, Vierzahl, das Rechteck; vgl. auch die Gegenbewegung ii 7.

[4]) Eine auffallende Analogie bilden die Reliefdarstellungen am Palast von Persepolis, wo die einzelnen Abteilungen des Prozessionszuges da und dort durch "schematisch gezeichnete Zypressen" gegliedert werden, so daß sie sozusagen 'zwischen den Zypressen' zu stehen kommen, vgl. F. Sarre, *Die Kunst des alten Persien, Die Kunst des Ostens* V, 1922, 14, Abb. T. 19 ff. (bes. 26);

Die Frage drängt sich auf: Was ist die Absicht bei der Verwendung eines Formprinzips, das vor allem in der Kunst der antiken Siegelornamentik und Reliefdarstellung zuhause ist und die Fülle der Einzelmotive zu ordnen hat? Die Frage ist durchaus offen. Vorläufig wird man soviel sagen können: Das Stilgesetz der Symmetrie [1]), das nach seiner Herkunft dem geometrisch Ornamentalen verpflichtet ist, verleiht der lebendigen Bewegtheit der Bildszenen, der zielgerichteten Geschäftigkeit der Einzelaktionen ein Moment des planvoll Konstruierten, ja des Kunstvollen — Ausdruck eines dahinter stehenden, planend koordinierenden Willens. So spiegelt sich in diesen Bildern, in ihrer durchsichtigen Rationalität und Proportionalität [2]) und zugleich szenischen Figuration [3]), eine andere Gesetzmäßigkeit und die gezielte Programmatik des erkannten göttlichen Heilsvorhabens. — Hier wird ein Ansatzpunkt für eine vergleichende *kunstgeschichtliche* Betrachtung sichtbar, welche das Theologische tangiert.

3. Die Bildfolge repräsentiert *Progression* in der sachlichen Aussage [4]). Schon dadurch, daß der Aktionsanteil in der Visionsschilderung zunehmend größer wird, bis er zuletzt die ganze Szene umfaßt, aber auch darin, daß der gezeigte Vorgang jeweils im Deutegespräch weiterverfolgt wird, ergibt sich ein Fortschritt des Geschehens bis zu einem anvisierten Ziel [5]). Ganz gleich aus welcher Situation die Visionen im einzelnen stammen — eine Frage, der sich zuletzt K. GALLING und S. AMSLER [6]) gestellt haben, der Zyklus ist in sich geschlossen und symbolisiert die in Sendungen und Wirkungen angezeigte, großangelegte Jahwe-Initiative, das bildhaft vermittelte

R. GHIRSHMAN, *Iran, Universum der Kunst*, 1964, 154 ff. (bes. Abb. 211, 216 f., 228 f.); H. FRANKFORT, *The Art and Architecture of the Ancient Orient*, [4]1969, T. 182 f.; K. ERDMANN, "Persepolis: Daten und Deutungen", MDOG 92, 1960, 21 ff.

[1]) Zur Herkunft, Verbreitung und Bedeutung dieses Formgesetzes in der Glyptik vgl. H. FRANKFORT, *Cylinder Seals*, 1939, bes. 185 ff., 204 f., 256, 311 ff.; L. WOOLLEY, *Mesopotamien und Vorderasien, Kunst der Welt*, [2]1962, 80 f.

[2]) Vergleichbar ist die Tempelvision Hes xl ff.; zur "geheimen Symmetrie" der Grundrisse W. ZIMMERLI, a.a.O. 992 f.

[3]) Zur Tiefenwirkung in der persischen Siegelkunst H. FRANKFORT, a.a.O. 221 ff.

[4]) Vgl. K. GALLING, "Die Exilswende", 123 ff.

[5]) Die Nacht kann kein einheitsbildender Rahmen der Gesichte sein. 1. gehört die Angabe i 8 zur Einführung und nicht zur Visionsschilderung (vor dem eröffnenden *w^ehinnē*); 2. ist die Angabe zunächst nur auf die 1. Vision bezogen und nur indirekt durch die einleitenden Verknüpfungen auf den ganzen Zyklus auszudehnen; 3. hängt die Beziehung zum "aufgehenden Morgen" der 7. Vision an einer bestimmten, nicht unbestreitbaren Deutung der Erzberge.

[6]) S.o. 92 Anm.3.

Relief eines Programms [1]) für die Errichtung und Verwaltung eines universalen Reiches, welches das achämenidische Großreich — in vieler Hinsicht als Gegen-Bild verwendet — ablösen soll. Die Erwartung des in der alten und neuen Jahweresidenz zu errichtenden Gottesreiches in der, jedoch nur im Ansatz erkennbaren, Dimensionierung und Periodisierung ist der Punkt, wo Sacharja mit seinem Bildzyklus der Bilderwelt des *apokalyptischen* Schrifttums am nächsten kommt. Daß dieser Visionszyklus als älteste uns bekannte "vollständige Apokalypse" [2]) anzusehen ist, läßt sich von der Bildsymbolik und ihrer Aussageintention her schwerlich begründen.

4. Denn — und damit werfen wir am Ende noch einen Blick auf die *literarische* Frage — mit der *Intention* der *Niederschrift* der Bildgesichte bleibt Sacharja in der prophetischen Tradition, wo Visionsberichte in erster Linie zu Zwecken der Legitimation verfaßt wurden [3]). Sacharjas 1. Gesicht hat man eine Berufungsvision genannt [4]). Ob 'Berufung' hier wie anderswo der zutreffende Terminus ist, ist fraglich; ohne Frage aber ist, daß die (erweiterte) Visionsschrift mit den Grundlagen und Grundvoraussetzungen der prophetischen Verkündigung zu tun hat: Indem der Prophet sich selbst mit dem Wort von Jahwes "großen Eifer" und "großem Zorn" beauftragt weiß und sich neben und mit den dienstbaren Wesen ins Bild bringt, stellt

---

[1]) Die Beziehungen zum visionären Zukunftsentwurf sind offensichtlich, s. 108 Anm 2; vgl. auch C. MacKay, "Zechariah in Relation to Ezekiel 40-48", EvQ 40, 1968, 197-210.

[2]) Auch H. Geses, auf E. Sellin und B. Duhm zurückgehende, jedoch neu begründete These, daß in den Visionen die erste vollständige Apokalypse, in Sacharja der "erste Apokalyptiker" zu sehen sei, bestätigt im Grunde die vor allem von R. North, S. Amsler, R. G. Hamerton-Kelly, auch H. P. Müller, "Mantische Weisheit und Apokalyptik", Congress Volume Uppsala 1971, SVT 22, 1972, 268-293, beschriebene Zwischenstellung des Visionenzyklus. Die auf S. 38 f. erörterte Indizienreihe aber scheint mir in fast allen Punkten für Sacharja nur ansatzweise und sehr bedingt zuzutreffen (z.B. Stichwort: Pseudonymität, Geheimwissenschaft — bei einem schriftlich verfaßten, nach i 7 datierten und autorisierten Bericht? Zweiäonenlehre? Geschichtsüberblicke?). Was aufweisbar bei Sacharja vorhanden ist: Visionsschilderung, Bild- und Symbolsprache, Engeldeutung, sind doch vor allem Züge und Motive der Tradition der prophetischen Visionsberichte. So scheinen zunächst die Sacharjavisionen mit den Visionen eines Amos, Jesaja, Hesekiel in einer Linie zu stehen. Wo der Punkt zu markieren ist, von dem ab man von "Apokalyptik" sprechen kann, ist offener denn je.

[3]) Zu Traum- und Visionsberichten als "legitimating devices" vgl. B. O. Long, a.a.O. 494 ff. und vor allem A. L. Oppenheim, *The Interpretation of Dreams in the Ancient Near East*, *Transactions of the American Philosophical Society*, NS 46, 3, 1956.

[4]) R. Press, "Das erste Nachtgesicht des Propheten Sacharja", ZAW 54, 1936, 43 ff.; A. Jepsen, a.a.O. 98 f.; W. A. M. Beuken, a.a.O. 241 ff.

er sich und seine Verkündigung mitten hinein in den weltweiten Aufbruch und bringt auf seine Weise in den symbolischen Formen ungemalter Bilder zum Ausdruck, wie die göttliche Bewegung hineindrängt in die Sichtbarkeit der menschlichen Realität.

WHY WAS JEREMIAH'S NEW COVENANT NEW?

BY

JAMES SWETNAM

Rome

Jer. xxxi 31-34 is a text perennially cited by Old and New Testament scholars alike as well as by preachers of all persuasions, and it is particularly in vogue today because of its stress on interiority:

> 31 The days are coming, says the Lord, when I will make a new covenant with the house of Israel and the house of Judah. 32 It will not be like the covenant I made with their fathers the day I took them by the hand to lead them forth from the land of Egypt; for they broke my covenant and I had to show myself their master, says the Lord. 33 But this is the covenant which I will make with the house of Israel after those days, says the Lord. I will place my law within them, and write it upon their hearts; I will be their God and they shall be my people. 34 No longer will they have need to teach their friends and kinsmen how to know the Lord. All, from least to greatest, shall know me, says the Lord, for I will forgive their evildoing and remember their sin no more [1]).

Stress is often put on the newness of the covenant which is announced. But when an attempt is made to specify in just what this newness consists viewpoints differ.

One approach to the problem of newness is to say that Jeremiah was speaking about the new covenant brought by Jesus Christ, i.e., the oracle was not verified until the coming of Christ more than five hundred years after the oracle was first uttered [2]). Although it seems evident that the prophecy of Jeremiah is immediately relevant to the covenant of Christ (cf. the allusion in 1 Cor. xi 25 and Lk. xxii 20), this first approach does not seem a particularly happy one. The reason is that other texts of Jeremiah which use ideas and language similar to those found in Jer. xxxi 31-34 refer to events at the time of the return from the Exile [3]).

---

[1]) Translation taken from the *New American Bible*. For a discussion of various problems connected with the Hebrew text and its interpretation cf. J. Coppens, "La Nouvelle Alliance en Jer. 31, 31-34", *CBQ*. XXV 1963, pp. 12-21.

[2]) Cf. F. Schröger, *Der Verfasser des Hebräerbriefes als Schriftausleger*, Regensburg 1968, pp. 167-68.

[3]) Cf. Jer. xxiv 4-7 and xxxii 37-41.

A more common approach toward specifying the newness of Jeremiah's new covenant is to say that it is new in the sense that the manner in which the covenant contents are communicated is new [1]). This is simply a corollary of the view that the covenant which Jeremiah is speaking about is the Mosaic covenant [2]): if the content is not new, the manner in which that content is presented must be [3]).

The present note explores the newness of the new covenant along the lines of newness of manner in presentation and not of newness in content.

The text itself indicates the manner in which the new covenant will operate: it puts emphasis on interiority ("I will place my law within them, and write it upon their hearts"). A preliminary indication of how this interiority is to be understood comes from the immediate context, for the prophecy goes on to say that "all, from least to greatest, shall know me, says the Lord". And how are they to know the Lord? "No longer will they have need to teach their friends and kinsmen how to know the Lord". Interiority is thus understood as implying a direct contact between the covenant and the individual. This is a veiled but unmistakable reference to the shortcomings of

---

[1]) "In Zukunft ... will Jahwe einen neuen Bund mit dem Volk aufrichten. Das bezieht sich nicht auf seinen Inhalt, denn der bleibt derselbe (*twrty* 33a) and setzt sich aus denselben beiden Stücken zusammen wie der alte: Jahwe Israels Gott, Israel Jahwes Volk (33b); das alte Mosegesetz ist unverbrüchlich sowohl in der Verheissung des göttlichen Schutzes als auch in der Forderung des Gehorsams, der Erfüllung des göttlichen Willens. Neu aber ist daran, dass nun eben diesen letztere restlos verwirklicht und damit die Bitte von 31:18b erfüllt werden wird: alle ohne Ausnahme werden die *daʿat Jahwe*, die rechte Gotteserkenntnis besitzen (34b, vgl. Jes. 11:9; 54:13) ..." (W. RUDOLPH, *Jeremia*[2], *HAT*. Erste Reihe 12, Tübingen 1958, pp. 184-85).

For further views cf.: S. HERMANN, *Die prophetischen Heilserwartungen im Alten Testament*, *BWANT*. 85, Stuttgart 1965, pp. 195-203; R. MARTIN-ACHARD, "La nouvelle alliance, selon Jérémie", *RTP*. XII 1962, p. 82.

[2]) Cf. P. BUIS, "La nouvelle alliance", *VT*. XVIII 1968, p. 5; W. D. DAVIES, *Paul and Rabbinic Judaism*, London 1948, pp. 104 and 224

[3]) "On s'est parfois demandé à quelle première alliance l'hagiographe fait allusion. S'agirait-il par example d'un pacte conclu au moment même du départ de l'Egypte? Ou importe-t-il d'identifier sans plus la première alliance avec celle de Sinaï? La réponse ne nous paraît pas douteuse. Rien ne nous invite à ne pas songer au pacte sinaïtique. En particulier, la mention de l'écriture sur le cœur se comprend le mieux si elle s'énonce en opposition à la loi du Sinaï sculptée sur des tables de pierre" (COPPENS, *art. cit.*, p. 15). The thesis of the present note is that the "first covenant" is not simply the Sinai covenant which was written on tablets of stone but the Sinai covenant *insofar as* it was written on tablets of stone and remote from immediate contact with the individual Israelite.

those who had previously been charged with transmitting the Mosaic Law to the people [1]).

The preceding considerations are important for trying to understand how the interiority of the new covenant is to be achieved. But the decisive clue as to how the interiority is to be achieved may well be the simple phrase "write it upon their hearts" (*w^{e}ʿal-libbām ʾektabennâ*). This phrase is ordinarily taken as a metaphorical way of expressing interior communication [2]). It is certainly that. But something additional may well be indicated. At Deut. vi 6 the phrase "on your hearts" (*ʿal-l^{e}bābeka*) is used in connection with a stress on direct contact between the individual and the Law. At xi 18 the phrase is also used (*ʿal-l^{e}bab^{e}kem*). What is striking in each of these two texts is that the context uses a strong metaphor to illustrate what is meant. Deut. vi 6-8: "Take to heart these words which I enjoin on you today. Drill them into your children. Speak of them at home and abroad, whether you are busy or at rest. Bind them at your wrist as a sign and let them be as a pendant on your forehead". Deut. xi 18: "Therefore, take these words of mine into your heart and soul. Bind them at your wrist as a sign and let them be a pendant on your forehead". Much modern critical interpretation sees in these strong metaphors strong metaphors and nothing else: they are simply vivid the idea that the Law should be remembered. Rabbinic interpreters do ways of conveying not agree. They say that these texts were originally intended to be understood literally and hence are the biblical grounding for the use of phylacteries [3]). Not all critical scholars reject this view completely, but the thrust of contemporary critical interpretation is against the literal rabbinic exegesis [4]).

---

1) Cf. Jer. viii 7-9.

2) COPPENS invokes Jer. xxiv 7 as the best text to illustrate this interior communication, a text using the imagery of the heart. Here the word "heart" seems to be unequivocally metaphorical. But when the word *lēb* is used with the preposition *ʿal* in the expression *dabbēr ʿal lēb* (e.g., in Gen. l 21 and Is. xl 2) it seems to demand the meaning of "breast" (cf. P. JOÜON, "Locutions hébraïques avec la préposition *ʿal* devant *lēb*, *lēbāb*", *Bib.* V 1924, p. 51). The use of the preposition *ʿal* in Jer. xxxi 31-34 thus lends support to a literal interpretation of *lēb*, though the metaphorical interpretation is certainly implied. Coppens, in other words, might be skipping the literal meaning in his invoking Jer. xxiv 7 as the best text to illustrate Jer. xxxi 31-34.

3) "Of all the [rabbinic] commentators on the Bible only the 12th-century commentator Samuel b. Meir takes this command as a figurative one" (L. I. RABINOWITZ, art. "Tefillin", *Encyclopaedia Judaica*, Jerusalem 1971, vol. XV, col. 898).

4) Cf. the remarks of one critical scholar: "It is doubtful if the commands of

But once the texts of Deut. vi 6-8 and xi 18 are placed alongside Jer. xxxi 31-34 on the basis of the heart imagery a new element comes into consideration: the possibility of mutual illumination. The texts from Deuteronomy may be indicating that there is a physical counterpart to the metaphor of the heart in Jer. xxxi 31-34, and the text from Jeremiah may provide a specific historical context for the texts from Deuteronomy. A line of reasoning based on the supposition of mutual illumination would run as follows: Jer. xxxi 31-34 dates from roughly the time when the synagogue seems to have become a significant part of worship in Israel [1]). And one of the principal functions of the synagogue seems to have been the imparting of knowledge about the Torah [2]). If Jer. xxxi 31-34 is to have some reference to a concrete way of impressing upon the heart of all Israelites knowledge of the Torah, this coming to the fore of the synagogue would supply that reference admirably. And, conversely, the use of phylacteries in daily worship would be a natural counterpart to the institution of the synagogue: if Jer. xxxi 31-34 refers to knowledge of the Torah as read in the synagogue service, Deut. vi 6-8 and xi 18 are plausibly seen as referring to knowledge of the Torah as aided by the liturgy of the binding of symbolic texts on the wrists and forehead.

The background of this supposition is the criticism directed by Jeremiah against the priesthood officially charged with making the Law known to the people. In Jer. viii 7 the people's ignorance of the Law is mentioned, and then in the two following verses the responsibility for this state of affairs is attributed to the official

---

Exodus and Deuteronomy [sc., regarding the remembrance of words or rites in the texts alleged by the rabbis as grounding the use of the phylacteries] were intended literally in the first instance, but it is equally doubtful if the literal fulfillment is to be dated as late as the postexilic period. The cultic reappraisal of religion in Israel predisposes an earlier date for the transformation of the command into a custom" (G. Henton Davies, art. "Phylacteries", *IDB*. III, p. 809.

[1]) The passage is dated at about 587 "or shortly afterward" by M. McNamara in "Jeremiah", *A New Catholic Commentary on Holy Scripture*, London 1969, §498a (p. 617). Cf. also the view of J. Bright: "so far as I can see ..., nothing in these chapters [sc., xxx-xxxi] need date after approximately the middle of the Exilic period" (*Jeremiah, The Anchor Bible* 21, Garden City, New York 1965, p. 285). "It is to the period of the Babylonian Exile that one must look for the origin of the synagogue" (I. L. Rabinowitz, art. "Synagogue", *Encyclopaedia Judaica, op. cit.*, vol. XV, col. 580). H. H. Rowley also held for a date during the Exile (*Worship in Israel*, London 1967, pp. 222-24. But some authors have held for a pre-Exilic date. So E. Janssen, *Juda in der Exilszeit*, *FRLANT*. 51, Göttingen 1956, pp. 108-115, and the late R. de Vaux in his review of Rowley's book, *RB*. LXXV 1968, p. 588.

[2]) Rowley, *op. cit.*, pp. 229-30.

priesthood [1]). The "newness" of Jeremiah's new covenant consists in the fact that copies of the Mosaic Law are officially to be made available wherever Israelites are to be found, and that these copies are to figure in a liturgy in which knowledge of the Law is directly communicated to all. Thus the "interiority" consists in a direct contact between Torah and Israelite: God's Word acts immediately upon the faithful as individuals and as a group.

In the post-Gutenberg age this interpretation is not one which comes instinctively to mind: when copies of texts are produced by the millions in a matter of hours it seems natural and inevitable that newness refer to content and not to physical copies. Or to some metaphor for indicating that a given content is to be assimilated in a different way. And this is possibly the reason why the newness of the new covenant has been an enigma: it is very difficult to think one's way back to a time when physical copies were the results of long and laborious processes of transcription and when the physical copies were the object of explicit provisions in treaties [2]).

One central consideration commends the above suggestion about Jer. xxxi 31-34: up to now no clear reference to the origins of the synagogue has been identified in the Old Testament [3]). Though this lack of reference cannot be said a priori to be impossible, it is certainly surprising in view of the antiquity of the synagogue and in view of its importance in regard to the Old Testament. The present suggestion would repair this anomaly by assigning to the synagogue a text which is of admitted importance [4]).

One of the truisms of contemporary biblical scholarship is that the Hebrew mind thought and expressed itself concretely. The present note takes that truism seriously.

[1]) Cf. also Jer. ii 8.

[2]) G. E. Mendenhall, *Law and Covenant in Israel and the Ancient Near East*, Pittsburgh 1955, p. 34 (= *BA*. XVII 1954, p. 60); K. Baltzer, *Das Bundesformular*², *WMANT*. 4, Neukirchen 1960, pp. 28-8.

A passage in rabbinic literature helps to throw light on the pre-Gutenberg mentality. The Hebrew verb *šnh* in the Hithpaʿel, "to be changed", is used to describe a change of the Torah not from the standpoint of content but from the standpoint of the script in which the Torah was written (*Tosefta*, *Sanhedrin* iv 3 ff.). Cf. the discussion in W. D. Davies, *Torah in the Messianic Age and/or the Age to Come*, *JBL*. Monograph Series, vol. VII, Philadelphia 1952, pp. 61-3.

[3]) Rowley, *op. cit.*, pp. 221-22.

[4]) The fact that sections of Jeremiah have been related to the synagogue by a number of authors in recent years tends to lend credit to an interpretation which would link Jer. xxxi 31-34 to the synagogue. Cf. T. R. Hobbs, "Some Remarks on the Structure and Composition of the Book of Jeremiah", *CBQ*. XXXIV 1972, pp. 270-1.

DIE ESCHATOLOGIE DER PROPHETEN DES ALTEN TESTAMENTS UND IHRE WANDLUNG IN EXILISCH-NACHEXILISCHER ZEIT [1]

VON

KLAUS-DIETRICH SCHUNCK

Rostock

Die Eschatologie ist ein Thema, das zu den aktuellsten Themen in der gegenwärtigen theologischen Arbeit gehört. Man braucht sich nur die stattliche Zahl von Monographien sowie von größeren oder kleineren Beiträgen aus dem Bereich der systematischen Theologie zu vergegenwärtigen, die allein in den letzten 15 Jahren zu dieser Thematik erschienen sind, um diese Feststellung sehr schnell bestätigt zu finden. Schaut man sich diese Untersuchungen einmal etwas genauer an, so stellt man unschwer fest, daß sie fast alle bei der Eschatologie des Alten Testaments, genauer bei der Eschatologie der Propheten des Alten Testaments, einsetzen oder dieser zumindest grundlegende Bedeutung zumessen. Mit Recht, — ist doch das AT nicht nur ebenso wie das NT Grundlage unseres Glaubens und Redens von Gott, sondern dabei zugleich auch noch die ältere und erste Quelle.

Eben darum ist es nun aber auch so wichtig zu klären, was denn das AT, speziell die Propheten, unter Eschatologie eigentlich verstehen, wann und wie sich ereignend sie sich das Eschaton vorstellen. Die Klärung dieser Fragen ist zumal in den letzten 15 Jahren immer wieder versucht worden, nachdem man dieses Problem nach Hugo GRESSMANNS großer Untersuchung über den Ursprung der israelitisch-jüdischen Eschatologie vom Jahre 1905 [2]) lange Zeit hindurch für eindeutig entschieden erachtet hatte, — mit dem Ergebnis, daß sich in der gegenwärtigen alttestamentlichen Arbeit nun zwei Auffassungen gegenüberstehen, zwischen denen derjenige, der nicht Fachmann auf dem Gebiet des AT ist, mehr oder weniger nach persönlicher Neigung bzw. Sympathie für ihm bekannte Namen auswählen wird. Was beinhalten also diese beiden Auffassungen? Ich will im folgenden

[1]) Gastvorlesung, gehalten an den Theologischen Fakultäten der Universitäten Aarhus und Kopenhagen im September/Oktober 1972.

[2]) H. GRESSMANN, *Der Ursprung der israelitisch-jüdischen Eschatologie*, 1905.

zunächst kurz das Verständnis von Eschatologie, das ich selbst nicht für sachgemäß halte, umschreiben, um auf diesem Hintergrund dann die Auffassung, die ich für ursprünglich erachte, darzulegen. Danach will ich in einem zweiten Teil diese m.E. richtige Auffassung an ausgewählten Texten genauer belegen und endlich in einem dritten Teil den in exilisch-nachexilischer Zeit eintretenden Wander der ursprünglichen Auffassung erläutern und begründen. Daß es dabei zunächst vor allem um eine Begriffserklärung gehen muß, liegt in der Natur der Sache.

I.

Die erste Auffassung, die zugleich als die ältere gelten darf, könnte man in verkürzter Form auch als die der religionsgeschichtlichen Schule und ihrer Nachfolger bezeichnen; es sind Gelehrte wie Gustav Hölscher, Sigmund Mowinckel oder Georg Fohrer, die in Anknüpfung an Hugo Gressmann die Auffassung vertreten, daß man von Eschatologie nur dort reden könne, wo das AT ein vom jetzigen Weltalter geradezu dualistisch abgehobenes zweites Weltalter im Auge habe, das auf das mit einer totalen Vernichtung endende jetzige Zeitalter folgt [1]. Für die genannten Theologen gelten dementsprechend nur solche Aussagen des AT als eschatologisch, die außerhalb des eigentlich Geschichtlichen liegen, und das bedeutet dann praktisch, daß man meint, Eschatologie nur bei einigen späten, d.h. nachexilischen prophetischen Texten, die kosmologisches bzw. transzendentales Geschehen zum Inhalt haben, finden zu können.

Ist diese Sicht, die die Eschatologie faktisch auf eine dualistische Apokalyptik beschränkt, aber wirklich haltbar? Sie krankt m.E. daran, daß sie auf zwei keineswegs eindeutig gesicherten Voraussetzungen aufbaut, was sich gut an der Konzeption von G. Fohrer zeigen läßt. Ich meine folgende Voraussetzungen:

1. Nach G. Fohrer soll es vor dem Exil prinzipiell keine Heilsprophetie gegeben haben, d.h. alle eschatologischen Heilsworte und messianischen Weissagungen bei Jesaja und den anderen vorexilischen Propheten seit Amos sollen unechte, spätere Eintragungen sein [2].

---

[1]) G. Hölscher, *Die Ursprünge der jüdischen Eschatologie*, 1925, S. 3; S. Mowinckel, *He that cometh*, 1965, S. 149; G. Fohrer, *Ezechiel* (*HAT I, 13*), 1955, S. XXIX. 216; ders., *Das Alte Testament, Einführung in Bibelkunde und Literatur des ATs und in Geschichte und Religion Israels II/III*, 1970, S. 93 ff.

[2]) G. Fohrer, *Das Buch Jesaja I*, ²1966, S. 16; ders., *Das Alte Testament II/III*, 1970, S. 21.85-87.

Diese These ist exegetisch aber keinesfalls beweisbar, und sie wird noch problematischer, wenn man bedenkt, daß der ganze tiefere Sinn der vorexilischen Prophetie doch gerade in der Verkündigung von Gericht und Heil im Sinn eines Entweder-Oder liegt.

2. In seinem 1967 erneut abgedruckten Aufsatz über *Die Struktur der alttestamentlichen Eschatologie* vertritt G. FOHRER dementsprechend die Ansicht, daß die eschatologische Prophetie geradezu als das Gegenstück zu der vorexilischen Prophetie zu verstehen sei; die eschatologische Verkündigung der Propheten soll „das Ergebnis der epigonalen Entartung der vorexilischen Prophetie" sein [1]). Eine solche krasse Scheidung zwischen vorexilischer Prophetie einerseits und nachexilischer Prophetie bzw. Eschatologie und Apokalyptik andererseits ist aber schwerlich sachgemäß. Selbst die Apokalyptik hängt ja wesensmäßig mit dem Geschichtsverständnis der vorexilischen Prophetie noch legitim zusammen, auch die Apokalyptik verbindet mit den vorexilischen Propheten die allgemeine Zukunftsbezogenheit des Jahweglaubens. Somit läßt sich keine so totale Diskontinuität, kein so entscheidender Bruch zur vorexilischen Verkündigung nachweisen, wie G. FOHRER es tun möchte.

Damit ist bereits gesagt, daß es m.E. nicht möglich ist anzunehmen, daß die Eschatologie des AT es nur mit dem Ende von Weltzeit und Geschichte (= Unheilszeit) sowie einer darauf folgenden transzendenten Heilszeit zu tun habe. Das heißt positiv gewendet: Es muß in der Eschatologie auch schon das aufgefangen und eingeschlossen sein, was die prophetische Verkündigung von der Erwartung des durch Gericht und Gnade kommenden Heils zu sagen weiß, es muß in der Eschatologie auch schon die immer neue Entscheidung des Menschen, an die die Propheten mit ihrer Aufforderung zur Umkehr appellieren, berücksichtigt sein.

Doch nun mag vielleicht der Einwand erhoben werden: Das ist eine gewiß gute und einleuchtende Forderung, aber wo liegt der Beweis dafür, daß dieses zweifellos entscheidend wichtige prophetische Anliegen auch als eschatologisch zu bezeichnen ist? Wir müssen uns daher diesen Begriff kurz etwas genauer ansehen, was uns zugleich zu der anderen Auffassung von Eschatologie hinüberführen wird.

In dem Begriff „Eschatologie" ist das griechische Wort τὸ ἔσχατον enthalten, das örtlich wie zeitlich das Letzte, das Äußerste bezeichnet.

---

[1]) G. FOHRER, *Die Struktur der alttestamentlichen Eschatologie*, in: *Studien zur alttestamentlichen Prophetie* (*1949-1965*) (*BZAW 99*), 1967, S. 58.

Gibt es dafür aber im Semitischen, speziell im Hebräischen ein genau entsprechendes, deckungsgleiches Wort? Ich meine, hier kommt der Unterschied zwischen griechischem und hebräischem Denken entscheidend ins Spiel. Das hebräische Wort, das dem griechischen ἔσχατον am nächsten kommt, ist אַחֲרִית; dieses Wort aber bezeichnet im Hebräischen nicht nur das Ende und Letzte, sondern zugleich auch das Zukünftige und Neue (vgl. Jer. xxxi 17, wo schon F. Nötscher übersetzt: „Hoffnung winkt deiner Zukunft — Spruch Jahwes" [1])). Dementsprechend hat man anzunehmen, daß für hebräisches Denken „Letztes" und „Neues" zusammengehören, daß also für das „Letzte" das Prädikat des „Neuen" entscheidend ist, nicht aber die Zuweisung zu dieser Geschichte bzw. dieser Zeit oder einer anderen außergeschichtlichen Zeit. Für den Israeliten gab es keine Unterscheidung zwischen innerzeitlichem und außerzeitlichem (bzw. außergeschichtlichem bzw. transzendentalem) Geschehen; er kannte nicht unsere Zeitbegriffe, für ihn war vielmehr immer und überall dort Geschichte, wo Gott mit den Menschen handelt. Zugespitzt könnte man den Sachverhalt deshalb vielleicht auch so formulieren: Nicht die Zeit war ihm wesentlich, sondern das neue Sein! Und so dürfen wir nun festhalten, daß es legitim ist, überall dort bei den Propheten des AT von Eschatologie zu sprechen, wo ein Neues, ein neues Sein, im Sinne eines letzten und endgültigen Seins in den Blick kommt.

Damit haben wir zugleich auch schon die Grundlage erkannt, auf der die Vertreter der Auffassung von Eschatologie stehen, der auch ich mich anschließen und auf deren Grundlage ich im Folgenden weiterbauen möchte. Zu dieser Gruppe ist einmal Gerhard v. Rad mit seinem Schülerkreis zu zählen, dann aber auch ein so angesehener skandinavischer Alttestamentler und gründlicher Kenner der prophetischen Theologie wie Johannes Lindblom. Er umschreibt die Sachlage so: „Wenn die Propheten von einer Zukunft reden, die nicht nur eine Fortsetzung der in dieser Zeit waltenden Verhältnisse bedeutet, sondern etwas Neues und ganz anderes mit sich bringt, da haben wir das Recht, den Terminus Eschatologie zu verwenden" [2]). Und in Fortführung und Vertiefung dieser Feststellung sagt G. v. Rad: „Entscheidend ist ... vor allem die Feststellung des Bruches, der so

---

[1]) F. Nötscher, *Jeremias* (*Echter Bibel*), 1947, S. 105. Analog übersetzen auch die *Menge Bibel* und die *Zürcher Bibel*.

[2]) J. Lindblom, *StTh 6*, 1952, S. 88.

tief ist, daß das Neue jenseits davon nicht mehr als die Fortsetzung des Bisherigen verstanden werden kann" [1]).

Das Neue und ganz andere jenseits eines Bruches mit dem Bisherigen, — damit haben wir m.E. das entscheidende Kriterium für die prophetische Eschatologie der vorexilischen Zeit gewonnen. Ich möchte nur kurz noch die tiefgreifende Konsequenz aus dieser Erkenntnis aufzeigen und die Stellung dieser Eschatologie im Gesamtgefüge des Jahweglaubens beleuchten, ehe ich diese These an einzelnen Texten näher ausführe und belege.

Die Umschreibung des Wesens der Eschatologie als „Bruch mit dem bisherigen Sein und ganz neues Sein unabhängig von Zeitkategorien" — das verlagert den Schwerpunkt zunächst weg von den traditionellen Begriffen „Jüngstes Gericht", „Auferstehung" und „Ewiges Leben". Es aktualisiert die prophetische Eschatologie in einer ganz neuen Weise, denn das heißt ganz konkret: Wo der Bruch mit dem bisherigen, unter Gottes Gericht stehenden sündigen Sein vollzogen wurde und ein ganz neues Sein nach Gottes Willen und in Gemeinschaft mit ihm begonnen wurde, da ist das Eschaton bereits da, dort steht der betreffende Mensch bereits im Eschaton. Die Propheten des AT bringen uns das Eschaton — wenn man so sagen will — in unsere Zeit und Gegenwart hinein; es kann auch hier und heute schon dasein, so wie es auch bereits gestern und zur Zeit Jesu Christi dagewesen sein kann. Ja, es ist das NT, das dieses Verständnis der ursprünglichen prophetischen Eschatologie dann wohl auch deutlich bestätigt. Wenn es Lc. xvii 21 heißt: „Denn siehe, das Reich Gottes ist (bereits) unter euch" (bzw. „in euch" = ἐντὸς ὑμῶν), so zeigt sich hier, daß die Eschatologie des NT mit der Christologie als neuem Motiv doch nur die ursprüngliche Eschatologie der Propheten des AT wieder aufnimmt. Damit ist zugleich schon gesagt, daß das Eschaton keine ungeschichtliche Endphase sein kann; es gehört vielmehr eben zur Geschichte hinzu, so wie Geschichte und Zeit überall und solange vorliegen, wie Gott mit den Menschen handelt. Ich meine, daß man diese Konsequenzen aus der prophetischen Eschatologie Israels in der heutigen Verkündigung nicht hoch genug beachten und bewerten kann.

Wo aber liegen nun die Wurzeln für diese prophetische Auffassung vom Eschaton? Ich möchte antworten: Im Wesen des Jahweglaubens. Jahwe ist seit seiner Offenbarung und dem Bundesschluß am Sinai der

---

[1]) G. v. Rad, *Theologie des Alten Testaments II*, ²1961, S. 129.

Gott Israels, der sein Volk durch immer erneute Offenbarungen, direkte wie indirekte Eingriffe und Willensäußerungen zu einem unverrückbar feststehenden Ziel hinführen will. So ist nicht nur Jahwe immer wieder der neu Kommende und Zukünftige, sondern auch die ganze Geschichte Israels als fortlaufende Begegnung Israels mit Jahwe tendiert auf die Erwartung eines endgültigen Eingreifens Jahwes hin, das die endgültige Aufrichtung seiner Herrschaft über sein Volk und die ganze Welt bringen soll. Diese allgemeine Zukunfts- und Zielbezogenheit haben dann die vorexilischen Propheten durch ihre eigene Interpretation dieser Geschichte, ihre spezielle Wertung der Zeitsituation und ihre daraus folgende Gerichtsverkündigung legitim zu einer fest umrissenen Eschatologie ausgebaut. Die prophetische Eschatologie behält also das alte Ziel des Jahweglaubens, nämlich endgültige Aufrichtung der Herrschaft Jahwes über ihn ungebrochen anerkennende Menschen, voll bei, baut jedoch das vor diesem Ziel liegende Eingreifen Jahwes zu einem großen Gerichtshandeln aus (= Tag Jahwes), in dem nur ein Teil des Volkes bzw. der Menschheit bestehen wird (= Rest). Zugleich wird das Leben in dieser endgültigen Herrschaft Jahwes, aus der Erkenntnis der totalen Falschheit des gegenwärtigen Weges folgend, als etwas ganz Neues, durch einen tiefen Bruch vom bisherigen Sein Getrenntes, dargestellt und für dieses endgültige Reich nach Jahwes Willen ein besonderer Beauftragter Jahwes als dessen Regent eingeführt (= Messias).

Damit sind die drei spezifischen Entfaltungsformen der prophetischen Eschatologie genannt und wir stehen an der Stelle, wo wir unter Heranziehung von Texten, in denen die Begriffe „Tag Jahwes", „Rest" und „Messias" eine Rolle spielen, die Richtigkeit der eben dargelegten Auffassung der prophetischen Eschatologie vorexilischer Zeit überprüfen können.

II.

1. *Der „Tag Jahwes"* = יום יהוה

Wie ich soeben schon ausführte, setzen die vorexilischen Propheten, ihrer negativen Einschätzung des religiösen Verhaltens ihres Volkes und der daraus resultierenden Unheilsandrohung entsprechend, unmittelbar vor dem Beginn einer ganz neuen und endgültigen Heilsherrschaft Jahwes unter den Menschen ein Gerichtshandeln Jahwes an: den sog. Tag Jahwes. Er beendet das bisherige verderbte Sein und steht sozusagen auf der Brücke zum Eschaton, er ist als unumgängliche Passierstelle zu diesem von diesem nicht zu trennen. Das wird zunächst an einem Abschnitt, der von dem Propheten Jesaja stammt, sehr gut erkennbar. Der originale Text von Jes. ii 12-17 lautet in Übersetzung:

12: Denn es kommt ein Tag für Jahwe Zebaoth
über alles Stolze und Hohe
über alles Ragende und 'Große'
13: und über alle Zedern des Libanon '...'
und über alle Eichen in Basan
14: und über alle hohen Berge
und über alle ragenden Hügel
15: und über jeden hohen Turm
und über jede steile Mauer
16: und über alle Tarschischschiffe
und über alle Luxussegler.
17: Da beugt sich der Hochmut der Menschen
und es duckt sich die Hoffart der Männer.
Aber erhaben wird Jahwe sein, er allein, an jenem Tage.

Hier wird zunächst ganz deutlich, daß dieser „Tag Jahwes" ein großer, überall wirksam werdender und alle ansprechender Gerichtstag sein soll. Zugleich wird aber auch deutlich, daß dieser Gerichtstag keinerlei zeitliche Festlegung erfährt und schon gar nichts davon gesagt wird, daß er ein Ende der Geschichte und dieser Welt herbeiführen werde. Es ist vielmehr alles auf die Feststellung ausgerichtet, daß dieser Jahwetag eine Verurteilung, wenn nicht Vernichtung alles dessen beinhalten wird, was bisher den Stolz der Menschen auf sich selbst und ihr Vermögen ausmachte, was — wie v. 17 sagt — ihren Hochmut und ihre Hoffart unterstützte, was also ihr falsches, sündiges Sein ausmachte. Daraus aber ergibt sich dann ja als unumgängliche Folgerung: Das, was nach diesem Jahwetag sein wird, wird ganz anders, wird ganz neu sein. Wenn v. 17 sagt: Aber erhaben wird allein Jahwe sein an diesem Tage, dann heißt das doch, daß das neue Sein ein Sein unter totaler Anerkennung Jahwes, seiner Herrschaft und seines Willens sein muß.

Zu dem gleichen Ergebnis führt danach auch der wohl bekannteste Text des AT über den Tag Jahwes, der Abschnitt Zeph. i 14-16 (18a). Dieser Abschnitt, dessen altlateinische Nachdichtung 'Dies irae, dies illa solvet saeclum in favilla' dann auch GOETHE in seinen *Faust* aufnahm, lautet in Übersetzung des originalen Urtextes:

14: Es ist nahe der große Tag Jahwes,
er ist nahe und 'eilt' sehr.
Der Tag Jahwes 'ist schneller als ein Läufer'
'und rascher als ein Held'.

15: Ein Tag voll Grimm ist dieser Tag,
ein Tag voll Drangsal und Bedrückung,
ein Tag voll Tosen und Getöse,
ein Tag voll Finsternis und Dunkel,
ein Tag voll Wolken und Nebel,
16: ein Tag voll Trompeten und Schlachtgeschrei
gegen die befestigten Städte
und gegen die hochragenden Zinnen.

Auch hier wieder haben wir die Aussage von einer umfassenden Bedrängnis des Menschen und einer Zerstörung alles dessen, worauf er in Verkennung der Forderung Jahwes seinen Stolz und sein Vertrauen gesetzt hat (v. 16). Und wieder läuft die Folgerung aus dieser Schilderung des Tages Jahwes darauf hinaus, daß nur eine unbedingte, ausschließliche Unterordnung unter Jahwes Willen und seine Herrschaft, also ein gegenüber dem bisherigen Sein ganz neues, anderes Sein, aus diesem Gericht herausführen kann; — sagt doch der ebenfalls von Zephanja stammende v. 18a in negativer Formulierung: Weder ihr Silber noch ihr Gold vermag sie zu retten.

Aber darüber hinaus wird aus diesem Zephanjatext nun noch ein weiteres deutlich: Hier wird sogleich am Anfang zweimal vom Propheten betont, daß der Tag Jahwes nahe sei. Diese Aussage findet sich nach Zephanja auch noch bei weiteren Propheten, besonders bei Ezechiel (xxx 3), Obadja (15) und Joel (i 15; ii 1; iv 14). Man geht daher wohl nicht zu weit, wenn man behauptet, daß erstmals bei Zephanja um 630 v. Chr. nun auch das Zeitproblem in Verbindung mit der Eschatologie in den Blick kommt. Aber freilich: Hier geht es um das Problem, *wann* das Eschaton *beginnt*; die Frage, ob damit ein Ende der Zeit und Geschichte und also dieser Welt verbunden sein sollte, ist eine andere, die auch Zephanja noch nicht kennt und nicht beantwortet.

2. Der „Rest" = שְׁאָר, שְׁאֵרִית

Was ich anhand zweier bedeutsamer Sprüche des Jesaja und des Zephanja über den „Tag Jahwes" ausführte, erfährt seine Bestätigung und Ausweitung durch prophetische Aussagen über einen „Rest", der diesen Gerichtstag Jahwes überdauern soll. Ebensowenig wie beim Tag Jahwes braucht uns hier die Frage zu beschäftigen, woher die Propheten den Begriff „Rest" übernommen haben und was er ursprünglich bezeichnete; — genauso wie es in diesem Zusammenhang ohne Bedeutung ist, daß die Begriffe „Rest" und „Tag Jahwes" im AT auch noch in einem nicht-eschatologischen Gebrauch begegnen.

Hier geht es vielmehr allein um den Nachweis, daß den Propheten der Begriff „Rest" sehr gern zur Umschreibung der nach dem Jahwetag im Eschaton existierenden Menschen dient und dabei keineswegs auf eine außerhalb von Zeit und Geschichte stehende Idealgemeinde führt.

Das wird bereits an einem kurzen Mahnwort des ältesten Schriftpropheten, Amos, deutlich, das zugleich in enger Verbindung mit der klassischen Aussage des Amos über den Tag Jahwes überliefert ist. Es steht in Am. v 14-15 und lautet:

14: Suchet das Gute und nicht das Böse, damit ihr lebt,
und so wird Jahwe '...' mit euch sein, wie ihr sagt.
15: Hasset das Böse und liebet das Gute
und richtet das Recht auf im Tor, —
vielleicht wird Jahwe '...' (dann) dem Rest Josephs gnädig sein.

Diese Aussage ist ganz eindeutig: Amos rechnet mit der Existenz eines Restes des Volkes — das Wort Joseph ist hier ja Synonym für Israel bzw. die Bewohner des Nordreiches —, nämlich mit der Existenz jenes Restes, dem Jahwe seine Gnade zuteil werden ließ. Und diese Gnadenerzeigung soll abhängig sein von dem ganz konkreten Handeln der Menschen, jedes Einzelnen an seinem Mitmenschen. Gutes tun und Gerechtigkeit üben sind Verhaltensweisen nach Jahwes Willen, und wer diesem folgt, soll leben (v. 14). Dieses „leben" — W. Rudolph übersetzt sogar „am Leben bleiben" [1] — kann aber kaum anders verstanden werden als Bewahrtwerden im Gericht Jahwes, am Tage Jahwes, und weist so wieder auf das neue Leben im Eschaton hin und bestätigt die Vokabel שְׁאֵרִית = „Rest" in v. 15 als eschatologisch. Das in diesem Zusammenhang gebrauchte Wörtchen „vielleicht" deutet dabei keinesfalls auf eine Unsicherheit in der Feststellung des Propheten hin; Amos wollte damit vielmehr die absolute Freiheit und Souveränität Jahwes bei seiner Entscheidung sicherstellen [2].

Somit ist dieses Amoswort ein klarer Beleg dafür, daß die eschatologische Gemeinschaft aus einem kleinen Teil des Volkes, eben denen, die Jahwes Willen taten bzw. aufrichtig zu tun strebten, bestehen soll. Zugleich belegt dieses Wort aber auch die Feststellung, daß für das Eschaton das neue, Jahwes Willen folgende Verhalten entscheidend

---

[1] W. Rudolph, *Joel — Amos — Obadja — Jona* (*KAT XIII*, 2), 1971, S. 189.
[2] Vgl. W. Rudolph, a.a.O., S. 193.

ist, nicht aber Vollendung der Geschichte und Endzeit; — Amos rechnete damit, daß bereits seine Zeitgenossen und Mitmenschen in diesem Eschaton leben könnten.

Dieselbe Auffassung findet sich in der Zeit nach Amos auch bei weiteren vorexilischen Propheten, so vor allem bei Zephanja, aber auch in den Büchern Jesaja und Micha, wieder. Zeph. iii 11-13 lautet in Übersetzung:

11: Ja, dann entferne ich aus deiner Mitte
deine hochmütig Frohlockenden.
Nicht wirst du weiterhin überheblich sein
auf meinem heiligen Berg.
12: Ich lasse übrig in deiner Mitte ein Volk
demütig und arm;
es wird Zuflucht suchen beim Namen Jahwes, —
der Rest Israels.
13: Nicht werden sie Unrecht tun
und nicht werden sie Lüge reden,
und nicht wird man finden in ihrem Mund
eine trügerische Zunge.
Ja, sie werden weiden und sich lagern
und niemand scheucht auf.

In diesem Heilswort, in die Form einer göttlichen Verheißungsrede gekleidet, geht es um das Gegenüber von überheblichen, Jahwe nicht Ernst nehmenden Menschen in Jerusalem, denen das Gericht Jahwes angedroht wird, und einem Rest des Volkes, der bei diesem Gericht übrig gelassen werden soll. Dieser Rest wird von Jahwe verschont — offenbar am Tag Jahwes —, weil er Demut übte und bei Jahwe Zuflucht suchte (v. 12), sich also an Jahwe und seine Weisung gehalten und auf ihn allein vertraut hat. Kann es schon auf Grund dieser Aussage keinem Zweifel unterliegen, daß hier wieder die Existenz einer Gemeinde im Eschaton umschrieben wird, so wird das durch v. 13 noch weiter ausgezogen und bestätigt. Im Unterschied zu dem bisherigen falschen Sein soll es unter diesen Menschen kein Unrechttun, keine Lüge und keine Verleumdung geben, ja, es wird sie auch niemand von ihren Weide- und Wohnplätzen — wir würden heute sagen: vom Arbeitsplatz und aus der Wohnung — vertreiben. Hier wird deutlich eine ganz neue Seinsweise umrissen, die für diese Menschen des „Restes" gelten soll, wobei, über das Verhalten dieser Menschen untereinander hinausgehend, in v. 13b bereits Vorstellungen von einem allgemeinen Friedensreich, wie es die endgültige Herrschaft Jahwes bewirken soll, mit einfließen. Vor allem aber ist wieder deutlich: Die Anerkennung Jahwes und die Befolgung seines Willens konstituieren das Eschaton, — unabhängig von Zeitfaktoren.

Weitere prophetische Aussagen über einen eschatologischen „Rest" können diese Feststellung m.E. nur noch erhärten. Ich will deshalb hier nur noch auf einen mir besonders aufschlußreich erscheinenden Text eingehen, nämlich Mi. v 6-8. Dieser Abschnitt, ein wohl sekundär in das Michabuch eingetragenes Prophetenwort spätvorexilisch-exilischer Zeit, rühmt die Stellung der eschatologischen Gemeinde unter den anderen Völkern und Menschen. Dabei werden v. 6 und v. 7 betont und übereinstimmend mit der Feststellung eingeleitet: „Es wird sein der Rest Jakobs inmitten vieler Völker ...". Diese Aussage macht es m.E. ganz deutlich, daß die Bildung des Eschaton kein schlagartig sich vollziehender Vorgang sein kann, der sofort die ganze Menschheit und Welt in ein eschatologisches Sein versetzt, so wie dies ja gern bei einer Beschränkung des Eschatons auf ein endzeitliches, außerhalb der Geschichte stehendes transzendentales Geschehen angenommen wird. Vielmehr können die einen bereits im Eschaton stehen und leben, während die anderen dem Eschaton noch ganz fern sind.

3. Der Messias und seine Herrschaft = מָשִׁיחַ

Es versteht sich von selbst, daß es im Zusammenhang dieser Vorlesung nicht darum gehen kann, die ganze Problematik von Messianität und messianischen Weissagungen im AT aufzurollen. Hier soll es vielmehr allein darum gehen aufzuzeigen, welche Rolle eine messianische Herrschergestalt in dem Eschaton, wie ich es zuvor umschrieben habe, spielt und wie diese Gestalt innerhalb eines so verstandenen Eschaton zu deuten ist. Bestätigen die prophetischen Aussagen auch in diesem Punkt die vorgetragene Auffassung?

Bevor wir die entsprechenden Texte befragen, muß ich freilich zunächst darauf hinweisen, daß das AT das Wort מָשִׁיחַ für eine eschatologische Gestalt niemals ausdrücklich verwendet. Ist das Zufall oder Absicht? Jedenfalls ist nicht zu bestreiten, daß prophetische Texte eindeutig von einem eschatologischen Herrscher sprechen, der von Jahwe eingesetzt wurde und in dessen Vollmacht handelt. Insofern ist das Wort Messias = „Gesalbter", das zunächst ja für den judäischen König als irdischen Regenten Jahwes Verwendung fand, hier sachlich voll berechtigt.

Aus dem Kreis der sog. messianischen Weissagungen möchte ich nun drei auswählen, um meine These zu belegen: Jes. viii 23-ix 6;

Jer. xxiii 1-8 und Sach. ix 9-10. Zunächst zu Jes. viii 23-ix 6; der Text der für unsere Frage entscheidenden vv. 2a.4-6 lautet:

2a: Du machst den ‚Jubel' groß, du machst gewaltig die Freude.
.....
4 : Denn jeder Stiefel, der auftritt mit Dröhnen,
und 'jeder' Mantel, gewälzt in Blut,
wird werden zum Brand, eine Speise des Feuers.
5 : Denn uns ist ein Kind geboren, ein Sohn ist uns gegeben,
und es ist die Herrschaft auf seine Schulter gelegt.
Und er nannte seinen Namen: Wunderbares Planer, Mächtiger Gott, Beute-Vater, Friede-Fürst, 'Ewiger Richter' [1]).
6 : Mächtig ist die Herrschaft und des Friedens kein Ende
auf Davids Thron und in seinem Königreich,
indem er es aufrichtet und stützt durch Recht und Gerechtigkeit
von nun an bis in Ewigkeit....

Daß es hier um das ganz neue Sein in einer endgültigen Herrschaft Jahwes, also um das Eschaton geht, machen zunächst die vv. 4 und 6 ganz klar: Es soll dann nicht mehr Kriegsgerät geben, sondern Frieden ohne Ende, und Recht und Gerechtigkeit sollen für immer herrschen. Aber in dieser Herrschaft Jahwes soll nun nach v. 5 jemand regieren, der z.Zt. zwar noch ein Kind ist, dem aber die Herrschaft schon auf die Schulter gelegt ist; daß es sich dabei um einen wirklichen Regenten handeln soll, zeigen die ihm zugelegten fünf Thronnamen, die analog auch dem Jerusalemer König bei seiner Inthronisation gegeben wurden [2]). Also ein von Jahwe beauftragter Herrscher für ein Leben im Eschaton! Wie sollen wir das verstehen? Spricht das nicht doch für die Annahme eines endgeschichtlichen Reiches in ferner Zukunft? Ich meine nicht; ich sehe hierin vielmehr eine Aussage darüber, daß auch das neue Leben im Eschaton, das sich ja in dieser Welt vollzieht, eben deswegen auch einer Leitung bedarf. Es versteht sich von selbst, daß dieser Leiter der irdischen eschatologischen Gemeinde eine von Jahwe beauftragte, ihm in einzigartiger Weise besonders nahestehende Person sein mußte; man braucht hier nur an den Thronnamen „Mächtiger Gott" zu erinnern. Und ebenso klar ist es, daß hier der Prophet Jesaja ganz nahe am NT steht; für uns als Christen schließt sich hier der Kreis: Der verheißene Beauftragte Gottes und Regent in der irdischen eschatologischen Gemeinde ist Christus!

---

[1]) Zur Ergänzung des fünften Thronnamens vgl. K.-D. SCHUNCK, *VT 23*, 1973, S. 108-110.

[2]) Vgl. dazu genauer S. MORENZ, *ZÄS 79*, 1954, S. 73-74; G. v. RAD, *Das judäische Königsritual*, in: *Gesammelte Studien zum AT*, 1965, S. 211 ff.

Die weitere messianische Weissagung in Jer. xxiii 1-8 führt danach die Beschreibung der Eigenschaften und des Verhaltens des Regenten im Eschaton noch weiter aus. Die entsprechenden vv. 3.5-6 lauten:

3: Ich selbst sammle den Rest meiner Schafe aus allen Ländern,
wohin ich sie verstoßen habe,
und bringe sie zurück auf ihre Auen;
und sie sollen fruchtbar sein und sich mehren.
. . . .
5: Siehe, es kommen Tage — Spruch Jahwes —,
da will ich dem David einen gerechten Sproß erstehen lassen,
der wird als König herrschen und weise handeln
und er wird Recht und Gerechtigkeit üben im Lande.
6: In seinen Tagen wird Juda Heil erfahren
und Israel in Sicherheit wohnen.
Und das wird sein Name sein, mit dem 'man ihn nennt':
Jahwe unsere Gerechtigkeit.

Hie wird zunächst deutlich, daß der Regent in der nun nach Jahwes Willen lebenden neuen und endgültigen menschlichen Gemeinschaft als König herrschen soll. Er soll also ein wirklicher Herrscher sein. Aber noch mehr: Er soll weise handeln, — ein Ergebnis seiner besonders engen Verbindung mit Jahwe, des besonderen Besitzes von Jahwes Geist. Vor allem aber: Er wird Recht und Gerechtigkeit üben, so daß immer Friede und Sicherheit herrschen. Hier tritt die gleiche Vorstellung wie in Jes. ix 6 ins Blickfeld, die diese richterliche Tätigkeit nicht etwa auf das mit dem Tag Jahwes verbundene Gericht vor dem Eintritt in das Eschaton bezieht, sondern die eine Rechtsprechung innerhalb der eschatologischen Gemeinde im Auge hat. Eine richterliche Tätigkeit innerhalb der eschatologischen Gemeinde aber, — das läßt sich nicht mit einer im paradiesischen Zustand lebenden Endzeitgemeinde verbinden, sondern nur mit einer mitten in der Zeit und Welt stehenden Gemeinde, die trotz ihrer Bindung an Jahwes Gebote doch allen Einflüssen der Welt immer wieder ausgesetzt ist.

Als letzter Textzeuge sei nun noch Sach. ix 9-10 herangezogen, ein Spruch eines unbekannten Propheten, der jedoch noch vor dem Exil, etwa z.Zt. König Josias von Juda, gelebt hat, wie Benedikt Otzen in seiner Arbeit über Deuterosacharja überzeugend darlegen konnte [1]):

---

[1]) B. Otzen, *Studien über Deuterosacharja*, 1964, S. 134-142. Ähnlich urteilen F. Horst, *Die Zwölf Kleinen Propheten, Nahum bis Maleachi* (*HAT I, 14*), [3]1964, S. 247 und wohl auch H. Ringgren, *The Messiah*, 1956, S. 37-38.

9: Du Tochter Zion, freue dich sehr, und du Tochter Jerusalem, jauchze!
Siehe, dein König kommt zu dir, ein Gerechter und ein Helfer,
'triumphierend' und reitend auf einem Esel, auf dem Füllen einer Eselin.
10: 'Er' schafft ab die Wagen aus Ephraim und die Rosse aus Jerusalem.
Die Kriegsbogen werden abgeschafft, und er verkündet Frieden den Völkern.
Und er herrscht von Meer zu Meer und vom Strom bis an die Enden der Erde.

Zunächst macht es die Aussage von v. 9 „Dein König kommt zu dir" ganz deutlich, daß dieser Text vom messianischen Herrscher spricht. Dann aber trägt dieser Text zweierlei zu unserem Problem bei: Einmal wieder, wie schon Jer. xxiii, die Feststellung, daß der eschatologische Herrscher ein echter Herrscher wie ein König sein wird; er reitet auf einem Esel als dem Reittier des Herrschers (vgl. 1 Kg. i 33) und er triumphiert über alle Gegner — wenn die neue Ableitung des bisher mit „arm" übersetzten hebr. Wortes von ענה = „triumphieren" richtig ist [1]). Zum anderen aber zeigt dieser Text, daß die Herrschaft des Herrschers im Eschaton sich über die ganze Welt erstrecken soll. Ist das nun nicht doch unvereinbar mit unserer Auffassung vom Eschaton? Ich meine nicht, denn weltumspannende Herrschaft dieses Herrschers schließt nicht aus, daß es neben der Existenz von Menschen, die im Eschaton leben, über die ganze Welt hin auch Menschen gibt, die nicht im Eschaton stehen, so wie das schon aus Mi. v 6-8 deutlich wurde. Herrschaft bis an die Enden der Erde dürfen wir legitim als einen Hinweis darauf verstehen, daß es über die ganze Welt hin Menschen geben soll, die im Eschaton und unter der Herrschaft seines Regenten leben. Eine Aussage, deren Richtigkeit wir im Zeitalter der Ökumene nur voll bestätigen können.

Somit darf wohl die Hauptthese meiner bisherigen Ausführungen als hinreichend belegt gelten: Das Eschaton liegt nach dem Verständnis der vorexilischen Propheten des AT überall dort vor, wo jenseits eines tiefen Bruches mit dem bisherigen Sein ein ganz neues anderes Sein beginnt und sich ereignet, und das unabhängig von Zeitkategorien. Doch was wird dann aus so bekannten und auch gewichtigen Vorstellungen wie „Jüngstes Gericht", „Auferstehung" und „Ewiges Leben"? Die Beantwortung dieser Frage führt uns in die exilisch-

[1]) Vgl. E. Lipinski, *VT* 20, 1970, S. 50-53 und B. Köhler, *VT 21*, 1971, S. 370.

nachexilische Zeit und zu dem Wandel, den die bisher dargelegte vorexilische Auffassung vom Eschaton in dieser Zeit durchgemacht hat.

III.

Wie allgemein bekannt ist, haben wir grundsätzlich innerhalb der Theologie des AT, und also auch innerhalb der Theologie der Propheten, mit einer zeitbedingten Entwicklung zu rechnen. Zumal das Exil und sein Erleben bedeuteten in dieser Hinsicht einen ganz wesentlichen Einschnitt, der eine neue Verarbeitung der alten Traditionen veranlaßte. Dabei kam es insbesondere auch zu einer weit stärkeren Beachtung und Bedeutung des Individuums. Das, was die vorexilischen Propheten als die Begründer und originalen Vertreter der prophetischen Theologie vertraten, dürfte also in exilisch-nachexilischer Zeit, zumal im Hinblick auf eine stärkere Beachtung des Einzelnen und seines Ergehens, neu durchdacht worden sein. Das heißt konkret: Was ich bisher als Eschatologie der Propheten herausgearbeitet habe, kann in dieser Spätzeit durchaus Umdeutungen erfahren haben.

Das wird zunächst an dem Auferstehungsgedanken deutlich. Die Vorstellung von der Auferstehung eines einzelnen Menschen lag dem kollektiven Denken des alten Israel ganz fern; das bestätigt auch die Archäologie, denn Ausgrabungen altisraelitischer Grabanlagen, die als Familiengräber dienten, lassen nur 1-3 Steinbänke neben einer Fülle von Gebeinen in einer im Grab angelegten Grube erkennen [1]). Offenbar wurden die Gebeine eines Toten, nachdem das Fleischliche auf der Steinbank vergangen war, wahllos zu denen seiner vor ihm verstorbenen Verwandten geworfen. Hinter diesem Verhalten steht deutlich die Vorstellung, daß das, was göttlich war am Menschen, im Augenblick seines Sterbens zu Jahwe zurückgekehrt ist, das übrige vergeht wieder zu Staub (vgl. Gen. ii 7; iii 19). Daran änderten auch gelegentliche Totenauferweckungen, wie sie von Elia und Elisa berichtet werden, nichts; sie verlängerten nur das diesseitige Leben um einige Zeit.

Erst der durch das Exilserleben gesteigerte Glaube an Jahwe als einen lebendigen Gott, dem nichts unmöglich ist, und das Ausbleiben einer Vergeltung für den Frommen und den unschuldig Leidenden führten dazu, den Auferstehungsgedanken allmählich zu reflektieren

[1]) Vgl. dazu L. Rost, *Alttestamentliche Wurzeln der ersten Auferstehung*, in: *In memoriam E. Lohmeyer*, 1951, S. 67-72.

und in die israelitische Glaubenswelt einzubauen; Ez. xxxvii ist ein erster Schritt auf diesem Wege. Ist Jahwe nichts unmöglich, so mußte sich seine Herrschaft auch auf die Totenwelt erstrecken und ihm eine Änderung des traurigen Loses des Toten möglich sein (vgl. Jes. xxiv 21; xxv 8; xxvii), und leidet der Fromme dennoch in dieser Welt, so mußte das durch eine jenseitige Vergeltung ausgeglichen werden (vgl. Jes. liii 10-12; xxvi 19; Dan. xii 1 ff.).

Dennoch geht das AT niemals so weit, eine Auferstehung aller Menschen anzunehmen; noch die Sadduzäer zur Zeit Jesu leugnen diese ja entschieden.

Diese Entwicklung einer Auferstehungserwartung mußte dann aber auch eine Umdeutung und Weiterentwicklung der alten vorexilischen Vorstellung vom Tag Jahwes als eines vor dem Beginn des Eschatons liegenden Gerichtstages für das bisherige falsche Sein zu einem weltumspannenden Vernichtungstag apokalyptisch-kosmischen Gepräges voraussetzen. Aussagen wie die von Joel ii 1-11; iii 3-4 und iv 14, aber auch der spätexilische Abschnitt Jes. xiii, lassen diese Wandlung deutlich erkennen. In dem Augenblick, wo man für einzelne Menschen als Strafe oder zur Belohnung eine Auferstehung annimmt, muß man auch ein Gericht über ihr Verhalten vor dieser Auferstehung ansetzen. Und da die Auferstehung ja ein Geschehen war, das sich nicht in die Gegenwart — und somit auch nicht in das Eschaton, so wie es die vorexilischen Propheten verstanden hatten — einbauen ließ, blieb gar kein anderer Weg, als den Tag Jahwes aus dem bisherigen eschatologischen Rahmen zu lösen und zu einem nun wirklich endzeitlichen bzw. endgeschichtlichen Geschehen zu machen. Jetzt erst wurde er wirklich zu einem „Jüngsten Tag" bzw. „Jüngsten Gericht". Und damit wieder im Zusammenhang wurde nun auch eine Geistausschüttung an *alle* Menschen vor diesem „Jüngsten Tag" vertreten (Joel iii 1-5), denn jeder Mensch sollte die Chance erhalten, sich auf diesen „Jüngsten Tag" noch recht vorzubereiten. Erst die nachexilische Prophetie entwickelt somit diejenige Auffassung vom Eschaton, die das NT dann in Mc. xiii (bzw. Mt. xxiv; Lc. xxi) wiedergibt, — und von der her nun auch die vorexilischen Texte verstanden bzw. neu interpretiert wurden.

In Verbindung mit der Umprägung des Tages Jahwes zu einem Zeit und Geschichte beendenden Gerichtstag dürfte dann schließlich auch die vorexilische Auffassung vom endgültigen eschatologischen Reich zu der Auffassung von einem endzeitlichen Friedensreich paradiesischen Gepräges umgewandelt worden sein. Jes. lxv 17-25 oder

der nachexilische Zusatz Jes. xi 6-8 zeichnen ein Bild von diesem Reich, in dem nun totaler Friede zwischen den Tieren sowie zwischen Mensch und Tier herrschen soll. Es ist eine außerhalb der Geschichte stehende ganz andere Welt, in der man ewiges Leben haben kann (Dan. xii 2).

Daß bei dieser Umdeutung des Tages Jahwes und der auf ihn folgenden Heilsherrschaft auch griechisches Denken und griechisches Zeitverständnis von Einfluß waren, erscheint mir als sehr wahrscheinlich, doch muß dies hier offen bleiben. Auf jeden Fall aber wird an dieser Wandlung der ursprünglichen prophetischen Auffassung vom Eschaton wieder einmal nachdrücklich deutlich, daß eine sekundäre Weiterentwicklung einer Vorstellung zwar eine Jahrhunderte alte Tradition erzeugen kann, damit aber für unsere Verkündigung heute noch lange nicht die beste und gar einzige Grundlage zu sein braucht. „Zurück zu den Anfängen" dürfte somit auch bei dem Thema Eschatologie eine Losung sein, die zu bedenken und der von Fall zu Fall zu folgen sich gerade für die Verkündigung der Kirche in unserer Zeit lohnen sollte.

ON WIZARDS AND PROPHETS

BY

J. LUST
Louvain

According to 1 Sam. xxviii 3-9 Saul had turned the *'ōbôt* and the *jidde'ōnîm* out of the land. The short notice in verse 3 may be a later addition to the text, since it interrupts the story. The same theme however occurs in verse 9 where it certainly belongs to the original narration. It offers us the earliest reference to an action against divination in Israel. Notwithstanding their illegitimacy, the forbidden practices subsisted. Even Saul himself had recourse to them. The structure and the terminology of the story are important for a comparison with the later narratives concerning prophetic consultation. The occasion for the consultation is a situation of crisis: War is at hand (v. 4-5). One goes to the medium (v. 7-8) for information and guidance (v. 15). An answer is given, foretelling what is going to happen (v. 16 ff.). The specific terminology for the description of such an event is to be found in verse 7: *hālak 'el* and *dāraš*: one goes to the deviner to inquire through him. In a prophetic consultation the same elements occur [1]). The only difference is that Jahweh is the object of the consultation and not the *'ōbôt* or *jidde'ōnîm*.

A. The Etymology

What do we know about those, *'ōbôt* and *jidde'ōnîm*?

Very few. They belong to the mysterious world of a belief about spirits and the dead, similar to that which can be found in modern spiritualism. It is a feature of this subject that there is little open mention of it in literature [2]). A comparison with Hittite, Assyrian and Sumerian parallels has called to attention a vocable *ab* with the meaning of a ritual hole in the ground, dug to give infernal deities or

---

[1]) C. Westermann, "Die Begriffe für Fragen und Suchen im A.T.", *KuD* VI, 1960, p. 17 ff.

[2]) H. W. Hertzberg, *I & II Samuel, Old Test. Library*, London, 1964, p. 217 = *Die Samuelbücher*, *ATD* 10, Göttingen, sec. rev. ed. 1960.

spirits of the deceased access to the upper world for a brief interval of time [1]).

H.A. HOFFNER reconstructs the *modus operandi* for officiating at these pits. The pit was visited at night. The possessor, called *baʿalat ʾôb* [2]) unsealed it, so that the spirit could come up out of the earth [3]). When the interview was over she (or he) resealed the pit with loose soil, sacrificial loaves or even a cloth. In time the term *ab* which at first designated only the pit itself came to be applied to the spirits who issued from it and also to the owner of the pit. The spirits were supposed to offer knowledge and information and could thus easily be paired with the *jiddeʿōnîm* a term derived from *jadaʿ*, to know [4]).

HOFFNER's interpretation is very tempting. However, some difficulties arise, mainly in connection with the etymology First, in the Hebrew Bible the *ʾōbôt* appear very often in a plural form [5]) which is, as far as we can see, never the case for the *ab* (pit) in the non-biblical parallels [6]). Second, the consonant *b* in *ab* is somewhat dubious. Most probably we have to suppose a root *ap* instead of *ab* since the ending vowel in the Hittite and Assyrian term is an î: *âpi* [7]). If this is true it is very unlikely that *ap* became *ʾôb* in Hebrew. Third, it is difficult to accept that a name which at first designated only a pit came to be applied to the spirit arising from the pit and to the necromancer consulting the spirit [8]). The least we can say is that such a development in the significance of one and the same word would be rather amazing. Finally, if Hebrew *ʾôb* is derived form *ab*, *api*, then we have to explain the appearence of the *ô*. According to HOFFNER the ô-vowel in the Hebrew noun must be considered as a reflex of either a long pure *a*-vowel affected by the 'Canaanite shift' or accented short *a* following

---

[1]) H. A. HOFFNER, "Second Millenium Antecedents to the Hebrew *ʾôb*", *JBL* LXXXVI, 1967, 385-401, cit. p. 401. ID., *ʾôb* in *TWAT*, Stuttgart, 1971, k. 141-145; based upon M. VIEYRA, "Les noms du 'mundus' en hittite et en assyrien et la pythonisse d'Endor", *RHA* XIX, 1961, pp. 47-55 and C. J. GADD, *Ideas of Divine Rule in the Ancient East* London, 1948, p. 88 f. It is noteworthy that A. VAN HOONACKER, without having access to the Hittite sources, suggested a similar interpretation many years ago in: "Divination by the *ʾOb* amongst the Ancient Hebrews", in *Exp Tim* IX, 1897/1898, pp. 157-160.

[2]) 1 Sam. xxviii 7.

[3]) 1 Sam. xxviii 13.

[4]) HOFFNER, "Antecedents", p. 401.

[5]) Lev. xix 31; xx 6; 1 Sam. xxviii 3-9; 2 Reg. xxiii 24; Is. viii 19; xix 3.

[6]) See HOFFNER, "Antecedents", p. 389 ff.

[7]) In his transliteration of the Hittite texts HOFFNER writes *a-a-pi*. In his translation however he writes *a-a-bi*, which is rather significant.

[8]) HOFFNER, "Antecedents", p. 401.

the Phoenician pattern [1]). This may be true if the Hebrew *w* in *ʾwb* stands for a vowel and not for a consonant belonging to the root of the word [2]).

Other studies on the etymology and the antecedents of the Hebrew *ʾôb* brought forward different proposals which were never considered as being really convincing [3]). Many authors refer to Arabic *ʾwb*:to come back [4]) as the root of Hebrew *ʾôb*. For a scholar with a certain knowledge of the French language, this rings a bell: The *ʾōbôt* are to be considered as equal to the so called "revenants" or ghosts of the deceased who can be called up through a spiritist. We wonder however whether this interpretation would have been acceptable in the eighth century BC for a Hebrew who didn't know French [5]).

All exegetes agree that the *ʾōbôt* have some connection with the spirits of the deceased. Most scholars even think that they are to be identified with them, at least in some texts [6]). Isn't it amazing then

---

1) *Ibidem*, p. 388.

2) The foregoing criticism on HOFFNER's (and VIEYRA's) views was suggested to me by E. LIPIŃSKI. He is however not responsible for the inaccuracies which may have crept in the final wording of these objections.

3) A short but excellent survey is offered by H. WILDBERGER, "Jesaja", *BK* 10, 1, Neukirchen, 1972, pp. 349-350. Further bibliography: H. HOFFNER, *op. cit.*; F. SCHMIDTKE, "Traüme, Orakel und Totengeister als Künder der Zukunft in Israel und Babylonien", *BZ* XI, 1967 pp. 240-246; F. VATTIONI, "La necromanzia nell' Antico Testamento" *Aug* III, 1963, pp. 461-481; M. VIEYRA, *art. cit.*; H. WOHLSTEIN, "Zu den israelitischen Vorstellungen von Toten- und Ahnengeistern", *BZ* 1961, pp. 30-38; I. TRENCSÉNY-WALDAPFEL, "Die Hexe von Endor und die griechisch-römische Welt," *Acta Or. Budapest*, XII, 1961, pp. 201-222; H. SCHMIDT, *ʾôb*, in *Festschr. K. Marti*, *BZAW* XLI, 1925, pp. 253-261; A. JIRKU, *Die Dämonen und ihre Abwehr im AT*, Leipzig, 1912, pp. 5-II; A. LODS, *La croyance à la vie future et culte des morts*, I, Paris, 1906; A. VAN HOONACKER, *art. cit.* See also L. KOEHLER - W. BAUMGARTNER, *Lexikon*, 3ded., Leiden, 1967, p. 19.

4) Apart from our term *ʾôb*, the root *ʾwb*, to come back, is not found in the Bible. For *ʾôb* as derived from Arabic *ʾāba* see already STADE, KÖNIG, HITZIG; KAUTSCH etc., cfr. A. VAN HOONACKER, *art. cit.*, p. 157. See more recently W. EICHRODT, *Theologie des A.T.* II-III, Berlin, 1964, pp. 145-147. J. AISTLEITNER, (*Wörterbuch der Ugaritischen Sprache*, Berlin, 1963, p. 73) thinks he can find *ʾb = wieder* in Ugarit in II AB VII 43. He refers to Arab. *ʾāba*, and to Hebrew *ʾôb* 'revenant'. The text is as follows: *ʾmlk ʾblmlk*. J. AISTLEITNER translates: "Nun wurde ich wieder zum König . . ." As far as we can see he stands alone in this translation. (See J. AISTLEITNER, *Die Myhtologischen und kultischen Texte aus Ras Schamra*, Budapest, 1964, p. 45). C. H. GORDON, *Ugaritic Textbook*, Roma, 1965 transliterates *umlk ublmlk*. A. HERDNER, *Corpus des tablettes en cuneiformes alphabétiques. Mission de Ras Shamra X*, Paris, 1963, p. 30 has *ʾumlk. ʾubl mlk*. G. R. DRIVER, *Canaanite Myths and Legends*, Edinburgh, 1956, pp. 100-01 reads: *u mlk u bl mlk*.

5) Other etymological studies often see the term *ʾôb* "ghost" as a derivation from *ʾôb* "bag" a word which occurs only in Job xxxii 19. In KOEHLER-BAUMGARTNER, *Lexikon*, p. 19, it is listed as I *ʾôb*.

6) See H. WILDBERGER, op. cit., p. 350.

that, where the etymology of the term is concerned, the root *'âb*: "father", "ancestor", is seldom or never taken into consideration? And yet we know that, when important people died in the Biblical world, they were "gathered with the *'ōbôt* or went to "sleep with the *'ōbôt*" [1]). Those and similar expressions mean that the dead joined the spirits of their former deceased fathers [2]).

The only full report of a consultation of the *'ôb* preserved in the Bible (1 Sam. xxviii) describes how in fact one of the fathers, namely Samuel, was awakend from his "sleep" to answer the questions of the consultant [3]).

When we adduce *'āb*: father, in connection with the etymology of *'ôb*, we are up against a few problems. The first is the spelling. We have to explain how *'b* developped into *'wb*. The authors proposing Sumerian *ab*: pit, as the root of *'wb* had to face a similar problem among many others. The answer may be found along the same lines. The *ô* vowel in *'ôb* may be considered as a reflex of the long *ā* vowel in *'āb* affected by the "Canaanite shift" [4]).

The new vocalisation may also imply a theological interpretation: It may have been introduced to dissociate the highly respectable fathers from a severely condemned practice of devination. Similar procedures occur elsewhere in the Bible. For the servants of Jahweh and of the gods the same term is used: *ʿbd*; the vocalisation however is different [5]).

1) H. RINGGREN, *'āb*, in *TWAT* I 1, Stuttgart 1970, k. 10; B. ALFRINK, "L' expression *šākab 'im 'obōtāw*", in *OTS* 2, Leiden 1943, pp. 106-118. See e.g. Jud. ii 10; Deut. xxxi 16.

2) H. RINGGREN, *ibidem.*

3) "Then Samuel said to Saul: Why have you disturbed me by bringing me up"? 1 Sam. xxviii 15.

4) HOFFNER, "Antecedents", p. 388. More data in R. MEYER, *Hebräische Grammatik*, I, Berlin, 1966, p. 102 f.: "Naturlanges ā in der Drucksilbe wurde kanaanäisch zu ō. Daneben begegnet altes ā in *qām* . . . und zuweilen sind tiberisch ā und ô neben einander belegt: Part. M. Pl. *qômîm* (2 R. 16, 7) neben üblichem *qāmîm* . .". Compare with R. MACUCH, *Grammatik des samaritanischen hebräisch*, Berlin, 1969, p. 165: "Das Sam. Hebr. hat in mehreren Fällen das ursprüngliche ā bewahrt, das im MH in ō verwandelt worden ist . . . vgl. neben den Partizipien auch den Eigennamen *'mr* Gn 36: 11,15 *āmar* ggüb. M *'omār* (= LXX Oman, Omar)". We have to notice however that to MH *'ôb* corresponds SH *'ôb* in Kennicot's edition.

5) A servant of the Lord is called an *ʿebed* (subst.) whereas a servant of the gods is an *ʿōbed* (part.). This is most striking in 2 Reg. x 23 where the *ʿabᵉdê Jahweh* are clearly distinguished from the *ʿōbᵉdê habaʿal*. We never find *ʿebed* in connection with the gods but always *ʿobed*; see e.g. 2 Reg. x 19, 21, 22; xvii 33, 41. The title *ʿebed* in relation to Jahweh is most often applied to individuals like Mozes, Abraham, Jacob, David, Elisha. The full title "Ebed Jahweh" is pratically the prerogative of Moses: Deut. xxxiv 5, Jos. i 1, 13, 15; viii 31, 33; xi 12; xii 6. See H. M. ORLINSKY,

In this context it may be important to notice that in most passages where *ʾwb* is mentioned in its singular form, some manuscripts read *ʾb* without *w*, which suggests that the original text didn't have the *w* [1]). The plural form causes no problem [2]).

The second objection against accepting *ʾwb* as derived from *ʾb*: father, ancestor, may come up out of the context. Indeed, some verbs used with *ʾôb* or *ʾōbôt* as object hardly allow to recognise the *ʾôb* as a person or as a ghost. How can one "make" [3]) ghosts or how can one "destroy" [4]) them or "remove and burn down" [5])? Of course, all those verbs taken separetely have different meanings and could "à la rigueur" be applied to persons [6]). When considered together however they rather refer to a material object [7]). So one has to accept that *ʾôb* not only stands for "ghost" but also for an image representing the "ghost" or any other object used in the practice of consulting the spirits. According to H. WILDBERGER something similar is true for the *ʾašerâ* which designates not only a goddess but also a cultic pillar representing the goddess. The comparison is somewhat dubious [8]). It may be better to compare the *ʾobôt* with the gods. The same verbs are used indeed in connection with the *ʾelohîm* [9]) and this implies that

---

"The So-called 'Servant of the Lord' and 'Suffering Servant' in Second Isaiah", in *Studies on the Second part of the Book of Isaiah*, *VT Supp*. 14, Leiden, 1967, p. 7-11.

1) See B. KENNICOT, *Vet. Test. Hebr.* Oxford, 1776: 1 Sam. xxviii 7a has *ʾb* in mss. 96, 168; 1 Sam. xxviii 7b in mss. 2, 96, 168, 249, 253, 257, 260; 1 Sam. xxviii 8 in 3, 168, 182; Deut. xviii, 11 in 80, 107 and "forte" in 128; Is. xxix 4 in 72, 182; 1 Chron. x 13 in 80, 118, 223, 235.

2) *1Q Isa* has *ʾbwt* in Is. viii 19 and xix 13 but puts a *w* above the line between *ʾ* and *b*. KENNICOT mentions some mss having *ʾwbwt*. In general however most mss read *ʾbwt* as the plural of both *ʾwb* and *ʾb*.

3) *ʿśh* in 2 Reg. xxi 6 and 2 Chron. xxxiii 6. At a first look one may think that this supports HOFFNER's theory. However the verb *ʿśh* is no specific term indicating the digging of a pit. Hebrew vocabularly has more appropriate terms for this particular action. Moreover, the object of *ʿśh* in the discussed texts is not only *ʾôb* but also *jiddeʿōnî*. The latter cannot be considered as an other name for a holy pit.

4) *krt* (hifil) in 1 Sam. xxviii 9.

5) *bʿr* (piel) in 2 Reg. xxiii 24.

6) E.g. *ʿśh* can have the meaning of "acquire": Gen. xii 5 (slaves); see KOEHLER-BAUMGARTNER, *op. cit.* p. 740.

7) Thus recently H. WILDBERGER, *op. cit.* p. 350; H. WOHLSTEIN, *art. cit.*, p. 33 f. Against KOEHLER-BAUMGARTNER, *Lexikon*, p. 20.

8) *ʾAšērâ* (goddess) may be found in Jud. iii 7 and 1 Reg. xviii 19. See however E. LIPIŃSKI, "The Goddess Atirat", *Orientalia Lov. Periodica* III, 1972, pp. 101-119. This author made it clear that *ʾašērâ* in those texts is due to a scribal error. Originally the text read *ʾaštārôt* in stead of *ʾašērôt*. In the other texts *ʾašērâ* means a grove or cultic place and not a pillar representing the goddess.

9) See e.g. Jud. xviii 24: *ʿśh*; F. VATTIONI, *art. cit.*, p. 470 f. for a comparison between *ʾelohîm* and *ʾôb*.

this term indicates not only the gods but also their images [1]). Thus *'ôb* may have a double meaning. There is no need however for a third one, recognising in the *'ôb* a "necromancer" [2]). When a specialist in evoking the spirits is intended, he or she is called a *šo'el 'ôb* (Deut. xviii 11) or a *ba'alat 'ôb* (1 Sam. xxviii 7-8) not simply *'ôb*.

Our interpretation of *'ôb* as derived from *'ab* "father" is confirmed by the use of some parallel terms in the Bible. The *'ōbôt* are placed in one line with the *'ittim* or the spirits of the deceased in Is. xix 3. This noun occurs only once in the Scriptures and is apparently derived from the Accadian *etimmu*: ghost of a dead person [3]).

In Deut. xviii 11 and Is. viii 19 they appear in connection with the *metîm*, the dead [4]). We also find the *terafîm* or "images of the ancestors" [5]) listed as a synonym of the *'ōbôt* in 2 Reg. xxiii 24. Finally we have to mention the *jidde'ōnîm*. In our Biblical texts they are always paired with the *'ōbôt*. Nobody seems to have any doubts about the meaning of the term and about its etymology. It is generally hold as being a derivative of *jd'* to know. The *jidde'ōnî* is the "one who knows" [6]) Like *'ôb*, the name is usually applied both to the spirit who is to be consulted and to the soothsayer [7]). In fact, it refers to the spirit of the deceased only. Indeed, in many cultures the ghost of the dead is supposed to be the "one who knows" and who can give information about hidden matters [8]). This leads us to some remarks on non Biblical parallels of *'ôb* [9]).

---

1) This suggestion is also given by H. Wildberger, *op. cti.*, p. 349, but is has to give way for the comparisen with the *'ašēra* om p. 350.

2) Against most Bible translations and F. Zorell, *Lexicon*, Roma, 1968, p. 18.

3) Koehler-Baumgartner, *Lexicon*, 1967, p. 36; H. Wohlstein, *art. cit.*, p. 35-36; F. Schmidtke, *art. cit.*, p. 240-246.

4) Notice how the *'ôb* and the *metîm* appear in a parallel-structure: *šō'el 'ôb wejidd e'ōnî* and *dōreš 'el hammetîm* in Deut. xviii 11.

5) See e.g. H. Wohlstein, *art. cit.*, p. 37-38. The etymology and meaning of the term is not certain. A good survey is given by A. Johnson, *The Cultic Prophet*, Cardiff, sec. ed. 1962, p. 32-33. It is interesting to notice that in Gen. xxi, the term *terāfîm* (v. 19, 34, 35) alternates with *'elohîm*.

6) See e.g. van Hoonacker, *art. cit.*, p. 157, Hoffner, "Antecedents", p. 401; Wildberger, *op. cit.*, p. 351, who compares *jidde'onî* with an Arabic ghost *hawkim* (root *hkm*), cfr. *Wörterbuch der Mythologie* I, ed. H. Haussig, p. 510. It has to be noticed however that in Arabic, *hkm* rather refers to an activity of judgement. See *Wörterbuch der Mythol.*, p. 510.

7) See Koehler-Baumgartner, *Lexikon*, p. 367, with reference to Accadian *mudū*: learned men.

8) See notes 1 and 2 on p. 139.

9) Other Biblical parallels of *'ôb* are less relevant for the etymology of our term. They are listed in Deut. xviii 10-11: *qōsem qesamîm*; *me'ônen*; *menaheš*; *mehašef*; *ḥōber ḥaber*. It has to be noticed however that these terms stand as parallels for

Necromancy was well known and cherished among Israel's neighbours. We cannot make a complete study here of this widespread and complex phenomenon [1]). For the etymology of *'ôb* it may be interesting however to point to some Hittite texts in which the ghosts of the ancestors are consulted. The name given to those spirits seems to be "divinised father" which comes very close to biblical *'ôb* [2]).

We may sumarize as follows: The *'ōbôt* designated originally the spirits of the deceased fathers living in the Netherworld. This explains sufficiently how the voice of an *'ôb* is supposed "to come out of the ground (*'ereṣ*)": Is. xxix 4 and how the spirit [3]) of Samuel "came up from earth (*'ereṣ*)": 1 Sam. xxviii 14 [4]).

B. The Consultation and its Condemnation

The consultation of ghosts and gods described above is usually indicated by the verb *dāraš* [5]). This term never occurs in a context where priests inquire of God. It seems to be a specific term reserved

---

šō'el 'ôb and not for simpel *'ôb*. The early translations are not of great help. For *'ōbôt* and *jiddeʿōnîm* the Targums have respectively *bdjn* and *zkwrw*. The etymology is uncertain. For *bdjn* M. Jastrow, *Dictionary of Talmud . . . and Targumim*, New York 1950, refers to hebrew *bāddîm* and translates: "fictions" (p. 140). For *zkwrw* he refers to *zkr* and translates: "necromantic incantation by means of a membrum virile" (p. 398). Comp. with J. Levy, *Wörterbuch über die Talmudim und Midrachim* I, Darmstadt, 1963: "*bdjn* mögl. Weise zusammenhangend mit *pjtm*, gr. *puthoon*" (p. 193). "*Zkrw*: das Wort ist höchst wahrsch. gr. Urspr." (p. 537). The Greek text usually reads ἐγγαστρίμυθος for *'ôb*. In Is. xxix 4 it has οἱ φωνοῦντες ἐκ τῆς γῆς for *'ôb mē'ereṣ*. This is however not the only exception (as opposed to Hoffner in *TWAT*): In 2 Reg. xxi 6 and xxiii 24 we find Θελητης for *'ôb*. The term ἐγγαστριμυθος shows that the LXX had in mind a ventriloquist known in Greece: see *Plut.* 414e and *Luc. Lexiph.* 20.

1) See *La divination*, ed. A. Caquot M. Leibovici, 2 vol., Paris, 1968; *La divination en Mesopotamie ancienne et dans les régions voisines*, Paris, 1966; J. Fahd, *La divination arabe*, Strassbourg, 1966; A. L. Oppenheim, *Ancient Mesopotamia*, Chicago, 1970[4]: p. 206 ff.: *The Arts of the Diviner;* T. W. Davies, *Magic, Divination and Demonology among the Hebrews and their Neighbours*, New York, 1969.

2) For the cult of the "manes" among the Hittites, see H. W. Haussig, *Götter u. Mythen im Vordern Orient*, Stuttgart, 1965, especially p. 203 f. For the Hittite Texts see H. Otten, *Hethitische Totenrituale*, Berlin, 1958, p. 108 f. *KUB* XVI, 39.

3) The Ghost of Samuel is called an *'elohîm* which is just an other but less specific name for *'ôb*: compare with Deut. xii 30 and Is. viii 19.

4) The connection of the *'ôbot* with the Netherworld may explain why they are often mentioned and forbidden together with the offering of children in a Moloch-sacrifice. Indeed, those sacrifices took place in the Valley of Kidron, the valley of the dead and of contact with the Netherworld. Concerning the Moloch-sacrifices see R. de Vaux, *Les Sacrifices de l'A.T.*, Paris, 1964, p. 67 ff.

5) Deut. xii 30; xviii 11; 1 Sam. xxviii 7; 2 Reg. i 2, 3, 6, 13; 2 Chron. xvi 12; Is. viii 19. Less frequently other terms are used e.g. Deut. xviii 11: *šā'al* as a parallel to *dāraš*.

for the description of a consultation through necromancers and later on through prophets [1]).

Non priestly and non prophetic divination was heavily condemned: The books of law, Leviticus and Deuteronomy repeatedly insist on its illigitimacy: Lev. xix 31; xx 6, 27; Deut. xii 30; xviii 10-11. It is commonly accepted that those legal clauses belong to the original setting of both Leviticus and Deuteronomy.

The wording of Lev. xx 27 is even proper to older cultic sentences, taken up by the original redactor of Leviticus [2]). Something similar can be said of Deut. xviii 10-11 [3]). Why were those forms of divination so harshly forbidden? Why had they to be punished with the death sentence? Why on the other hand were priestly divination with the *Ephod* and the *Urim* and *Tummîm* allowed [4])? The main reason seems to have been that the practices of the charmers and wizards were *tôʿebâ* [5]) or abomination.

In Israel, every custom which could not be taken over from the neighbouring peoples and assimilated without endangering the specific essence of the chosen people, was called an abomination [6]). The *ʾōbôt* and the *jiddeʿōnîm* belonged to foreign cultures and religions. They contained a danger of syncretism which had to be avoided. Only

[1]) C. Westermann, "Die Begriffe für Fragen u. Suchen im A.T." *KuD* VI, 1960, 2-30; see also G. Turbessi, "Quaerere Deum", *Riviesta Biblica* X, 1962, pp. 282-296; E. Jenni, *dāraš* in *THAT* vol. I, München 1971, k. 460-467. The last two works are much indebted to C. Westermann. O. Gardia de la Fuente, *La búsqueda de Dios en el A.T.*; thesis dact. 1970, printed Madrid, 1971; Id., "La Figura de Moisés en Ex. 18, 15 y 33, 7". *Estudios Biblicos*, XXIX, 1970, pp. 353-350.

[2]) R. Kilian, *Literarische v. Formgeschichtliche Untersuchung des Heiligkeitsgesetzes*, *BBB* 19, Bonn 1963, pp. 68-71: "Eine alte kultische Reihe mit *mwt jmwt*" (p. 71).

[3]) R. P. Merendino, *Das deuteronomische Gesetz*, *BBB* 31, Bonn 1969, pp. 193-196: "Der deuteronomische Redaktor hat die Perikope in ihrer ursprünglichen Gestalt aufgenommen" (p. 195). According to Merendino v. 10 b concerning Moloch does not belong to the original text. Compare with our remark above. Comp. with J. L'Hour, "Les interdits toeba dans le Deutéronome", *RB* 71, 1964, p. 489 ff.

[4]) About the priestly oracle see A. Barucq "Oracle et divination", in *DBS* VI, k. 779-782 (Paris, 1960).

[5]) See e.g. Deut. xviii 12.

[6]) O. Bächli, *Israel und die Völker*, *ATANT* 41, Zürich 1962, p. 53. Except for the Proverbs, the meaning of the term *tôʿēbâ* is pretty constant, according to P. Humbert, "Le substantif *tôʿēbâ* et le verbe *tʿb* dans l'AT", *ZAW* LXXII, 1960, pp. 236: "Le mot *tôʿēbâ* . . . témoigne . . d'une grande variété d'applications . . .". A further analysis of the texts shows that this affirmation has no ground. See J. Lust, *Traditie, redactie en kerygma bij Ezechiël*, Brussel, 1969, pp. 113-118. See also J. L'Hour, "Les interdits *Toeba* dans le Deutéronome", *RB* LXXI, 1964, pp. 41-503.

the proper Israelite forms of divination could be accepted. Moreover, according to the official Jahwism, the dead could not be consulted since they were ignorant [1]).

They could not give any information about what was going to happen in the world. The only being who was able to give information was Jahweh imself. Israel had its own ways of divination [2]).

During the period of the judges and the early kingdom, the main practice seems to have been the casting of lots. The technical term indicating the question put to this oracle was *šā'al* (and not *dāraš*). It was so formulated that the answer could be a simple "yes" or a "no". This type of oracle most probably was turned into a priestly institution [3]).

For some reason the priestly casting of lots came to an end with Saul's dead. The term *šā'al* with the meaning of "to consult god" doesn't occur any more in the Books of the Bible after 1 Samuel. Priestly consultation seems to have been succeded by a prophetic one, characterised by the expression *dāraš Jahweh* which we find most often in 1 & 2 Kings [4]). Can we say that the dawnfall of Saul's kingdom and his sin against Jahweh caused the dissolution of this oracle [5])? There is no apparent reason for that. It is more probable that the destruction of the priestly house of Eli brought with it the end of the priestly institutionalised oracle. An other reason for the disappearence of the priestly oracle may have been the rise of a new type of Israelite divination more appropriated to function as a countrepart to the condemned practices around the *'ōbôt* and *jiddeᵉ 'ōnîm*. The new oracle was performed by seers and prophets. They never gave just a simple yes or no answer to the questions of their consultants. They gave a more elaborate answer wherein they spoke God's word in human language. We may accept that this corresponded better to the information given by the charmers and wizards who translated the "whispering" [6]) of the ghosts in human speech [7]).

---

1) Job xiv 21; Eccles. ix 5, 10. See A. van den Born, *Samuel*, *BOT* 4, Roermond 1956, p. 122.

2) See A. Caquot, "La divination dans l'ancien Israël", in *La divinition*, vol. I, Paris 1968, ed. A. Caquot. M. Leibovici, p. 83-1113; O. Eissfeldt, "Wahrsagung im Alten Testament", in *La divination en Mésopotamie ancienne*, Paris 1966, pp. 141-146.

3) See C. Westermann, *art. cit.*, p. 12 and 27.

4) See C. Westermann, *art. cit.*, p. II and 17 ff.

5) Thus C. Westermann, *art. cit.*, p. 29.

6) See Is. xxix 4, compare with the more denegrating terminology in Is. viii 19: chirping and muttering.

7) See 1 Sam. xxviii. From verse 13-14 we know that the ghost of Samuel

The structure and the wording of the accounts of prophetic consultation are practically the same as they are in the story about the witch of Endor [1]). Someone is in a situation of urgency such as illness or war [2]) and goes to the prophet [3]) or sends a messenger [4]). A question (*dāraš*) is put to Jahweh, through the prophet concerning the actual state of crisis. No help is asked for, only information [5]). The Man of God answers with an oracle [6]).

In fact the prophetic function was considered as the Israelite countrepart to the non Jahwistic practices of divination. This is most evident in Deuteronomy. Both Deuteronomic texts condemning the consultation (*dāraš*) of the *ʿōbôt*, the *jiddeʿōnîm* and the *ʾelohîm* are followed by considerations on the prophetic office [8]). This is the more striking since Deuteronomy nowhere else mentions the prophets explicitly[7]). It is clear that the prophets were opposed to the necromancers as the official Jahwistic diviners to the non Jahwistic ones.

We may conclude as follows: 1. *ʾobôt* and *jiddeʾônim* were no sacred pits nor wizards, but the ghosts of the deceased fathers and the instruments representing them. 2. The consultation of those ghosts was forbidden as a foreign practice. It was replaced by the typical Israelite practice of consulting Jahweh through the prophets.

---

appeared to the witch of Endor in a vision which was not seen by the consultant Saul. The words spoken by the ghost in v. 15 ff. must logically be considered as the witch's interpretation for Saul of what she heard in her vision. Comp. HOFFNER, *ʾôb*, k. 145.

[1]) See p. 133; WESTERMANN, *art. cit.*, p. 17 ff.

[2]) 1 Reg. xiv 5; 2 Reg. i; viii 8; 1 Reg. xxii 8; 2 Reg. iii 10; (xxii 13); comp. with 1 Sam. xxviii 5.

[3]) *hlk* or *bwʾ*; see e.g. 1 Reg. xiv 2-5; comp. with 1 Sam. xxviii 8.

[4]) 1 Reg. xiv 3; 2 Reg. viii 8; comp. with 1 Sam. xxviii 7.

[5]) See e.g. 1 Reg. xiv 1 ff. The son of king Jerobeam is sick. The king sends his wife to the prophet Ahiah. The prophet is supposed to reveal (*ngd*, hifil) what is going to happen to the child. No cure is asked for. See also 2 Reg. viii 7-10; 1 Reg. xxii 6; 1 Sam. ix 6-8; comp. with 1 Sam. xxviii 15. In opposition to WESTERMANN, *art. cit.* p. 18, we are convinced that this applies also to 2 Chron. xvi 12 where *rfʾm* is to be vocalised as *refāʾîm* in stead of Massoretic *rōfeʾîm*.

[6]) See Deut. xii 30 — xiii 5 and Deut. xviii 9-22.

[7]) In Deut. xxxiv 10, the conclusion of the book, there is no question of the prophetic function as such but only of Moses who is called a prophet. The remarks on the prophets in Deut. xiii and xviii probably belong to a later strand. See MERENDINO, *op. cit.*, p. 61 ff. and 197. The reason for their introduction is to be found in the context: They had to function as a countrepart to the foregoing passages on forbidden divination.

CLASSES IN THE PROPHETICAL STORIES: DIDACTIC LEGENDA AND PARABLE

BY

ALEXANDER ROFÉ

Jerusalem

In a recently published article I have advanced the thesis that the proper classification of the prophetical stories will not be achieved along the usual lines of formcriticism but rather through a study of the content of each narrative [1]) based upon the search for the creative activity inherent in the story [2]). Since this method of classification may appear vague, it seems necessary to state briefly how such content study should be done. I believe that the best procedure is to check the constitutive elements typical to this literature.

In the first place the perspective of the story should be examined. Does it describe a single episode or a whole sequence of events? Does it present concrete protagonists or only ephemeral figures? Does it deal with everyday life or with central issues of religion and politics? Such questions might help determine whether the narrative belongs to a stage of folktale or to that of more sophisticated literary activity. In the latter case, the main concern, whether artistic, political, or theological, may reveal both the origin and the stimulus behind the story.

A second element is the way the personality of the prophet is depicted. Veneration towards the holy man is the hallmark of the *legenda*, while other attitudes indicate a different origin and type. If veneration gives way to interest solely in the prophet's life, the story probably belongs to the class of biography but if veneration and biographical interest go hand in hand, the result will be a *vita*.

Realizing how much the prophetical narrative is pervaded by

---

[1]) A. Rofé, "The Classification of the Prophetical Stories", *JBL* 89 (1970), pp. 427-440. For a similar argument about NT material, cf. M. Smith, "Prolegomena to a Discussion of Aretalogies, Divine Men, the Gospels and Jesus", *JBL* 90 (1971), p. 196: "The aretalogy . . . has no precise formal definition but is determined by its content; it must have a hero whom it celebrates, by reporting one or more of his marvellous deeds."

[2]) A. Rofé, *op. cit.*, p. 440.

stories kindred to the *legenda* brings into focus the third constitutive element, the miracle. A tale about a miracle which is only a minor redemptive act is pure popular *legenda*. What, however, if the miracle's scope is greater than just floating an axe or curing a pottage? What if its purpose transcends the mere result of the prophet's intervention? Or, what if it is not done by the prophet, but performed *on* him or in his presence? A study of variations in the character of the miracle as well as a study of variations which appear in the other constitutive elements paves the way for the identification of additional classes of prophetical narrative.

The search for constitutive elements, however, is not free of perplexities. Although we characterize as "constitutive" those elements that are generally used in molding a narrative without which the narrative seems inconceivable, such constitutive elements are not indispensable. Theoretically, music or painting could be used to describe a prophet, although there is no extant evidence of these media having been used. More real is the possibility of a narrative having most of the usual patterns of a prophetical story about a *non-prophetic* hero. Paradoxically, it would seem that a prophetical story can exist even without a prophet [1]). No less probable is a situation where a prophet would be described without veneration as a purely secular figure, and, accordingly, would not perform any miracles. Such an account would in many respects be the very opposite of *legenda*. Thus one can maintain that the very absence of constitutive elements can be instrumental in classifying prophetical stories.

Here it is perhaps advisable to state exactly how this work-program differs from the form-critical method. Clearly, some of the usual guide-lines of form-critics such as stereotyped formulas, smallest literary units, original sitz im leben are declined as unhelpful in analysing prophetical literature. However, formcriticism also relies on what are called "Inhaltsmotive", "inhaltliche Elemente" or "in inhaltlicher Hinsicht gattungsmässig festgeprägte Überlieferungen" [2]). To use another's terminology, formcriticism uses the content's recurring characteristics which together form a "structure" [3]). This approach seems identical with our own "content study".

---

[1]) Some of the stories of the Book of Daniel seem to belong to this category.

[2]) K. H. BERNHARDT, *Die gattungsgeschichtliche Forschung am AT als exegetische Methode*, Berlin 1959, pp. 37 f.

[3]) B. O. LONG, "2 Kings iii and the Genres of Prophetic Narrative", V.T. xxiii, 3.

In my opinion, the difference lies in the direction of the investigation. Formcriticism has accustomed us to look for "das Festgeprägte", the constant "structure". Critics, therefore, tend to classify literary creations according to a few prototypes. While not denying the validity of these classifications in cases where the "structure" is based not merely on deduction or free conjecture, I believe that one should look beyond the structure for the individuality of the literary creation [1]). After all, prophetical narrative is not a piece of mass production but rather the creation of a living intellect. This intellect can sometimes relax into customary patterns of thought and expression, but if it is human — all the more so if it is divinely inspired — it soon rises to new efforts of imagination, invention and creation [2]). It is these efforts that we wish to assess by considering how the individual elements of a story have been developed. Classification is thus conceived as the final phase, to be undertaken only when a study of individual narratives demonstrates that a similar creative activity has been at work in different literary pieces.

The Didactic Legenda

This type is best represented by the story of Naaman, Elisha and Gehazi (2 Kings v). It is the account of two miracles: the healing of the leper Naaman and the affliction with leprosy of the disobedient Gehazi. Of the two, the first miracle is undeniably the more important. However, in contrast to the usual structure of the *legenda* [3]), it does not come as a surprise to anyone. The healing of Naaman is anticipated from the very beginning. A young maid instructs Naaman's wife on the matter (vs. 2). A moment of tension and despair is created by the reaction of the King of Israel to the emissaries from Aram (vs. 7). This, however, is not the despair of the needy: Elisha is there, ready to perform his miracle (vs. 8). The King's despair is not meant to magnify the dimensions of the miracle, but only to juxtapose

[1]) The difference between this kind of investigation and pure form criticism can be illustrated by comparing G. von Rad (*Genesis, a Commentary*, E.T., London 1961) with H. Gunkel (*Genesis, übersetzt und erklärt* [*GHAT*], 1910³) on Gen. xxii 1-19. One senses a clear shift of emphasis from the reconstruction of the original etiological legend to the exposition of the present narrative.

[2]) Cf. H. F. Hahn, *The OT in Modern Research*, Philadelphia 1966², p. 150: "By failing to follow up the search for the genesis of the original oral materials with an investigation of the subsequent processes of literary composition, the heirs of Gunkel had so far produced only limited results". But cf. also his evaluation of J. Hempel's and G. von Rad's work in the following pages.

[3]) A. Rofé, *op. cit.*, p. 431.

the King's helplessness with the Prophet's confidence [1]). The miracle, therefore, in not resolving an impossible situation, nor answering any real need of the Prophet's followers, transcends its immediate circumstances. Its aim is to prove to foreigners that "there is a prophet in Israel" (vs. 8). Actually, it proves even more: "that there is no God in all the earth, but in Israel" (vs. 15) [2]).

This miracle, performed for such a sublime purpose as propagating knowledge of the true God, must remain a pure testimony. It cannot be profaned by utilizing it for wordly advantages [3]). The Man of God will not accept any kind of remuneration (vs. 16) nor let his followers accept payment in his name (vs. 20-27) [4]). Furthermore, as pure testimony, the miracle must be enacted in a way that will prove its godly origin and differentiate it unequivocally from the sorcerous practices of the heathens. Therefore, contrary to the expectations of the Aramean fighter, Elisha does not perform any magic but simply commands the foreigner to bathe repeatedly in the Jordan River (vss. 9-11) [5]).

Indeed, the introduction of a moral element into the *legenda* i.e. bearing witness to God's oneness has infused the story with ideology, thus radically transforming its character. In the simple *legenda* the prophet accepts a gift (2 Kings iv 42); now he refuses it with disdain. In the simple *legenda* the miracle consistently happens through a visible, breath-taking spell; now such magic is dismissed as sheer

---

[1]) Cf. H. GRESSMANN, *Die älteste Geschichtsschreibung und Prophetie Israels* (*SATA*) Göttingen 1910 (1921²), *ad loc.*

[2]) This statement should be taken at face value as a monotheistic affirmation. In conformity to it, Naaman would no longer sacrifice to any other god (v. 17) and requests Elisha's indulgence for his expected participation in the heathen official cult of Aram (v. 18). Contrary to the opinion of R. KITTEL, *Die Bücher der Könige* (*GHAT*), Göttingen 1900, 206 f., the transporting of Israel's earth to Aram does not reflect the idea of the limitation of the Lord but of the holiness of the land of Israel; see *infra*, p. 148.

[3]) Against the wide acceptance of the LXX reading in v. 26ª, I retain most of the Massoretic reading as superior. עֵת means here "suitable time", "opportunity"; cf. Ho. x 12; Hg. i 4; Qoh. iii 2-8. The sentence reads: "Is this an opportunity to acquire money and to acquire with it gardens and oliveyards and vineyards and sheep and cattle and slaves and maids?" . . .

[4]) The function of Gehazi must have been similar to that of the *šammaš* in the Hasidic milieu (cf. A ROFÉ, *op. cit.*, p. 435). *Inter alia* he provided the means for making a living, collecting gifts and payments from his master's admirers.

[5]) H. GUNKEL seemed to have missed the significance of the story when he commented that "Elisha is the best sorcerer since he uses the simplest devices". Cf. his *Meisterwerke hebräischen Erzählungskunst, I: Geschichten von Elisa*, Berlin n.d. (1922?), pp. 31 ff.

frippery. The typical elements of primitive naivete have been discarded as the popular *legenda* has grown into a didactic one. Hence the didactic *legenda* should not be considered as a subtype of the *legenda* but as a type in itself.

The moral concepts, both positive (vss. 8, 15, 26) and negative (vss. 11,20), are expressed concisely in the dialogues of the story. These conceptual pronouncements constitute a substantial portion of the dialogues. Since they are mainly formulations of the author's beliefs, they cannot endow the characters with distinct personalities. Therefore, the protagonists of the story remain archetypal figures: the proud foreign conqueror, the greedy assistant, and the divine, both benign and terrifying, Elisha. Their particular personalities escape the reader because they were of no concern to the author. The didactic evolvement thus significantly differs from the literary elaboration of *legenda* such as the story of the Shunammite. The former is characterized by formulated creeds; the latter by the thoughts of individualized characters. The antinomy of art and doctrine could not be better epitomized.

One would like to know more about the origin of the doctrines expressed in the story of Naaman. Indeed, this question is fundamental for the student of Israelite literature and religion. One's first impulse is to regard these ideas as stemming from the teaching of classical prophecy Actually all of them — the anticipation of the conversion of the Gentiles, the negation of magical practices in proper prophetic activity and the censure of the prophet's acceptance of rewards — belong to the ideological stock of classical prophets. The fact that in other *legenda* Elisha is described as accepting gifts and performing magic seems to lend more strength to a late dating of the Naaman story. However, one must admit that we know too little of the ideology of Elisha and his followers. The analogy of the Hasidic *legenda* — whose relevance for the prophetical *legenda* has already been pointed out — [1]) proves that even within the framework of a devoted pietist movement, common vulgar legenda, not reflecting the ideology of the movement, could exist [2]).

A more reliable guide for dating the story are those beliefs which are assumed rather than preached. The concept of the holiness of the Land of Israel, expressed in the contrast of the Jordan with the rivers of Aram, seems to indicate an idealization of the Land of Israel, typical

---

[1]) Cf. *supra*, p. 146, n. 4. and the reference there.

[2]) Y. DAN, *HaNobēlāh HaḤasidit*, Jerusalem 1966, pp. 8 f.

of uprooted Israelites. In this milieu the altar of Naaman also acquires significance. Elisha's agreement to build an altar abroad with the holy earth of Israel [1]) seems to function as the justification of a cultic practice that spread out in the Israelite diaspora of the Assyrian Empire. All in all, a late eighth or early seventh century origin for the story of Naaman seems plausible.

Sometimes comparison of related material helps reveal the didactic elaboration in the *legenda*. For example, consider the stories about Elijah and the widow in Zarephath (1 Kings xvii 8-24).

The first story (xvii 8-16) is an integral part of a great literary composition, which, excluding the additional note in 1 Kings xvi 34 [2]) and the passage in xix 19-21 belonging to the cycle of Elisha [3]), comprises most of the material in 1 Kings xvi 29 - xix 18 [4]). It is the account of the fight of the Lord and His servant Elijah against Baal and his worshipers in Israel. The function of the *legenda* about the multiplication of meal and oil is clearly to explain the hiding and survival of Elijah in the second year of drought. Thus, on the basis of literary history, this *legenda* appears to be secondary to the independent tale of 2 Kings iv 1-7 [5]).

---

[1]) In the present form of the story, Elisha's approval is implicit. Was there an earlier text in which the building of the altar by Naaman met with Elisha's explicit endorsement? The movement of the story seems to lead to such approval, for otherwise it is unclear why Naaman asks for Elisha's sanction for taking a load of earth from the Land of Israel.

[2]) This verse is missing in the Lucianic recension of the LXX. It was probably transferred here from its original setting in Joshua vi 26 where it is still present in the LXX version. Cf. S. Holmes, *Joshua: The Hebrew and Greek Texts*, Cambridge 1914, *ad. loc.*

[3]) Cf. A. Alt, Die literarische Herkunft von I Reg 19: 19-21", *ZAW* 32 (1912), pp. 123-125.

[4]) It is difficult to explain why so many Biblical critics have failed to recognize the beginning of the Lord-Baal complex in 1 Kings xvi 29. The reason is probably because the question of the present literary unity was not well distinguished from that of its sources. Undoubtedly xvi 29 ff. belongs to another source than xvii 1 ff. However, with the same certainty one may say that they have been built together into one complex, no matter what the consequences are for the date of its composition. 1 Kings xvi 29-33 corresponds to 1 Kings xix 16-18. It also gives the grounds for xvii 1 and introduces Achab, who is taken as known in xvii 1 ff. xvii 1 is no more a beginning of a story than xi 11, xvi 1, 2 Kings vii 1 or xxi 10. The NEB translation rightly has a new heading at xvi 29. On the other hand, the procedure of O. Eissfeldt, "Die Komposition von I Reg 16:29 — II Reg 13:25", *Festschrift L. Rost* (*BZAW* 105) pp. 49-58, to start the analysis by excising from the literary complex the verses in 1 Kings xvi 29-34 is, in my opinion, unjustified.

[5]) As recognized already by O. Plöger, *Die Prophetengeschichten der Samuel — und Königbücher* (Dissertation), Greifswald 1937, p. 18. *Contra* I. Benzinger, *Die Bücher der Könige* (*KHAT*), Freiburg i.B. etc. 1899, p. 129.

The internal analysis of the *legenda* confirms this impression. A most significant difference between the stories is the conduct of the widow. In 2 Kings iv 1-7 were it not for her husband's righteousness, the widow would be entirely without merit. Not so the widow of Zarephath. First her good nature is tested (vss. 10[b]-11) and then her faith: she is asked to sacrifice part of her last meal to the stranger. Only after passing these two tests, is she rewarded with miraculous plenty [1]). Here again, in contrast to the miracle of Elisha, Elijah's miracle is not performed by any magical practice. It is enacted only by the utterance of the Word of the Lord, pronounced by His prophet. The author emphasizes this idea through repetition. Indeed, the different circumstances of the miracle suggest that this *legenda* is an improved, moralizing edition of its parallel in the cycle of Elisha.

The second story (xvii 17-24) is less integrated in the whole composition. It could be omitted without any damage to the whole. It does not share in the chronology of the narrative (cf. xvii 7, 14, 15; xviii 1). It digresses from the main theme which deals with the drought. Finally, its conclusion in vs. 24 is inconsistent with vss. 8-16.

Although loosely connected to the main narrative, this *legenda* can be shown to be a relatively late composition, once its dependence on the story of the Shunammite is realized. A trivial detail demonstrates this dependence. The Shunammite, being a rich woman, could afford to add a story to her house and provide Elisha with a special room. The widow of Zarephath is destitute, and yet she too is described as having an upper-chamber for Elijah's dwelling (vs. 19). Clearly, this pattern is transferred from the tale of the Shunammite.

The character of this story is illustrated by the description of the revival of the child, when compared with the parallel story in 2 Kings iv. The magical practice of affecting the child directly with the supernatural power of the prophet is reduced to a minimum (vs. 21[a]). In its place, the story insists upon the role of Elijah's prayer (vss. 20, 21[b]), and its acceptance by the Lord (vs. 22). The author had a clear concept of what is and what is not legitimate in prophetic activity and described his hero accordingly. Elijah is thus depicted as using the proper means, revealing himself as a great impetrator in the line of Moses and Samuel. The miracle has acquired an ethical meaning. This is also evident from its consequences. While the Shunammite

---

[1]) H. Gressmann, *op. cit.*, in his comments on 2 Kings iv 1-7 observed that the parallel story in 1 Kings xvii 8-16 was better told but did not try to define the relation between the parallels.

merely acknowledged the miraculous event with an act of renewed veneration, the widow of Zarephath responds with a confession of faith: Elijah is a man of God and the word of the Lord, which he pronounces, is true (vs. 24). She seems to be echoing the truths expressed in the story of Naaman.

Again, the author seems weak in molding his characters and in building his plot. One need only compare the primitive reproach of the widow from Zarephath (vs. 18) [1]) and the vague situation of the child — is he sick or dead? — with the parallel features in the story of the Shunammite (2 Kings iv 28, 32). One may conclude that the story in 1 Kings xvii 17-24, while preserving many features of a simple, primitive *legenda* [2]), has also passed through the refinement of a didactic impulse.

The description of the didactic *legenda*, as evolved from the basic simple *legenda* explains the contradictions in the story of the healing of Hezekiah in 2 Kings xx 1-11 In this text, two miracles are actually narrated: the healing itself (vss. 1-7) and the turning back of the shadow (vss. 8-11). They were not written by the same hand. This is obvious from the fact that Hezekiah's request for a sign is meaningless after the account of his recovery. On the other hand, vss. 8-11 are not an independent account. Since they assume the circumstances of the first story, they must be an accretion to it [3]). Isaiah xxxviii, while adding the Psalm of Hezekiah (ibid. vss. 9-20), strung together the two accounts by omitting or inverting [4]) the position of those verses which disturbed the sequence.

However, even the first story alone (2 Kings xx 1-7) does not run smoothly. Isaiah's remedy comes rather abruptly. It comes as an anti-climax to the preceding sublime words of God giving Hezekiah an unconditional prophecy of consolation and assurance. Is Isaiah's thaumaturgy still necessary [5])? On the other hand, when we examine

---

[1]) Cf. J. A. Montgomery, *The Book of Kings* (ICC) New York 1951, p. 295.

[2]) Cf. H. Gunkel, *op. cit.* p. 28. However, I cannot accept his conclusions about the relation between the parallel stories. The same applies to R. Kilian, "Die Totenerweckung Elias and Elisas — eine Motivwanderung?", *BZ* 10 (1966), pp. 44-56.

[3]) Cf. I. Benzinger, *op. cit.*, R. Kittel, *op. cit.*, and J. A. Montgomery, *op. cit.*

[4]) About inversion of passages as a redactional device, cf. my "The Composition of the Introduction to the Book of Judges" (Hebrew), *Tarbiz* 35 (1965/66), pp. 201-213.

[5]) Cf. I. Benzinger, *op. cit.*: "V 7 erzählt die Heilung als vollendete Thatsache

Isaiah's act, where are the expectation and suspension characteristic of the simple *legenda*? In the present story, they are surpassed by God's prophecy. The wondrous act of the prophet ceases to be the long awaited, single solution to an unbearable situation.

Possibly the literary problem of the whole pericope can be solved on the basis of the history of the type. The original story was a pure, simple *legenda*, told about Hezekiah's sickness and his healing through Isaiah's thaumaturgy. A second author enlarged the story with another *legenda* (vss. 8-11). In the latter, however, the miracle is not performed by Isaiah but only provoked by his prayer to the Lord. This second author, dissatisfied with the gross nature of his source, expanded it by an account of Hezekiah's prayer and the Lord's response (vss. 2-6) [1]. As in the story of the healing of the child by Elijah, the moral is that prayer prevails over magic. Yet, in the present story, the prayer is not that of a prophet, but of a secular figure like the king [2]. Apparently, this author wanted to point out the readiness of the Lord to answer the prayers of all, without hierarchical limitations.

A common denominator of the four didactic *legenda* here examined is the decline of magic in the holy man's performance of the miracle. This amounts to sheer repudiation of magic if one compares the didactic *legenda* with their parallels in the simple-*legenda* class (e.g. 1 Kings xvii 8-16 versus 2 Kings iv 1-7). As shown above, the rejection of magic is due to the emphasis on the Lord's intervention in the natural order. This intervention can be recorded either as the answer to a prayer (1 Kings xvii 21-22) or by human recognition of His action (ibid. 24; 2 Kings v 15) or, best of all, as the action of His spoken word (1 Kings xvii 14, 16) [3].

The comparison between didactic and simple *legenda* explains ade-

---

infolge der Arzneimittel, die Jesaja anwendet, *zugleich allerdings* (italics are mine, A.R.) auch eine wunderbare Erhörung von Hiskias Gebet."

[1] I arrived at this explanation of the history of the pericope as a result of discussions with Mr. Harvey Bock at Yale University.

[2] Cf., against contrary assertions about the character of the Israelite kingship, M. Noth, "God, King and Nation in the OT", *The Laws in the Pentateuch and Other Studies* (E.T.), Edinburgh and London 1966, pp. 145-78.

[3] B. Long, "2 Kings III and Genres of Prophetic Narrative" (Paper for the OT Form Criticism Seminar, October 1971, *V.T.* xxiii, 3). In my opinion 2 Kings ii 19-22; iv 42-44 should not be included in this class since their reworking is merely external and probably derives from an editorial hand. Note the similar case of 1 Kings xvi 34 where a late editor reinterpreted the *curse* of Joshua vi 26 as a *prophecy*.

quately the relation between two *legenda* of the Mosaic cycle: the stories of Massāh and (Me) Meribāh in Exodus xvii 1-7 and Numbers xx 1-13. [1]). The many parallels between the two stories prove beyond doubt that they are two records of the same tradition [2]). A trivial detail, again, demonstrates the dependence of the Priestly account in Numbers upon the account in Exodus. While in Ex. xvii the Lord commands Moses to take the rod and to smite the rock with it (vss. 5-6), in Num. xx He commands him to take the rod but only to speak to the rock (vs. 7). Thus, in the Lord's order to Moses, the rod remains hanging in the air without any clear function. It seems possible to prove, further, that the Priestly account in Num. xx recasted the other, older narrative with a theological intent or, in other words, that it is a didactic elaboration of a simple *legenda*. The simple *legenda* (Ex. xvii 1-7) relates, without blame, the extraction of water out of a rock by the magical means of Moses' rod. The didactic *legenda* of Num. xx 1-13 required that the miracle be performed by the Lord's command as uttered by Moses [3]). Moses' failure to utter the command is considered a severe sin because God was not "sanctified" by the miracle. His divine power was not reaffirmed and recognized through the incident [4]). Apparently, patterns, and trends of the prophetical narrative were at work in the creation of part of the Torah-literature [5]).

The didactic *legenda* deliberately assaults the belief in the magical origin of miracles. At the same time it also derogates inadvertently the import of the miracle itself. The miracle is either assumed from the beginning or minimized in the resolution of the plot. In any case, it has been displaced from its central role by another, deeper element, the

---

[1]) The following interpretation of the relation between the two stories comes near to the method put forward by Prof. Samuel SANDMEL in his "The Haggada Within Scripture", *JBL* 80 (1961), pp. 105-122.

[2]) This was already noted by R. Yosef BeKHOR SHOR, *Commentary on Leviticus and Numbers* (Hebrew), ed. by R. J. GAD, London 1960, p. 98 f.

[3]) Cf. S. E. LOEWENSTAMM, "The Death of Moses" (Hebrew), *Tarbiz* 27 (1957/8), p. 145.

[4]) This understanding of Numbers xx 1-13, advanced already by RASHI and BeKHOR SHOR (*op. cit.*) and recently by LOEWENSTAMM, seems not to have occured to modern exegetes.

[5]) M. BUBER, *Moses*, Heidelberg 1952, p. 76: " . . . ich vermute, dass die Ausgestaltung der Tradition zum Legendenkranz der ägyptischen Plagen sich zu einem wesentlichen Teil in den Kreisen der Elisa-Jünger vollzogen hat, die neben der Legende ihres Meisters auch die des Ahnen der Nebiim gedichtet haben". Prof. B. S. CHILDS called my attention to this reference in an OT Seminar at Yale University, 1969/70.

miracle's own significance [1]) which transcends its immediate circumstances. Therefore, excitement before the supernatural has been replaced by concern about the significance of divine intervention in the natural order. This process of mutation found a classical expression in the Hasidic teaching which is worth quoting: [2])

> "The miracle", Jaacob Yitzchak repeated, "is not of such great importance". "What then would you call important?", Naftali asked. "Did not the Rabbi himself say that the miracle bears witness to the indwelling of the Shechinah?" "That is what I said", answered the Yehudi, "important is weeping, important is repentance, important is love. It is important that the Rabbi set free good from evil and thus help to raise up the Shechinah from the dust of the road. The miracle merely bears witness; hence it is not important. How do you know whether the Rabbi does not hide himself behind all his miracles, in order that you may not see him, himself?"

The Parable

The fundamental purpose of the didactic *legenda* is to teach some truth. With this aim Biblical writers utilized the existing material of *legenda*, introducing their moral, but, simultaneously, disrupting the original structure of the popular, venerative story. Since the substance is the moral, the *legenda* itself does not matter. It could even have been dispensed with had the writer had enough imagination to invent his own story. Thus prophetical literature arrived at the parable, a story designed from its inception for its moral, differing from the fable by its association with the human world and its account of fictional, but mostly plausible, happenings.

The parable, a literary genre well attested in the wisdom literature of the Ancient Near East [3]), was used rather early by the prophets

---

[1]) Cf. G. von Rad, *Theologie des AT, II*, München[3] 1962, p. 441 (about the story of Naaman): "Diese Erzählung ist darin Bemerkenswert, dass sie Probleme andeutet, die jenseits der Heilung Naamans, ja eigentlich jenseits des Erzählten liegen".

[2]) M. Buber, *For the Sake of Heaven* (E.T. by Ludwig Lewisohn), Philadelphia 5705-1945, pp. 37 f. Quoted with the kind permission of the Jewish Publication Society of America. Some minor modifications have been introduced in the translation, according to the Hebrew and German texts.

[3]) Cf. S. N. Kramer, *From the Tablets of Sumer*, Indian Hills, Colorado, 1956, pp. 147-151. The "Tale of the Two Brothers" too has a parabolic character. Cf. J. M. Plumley's translation and notes in D. Winton Thomas (ed.), *Documents from Old Testament Times*, London etc. 1958, pp. 168-171. Another important instance is the *Story of Ahikar* (edited by F. C. Conybeare, J. Rendel Harris and A. S. Lewis, Cambridge 1913[2]; for its Aramaic version cf. A. C. Cowley, *Aramaic Papyri of the Fifth Century*, Oxford, 1923, pp. 204-248). For Israel, cf. R. N. Why-

themselves. Nathan's parable of the ewe-lamb of the poor and Isaiah's poem of the vineyard are familiar instances of its early use in their allocutions. Hence, its appearance in the secondary prophetic literature — i.e. the narratives in which the prophets' disciples relate about their masters — can scarcely be a surprise. Actually, parables and paradigms — i.e. *exempla*, a kindred class to be dealt separately — are present in the historical narrative of the OT.

What are the constitutive elements of the prophetical parable? The story is obviously built around a moral without which it has no existence. In this it differs sharply from the didactic *legenda*. For example, in the didactic *legenda* of 2 Kings v, the healing of Naaman could have been the subject of a story even without the moral attached to it. Conversely, in the Book of Jonah, acceptedly a parable, the plot itself is designed to convey a message. One must concede that as a tool for classification this definition seems too general. However, what makes things easier in the specific case of prophetical parables is that the ideas represented are doctrines or beliefs relevant to the prophetic activity and, consequently, can be detected elsewhere in the prophetic books. In this prophetic activity the most puzzling element has always been the relation of the prophet to God. Hence it is natural for most prophetical parables to deal with this aspect and not to dwell on relations between prophet and people. Furthermore, in a reflective genre such as the parable, there is not room for the veneration of the prophet typical of the *legenda* [1]). The prophet is no longer the awe-inspiring Holy Man of the popular fantasy. On the contrary, the confrontation with God naturally results in a lowering of the prophet's statute. The man of God can even be described as faulty or misled and hence called to account by the deity. The miracle — if present at all — is performed not by the prophet, but by the Lord Himself. The prophet remains on the scene as a mere spectator, sometimes even as the passive object of God's miracle.

BRAY, *The Succession Narrative*, London 1968, pp. 71 ff. In my opinion, his characterization of the Succession Document is rather one-sided. More justified is the definition of the Story of Joseph as a didactic tale. For the reworking of the fable as a parable, cf. W. SCHOTTROFF, "Das Weinbergslied Jesajas (Jes v 1-7). Ein Beitrag zur Geschichte der Parabel", *ZAW* 82 (1970), pp. 68-91.

[1]) A very interesting instance from the Hasidic milieu is the story told by Dov Baer of Leva about his ancestor, Dov Baer of Mezritch, the Great Maggid, who had been one of the founders of Hasidism; cf. M. BUBER, *Tales of the Hasidim: the Later Masters*, New York 1961, pp. 12 f. Actually the tale is not a legend, but a parable, as argued convincingly by BUBER. Its attitude can be characterized as one of anti-veneration.

Most of these patterns can be discerned in the stories of Jonah and the Man of God from Judah (1 Kings xii 33 — xiii 32).

That the Book of Jonah is a parable has long been recognized by the exegetes [1]). What, however, is its moral? A much followed interpretation holds that the book is the manifesto of the universalistic trend in Judaism, the heirs of Second Isaiah, striving in the fifth century B.C.E. against the particularistic bigots, the builders of Ezra and Nehemiah's wall [2]). The mere fact that the book does not mention any antagonism between Jews and Gentiles nor give any hint of the role of Nineveh in the national history of Israel [3]) should dispose of this theory. A traditional Jewish interpretation viewed the book as a sermon on the value of repentence and therefore made it, with the addition of the last three verses of the book of Micah, the hap̱tārāh of

---

[1]) However, even recently an attempt has been made to deny the parabolic character of this book; cf. G. Ch. Aalders, *The Problem of the Book of Jonah*, London 1948. But his fine arguments (on p. 10) were already disposed of by H. Gunkel, when he wrote ("Jonabuch," *RGG*², Vol. 3, col. 367): "Dem Erzähler, der nicht berichtet, was weiter mit Jona geschehen sei, ebenso wie er die Schiffer mitten auf dem Meer verlässt, kommt es nicht sowohl auf die berichteten Begebenheiten, sondern vielmehr auf die dargestellten Wahrheiten an". Another objection is that of G. Rinaldi, *I Profeti Minori* (*SB*), Torino 1960, p. 196: "Per constituire una classe di oggetti ci vuole un certo numero di quegli oggetti: ma il libro di Giona non ha un parallelo ne dentro, ne fuori della Bibbia". Cf. also A. Vaccari, "Il genere letterario del libro di Giona in recenti publicazioni", *Divinitas* 6 (1962) pp. 231-256. This exception might find an answer in the following discussion of two prophetical parables.

[2]) The following is a very partial list of adherents to this position: A. Kuenen, *The Religion of Israel* (E.T. by A.H. May), London 1875, p. 243 f.; E. König, art. "Jonah", *DB*, Vol. 2, col. 744-753; T. K. Cheyne, art. "Jonah", *EB*, Vol. 2, col. 2565-2571; J. A. Bewer, *The Book of Jonah* (*ICC*), New York 1912, pp. 6-11; K. Budde, art. "Jonah", *JE*, *Vol.* 7, col. 225-230; G. A. Barton, *The Religion of Ancient Israel*, 1928)Repr. New York 1961), pp. 237-240; A. Feuillet, "Les sources du livre de Jonas", *RB* 54 (1947), pp. 161-186; idem, "Le sens du livre de Jonas", *ibidem*, pp. 340-361 G. von Rad, *Der Prophet Jona*, Nürnberg 1950, p.12 (but in his *Theologie des AT*, II Müchen 1962³, p. 304, his position becomes rather ambivalent); B. S. Childs, "Jonah: A Study in OT Hermeneutics", *Scot. Jour. of Theol.* 11 (1958), pp. 53-61; O. Loretz, "Herkunft und Sinn der Jona-Erzählung", *BZ* (N.F.) 5 (1961), pp. 18-29; O. Eissfeldt, "Amos und Jona in volkstümlicher Überlieferung", *Barnikol-Festschrift* 1964, pp. 9-13 (*Kleine Schriften IV*, Tübingen 1968, pp. 137-142); H. W. Wolff, *Studien zum Jonabuch*, Neukirchen 1965, esp. p. 70; J. A. Soggin, *Introduzione all'Antico Testamento II*, Brescia 1969, p. 71.

[3]) This has been pointed out by U. Cassuto, art. "Jona", *EJ*, Vol. 9, col. 268-272 and S. D. Goitein, "Some Observations on Jonah", *JPOS* 17 (1937), pp. 63-77; but their arguments have been generally disregarded. E. Bickerman, *Four Strange Books of the Bible*, New York 1967, pp. 1-50, analyses the origin of the bias of modern scholars about the Book of Jonah.

Yom Kippur [1]). This view does not do justice to Chapter iv where the issue is not the conduct of men but the qualities of God. As a sermon on the importance of *t^e^šubāh*, the book should have ended with Chapter iii, but Chapter iv is certainly an integral part of the book because only with it is the flight of Jonah (Chapters i-ii) explained [2]). What is said in Chapter iv is actually clear enough. Jonah would have liked the Lord to keep His word, but as he knew that the Lord's quality is to repent of evil, he preferred escape to prophecy. Now that the prophecy has been belied, he is confirmed in his previous position. The Lord retorts taking His cue from Jonah's affection for the gourd. God too has some precious things besides His word, one of them being the city of Nineveh with its many souls. Therefore the Lord is justified in being "gracious and merciful, in repenting from evil" (iii 10; iv 2) and, consequently, in not keeping His word [3]). Nineveh has the right to exist on its own, independently of one's expectation the fulfillment of the word of God [4]).

This conclusion can be confirmed by inspecting the contemporary prophetic texts which deal with the problem of the fulfillment of prophecies. If we accept, mainly on the basis of the linguistic data, an early post-exilic date for the composition of the Book of Jonah [5]), then the contemporary records will include those written in the 7th-5th centuries B.C.E. Deut. xviii 21-22, which is a scholium to the law of the prophet (ibid. vss. 14-20 [6]), asserts that if the word is not

---

[1]) This opinion was also defended by Y. KAUFMANN, *The Religion of Israel*, (translated and abridged by M. GREENBERG), Chicago 1960, pp. 282-286, who tried to prove that the concept of repentance was a great innovation in the middle of the eighth century B.C.E. (which, in his opinion, is the period of composition of the book).

[2]) A better division of chapters in the story was proposed by N. LOHFINK, "Jona ging zur Stadt hinaus (Jona 4:5)", *BZ* (N.F.) 5 (1961) pp. 185-203. According to him the last episode in the tale begins in iv 5. In any case, this last episode is necessary to give the Lord's answer to Jonah's complaint (iv 2).

[3]) I thus return to the interpretation given by F. HITZIG, *Die zwölf kleinen Propheten* (*KEHAT*), Leipzig 1863^3, p. 161. See now E. BICKERMAN, *op. cit.*

[4]) I cannot help offering one more explanation for the name of Jonah based on his philosophy. Could it mean Destroyer (root y.n.h., cf. Jer. xlvi 16, 1 16) son of True? In any event, if the Book of Jonah still has a lesson for the religious man today, it is the following: No one is entitled to expect or rejoice in the calamity of another people or religious group in order to justify his own God.

[5]) The evidence is even more comprehensive than that adduced in the introductions, commentaries and encyclopedia articles.

[6]) Prof. I. L. SEELIGMANN in his seminar about prophecy (Hebrew University, Jerusalem, 1959/60). First hints in this direction were offered by A. B. EHRLICH, *Randglossen zur Hebräischen Bibel II* (1909), p. 305.

fulfilled, it can be dismissed as a human pretension, thus implying that all true prophecies are fulfilled. The term which refers to the false prophet (*lo' tāgur*) reminds one of Nehemiah vi 14 (*hāyu meyāreim 'oti*). Indeed, a fifth century B.C.E. date for Deut. xviii 21-22 is strongly suggested by the fact that the same type of scholium is present in Lev. xxv 20-22. By the middle of the sixth century, the Deuteronomistic redactor of the Book of Kings had already maintained the same view, by presenting the most remarkable events as exact fulfillments of the Lord's word [1]. There can be little doubt that the belief that the word of God is literally fulfilled was inherited by the Deuteronomistic historian from earlier writers because the same view appears in old Ephraimitic stories, such as 2 Kings vi 24 — vii 20, and is the main point of the first layer of the story of Sennacherib's siege of Jerusalem (2 Kings xviii 17-32[a], 36-37; xix 1-9, 36-37) written around the middle of the seventh century [2]. In the Book of Jeremiah, two distinct reactions to this doctrine can be detected. Jer. xxviii 7-9 distinguishes between prophets of calamities and prophets of peace, applying the Deuteronomistic norm only to the latter. Jer. xviii 7-10 refutes the Deuteronomistic doctrine altogether and makes the realization of God's word depend on the current conduct of man [3]. The same view is held by Ez. xxxiii 12-20 which elaborates on Ez. xviii 21-32, introducing in the latter allocution the element of God's outspoken commitment (vss. 13[a], 14[a]). The debate between Second Isaiah, who accepted the Deuteronomistic doctrine, and Trito-Isaiah, who opposed it, cannot be dealt with here, as it calls for a reexamination of the crucial passage Isa. lv 6-11 and its attribution to either prophet.

Even so, the above material illustrates how extensively the problem of the fulfillment of God's prophecy was debated in the period around the Exile. Jonah, as well as some (editorial?) [4] passages in the prophetic books, probably record the discussions on this topic between the disciples and admirers of the classical prophets.

---

1) Cf. G. von Rad, "The Deuteronomistic Theology of History in the Book of Kings", *Studies in Deuteronomy* (E.T. by D. Stalker), London 1953, pp. 74-91.

2) For the analysis and dating of this story, cf. my *Israelite Belief in Angels in the Pre-exilic Period, as Evidenced by Biblical Traditions*, Hebrew University Ph. D. Thesis, Jerusalem 1969, pp. 203-218.

3) Cf. Bickerman's essay, *op. cit.* A. Feuillet, *op. cit.*, gathered impressive material about the relation of Jonah to Jeremiah. It should be emphasized, however, that the Book of Jeremiah itself stands in a dialectical relation to the Deuteronomistic theology of history.

4) As seems to be suggested by the contradiction between Jer. xviii 7-10 and xxviii 7-9.

One story in the Book of Kings shows some affinity with the Book of Jonah. This is the story of the Man of God from Judah in 1 Kings xii 33 — xiii 32) [1]). In both stories the prophet, sent with a message to another place, disobeys God's order. In both, one of the protagonists—prophet or God—argues with the other, showing his dissatisfaction with the other's conduct (Jonah iv 2; 1 Kings xiii 20-22). In both, God deals with the prophet through the agency of a beast. In both, the beast, a better envoy than the man, carries out the divine order exactly, in spite of its animal nature. These similarities between the stories give a first hint that the genre of 1 Kings xiii must be sought in the parable [2]).

Actually, 1 Kings xiii cannot be a historical narrative because of the anonymity of its heroes and its fantastic miracles. It cannot be a *legenda* [3]) because there is no point in venerating an unknown holy-man and because the Man of God is not venerated but condemned. Furthermore, in most of the story he does not perform miracles. Obviously, the features of anonymity and unearthliness prove that the genre cannot be that of the biography either. Can it be a prophetical parable? The development of a plot involving prophet and God, the consequent adjustment of the prophet's stature and his serving as the object of the lion's miracle all seem to enforce the latter suggestion.

What really has prevented scholars from reaching this conclusion is the apparent lack of a clear moral [4]). Indeed, the story seems to have a rather dubious morality. The Man of God falls victim to a well planned deceit; nonetheless, he pays with his own life. On the other hand, the deceiver, an old prophet from Bethel, is rewarded with the

---

[1]) What follows is an abridgment of the study I dedicated to 1 Kings xiii in my dissertation, *op cit.*, pp. 313-329.

[2]) Hints in this direction can be found in W. E. BARNES, *The Two Books of Kings* (*CB*), Cambridge 1908, and A. ŠANDA, *Die Bücher der Könige* (*EHAT*), Münster i. Westf. 1911, *a 1*.

[3]) Contrary to the prevalent opinion. Cf. E. SELLIN, *Einleitung in das AT*, Leipzig 1910, p. 66; O. EISSFELDT, *The OT, an Introduction* (E.T.), Oxford 1965, p. 46; J. FICHTNER, *Das erste Buch von den Königen*, Stuttgart 1964, p. 203; K. KOCH, *Was ist Formgeschichte?*, Neukirchen 1954, p. 212; E. SELLIN-G. FOHRER, *Einleitung in das AT*[10], Heidelberg 1965, pp. 98 ff. I. PLEIN, (Erwägungen zur Überlieferung von I Reg 11^{26} — 14^{20}", *ZAW* 78 (1966), pp. 8-24) wrote as follows (p. 17): "Es scheint im I Reg 13 um die Verbindung einer an Bethel gebundenen Lokaltradition mit der Legende über einen wandernden "Gottesmann" zu handeln."

[4]) Cf. M. NOTH, *Könige, I Teilband* (BK), Neukirchen 1968, p. 306: "Gewiss darf man diese Erzählung, in die offenbar eine Betheler Lokaltradition (Prophetengrab) hineinspielt und die eine offensichtliche Freude an der Darstellung überraschender, wechselvoller Vorgänge und Szenen hat, nicht überfordern hinsichtlich der Konsequenz einer strengen Gedankenführung".

gift of prophecy (vss. 20-22) and with the assurance that his grave will not be desecrated on the day of visitation. Does such a story have a sublime lesson to teach [1]), or is it rather a "measure of the spiritual level of the dervish guild of Bethel" [2])?

To interpret the whole story properly one must understand the prohibitions imposed on the Man of God and their significance. Indeed, these prohibitions (and their transgressions) are repeated so many times (vss 9, 16, 17, 18, 19, 22) that their central role in the story is self evident. In other words, the importance of the prohibitions lies not only in their being orders of God, but also in their particular content: not to eat in Bethel, not to drink there, and in spite of vs. 10, also not to return there once having left [3]).

What, then, is the purpose of these prohibitions? Commentators generally believed that the interdictions of eating and drinking were designed to avoid any contact with the sinful, idolatrous Northeners, if not to reprimand them [4]). This interpretation, however, can scarcely be true. Bethel is not presented as a site of idolatry, and there is no hint that the inhabitants' food is impure (their water, too?). The Man of God is not prohibited from conversing with the inhabitants, and even God reveals Himself to their prophets (vss. 20-22). It has been thought that the prohibition against returning on the same road was designed to save the Man of God from ambush or capture, lest anyone try to force him to recant his prophecy [5]). However, this explanation is also inadequate, since the prohibition applies not only to the road from Judah and back but also to returning to Bethel for any purpose, not only for delivering a second prophecy.

The one who came closest to understanding this matter was, I believe, ŠANDA who argued that the Man of God's behavior was designed to sustain the impact of his appearance on the people. He was to disappear as a *Deus ex Machina* who shares no intimacy with the punished king, thereby strengthening the impression of unearthliness created by his sudden appearance [6]).

---

[1]) K. BARTH, *Exegese von I Könige* 13 (Biblische Studien, Heft 10), Neukirchen 1955.

[2]) J. GRAY, *I and II Kings* (*OTL*), London 1963, *ad loc.*

[3]) See the remarks of A. B. EHRLICH (cf. the next note) to vss. 9b-10. These verses, however, might be original.

[4]) Cf. the commentaries of R. D. KIMCHI, W. E. BARNES, *op. cit.*, H. GRESSMANN, *op. cit.*, and A. B. EHRLICH, *Mikrâ ki-Pheschutô*, II, Berlin 1900, a.l.

[5]) R. KITTEL, *op. cit.*, *ad loc.*

[6]) ŠANDA, *op. cit.*, p. 353: "Er (scil. der Prophet, A.R.) will die Wirkung der

In fact, if we search for a biblical analogy to a messenger who does not eat or drink with his addressees, we find only one such messenger, heavenly angels. Both the angels who appeared to Gideon and Manoah (Judg. vi 11-24; xiii) dit not eat the meals prepared for them by their hosts, but consumed them with fire. In the case of Manoah, the angel explicitly said that he would not eat "the bread" (Judg. xiii 16).

This concept of how angels behave is also found in the book of Tobit which, though deuterocanonical, could well be closer in time to the story of the Man of God than Judg. vi 11-24; xiii [1]). While parting from Tobias and Tobit, angel Raphael told them: "All these days did I appear unto you; and I did neither eat nor drink, but it was a vision ye yourselves saw" (Tob xii 19) [2]). In time, the concept became so entrenched in post-exilic Judaism that the ancient, half mythical story of the angels' visit to Abraham [3]) was reinterpreted to show that the angels did not actually eat [4]). We can therefore conclude that it was widely believed that angels refrain from eating and drinking with men on earth. Thus the prohibition against eating and drinking in 1 Kings xiii served to equate the Man of God with the heavenly angels of popular legends.

The stories about Gideon, Manoah and Tobit provide an additional analogy to the story of the Man of God. It is characteristic of angels to disappear suddenly (Judg. vi 21-22; xiii 21; To. xii 19) [5]). The conviction that one has dealt with angels partly derives from this attribute. This conforms to ŠANDA's interpretation cited above [6]); "the Man of God was to withdraw like a *Deus ex Machina* . . . hereby strengthening the impression of unearthliness created by his sudden appearance." The prohibition against returning to the places he had

---

Szene auf das Volk nicht abschwächen und wie ein Deus ex machina, der mit dem bestraften König keine Familiarität pflegt, rasch wieder verschwinden".

[1]) The low date of the present story will be argued *infra*. A relatively early date for the Book of Tobit was suggested by D. C. SIMPSON in (R. H. CHARLES ed.) *Apocrypha and Pseudoepigrapha of the OT*, *Vol. I*, London 1913. Cf. also M. M. SCHUMPP, *Das Buch Tobias* (*EHAT*), Münster i. W. 1933.

[2]) The translation is according to MSS A and B; MS S differs slightly.

[3]) For its mythical affinities cf. H. GUNKEL, *op. cit.* p. 200; J. SKINNER, *Genesis* (*ICC*), 1930[2]; *ad loc.*

[4]) For this re-interpretation, cf. *inter alia* Jubilees xvi 1-4; The Testament of Abraham (ed. by M. R. JAMES, Cambridge 1892); Josephus' Antiquities I, xi 2 (197); Targum Pseudo-Jonathan to Gen. xviii 8; Bat. T. Baba Meṣiʿa' 86[b]; Midrash Gen. Raba 48.

[5]) According to Ms. S.

[6]) *Supra*, p. 159.

already visited aimed at making the Man of God conform to popular legends about heavenly angels.

Now, what is the purpose of equating the Man of God with heavenly angels if not simply to identify him as God's angel? The careful terminology of the story confirms this interpretation. The prophet from Bethel is always referred to as "the prophet" while the man from Judah is always called *ʾîš haeʾlōhîm*. Titles do not interchange here as they do in the *legenda* about Elijah and Elisha. In this way, I believe, the author sought to emphasize that the man belonged to his God, much the same as a messenger belongs to his sender. The Man of God is God's *malʾāḵ*, his messenger or angel, although a mortal one.

We can now understand what was the sin of the Man of God. When he returned to Bethel and ate and drank there, he did not merely transgress a command — such an action could have been excused by his being deceived — but subverted categorically his essence as a human angel of God and thus denied the authority of his sender. Immediately God chose new emissaries (vss. 20b, 25-26) and deprived the old one of his own patronage The moral of this story — or better, this parable — is that the prophet is God's *malʾāk* and his behavior must conform to this role

This conclusion is confirmed by patterns of thought current in the prophetical writings. The dominant formulas כ׳ה אָמַר י׳ at the beginning of the prophetic message, and נְאֻם י׳ at its end, which have been recognized as typical of the messenger speech [1]), indicate how Israelite prophecy, especially in its classical period, conceived of itself. This conception is expressed in still clearer terms in the three major prophetical books, Isaiah, Jeremiah and Ezekiel whose inaugural visions employ the verb ש.ל.ח. (to send) to describe God's relation to them (Is. vi 8; Jer. i 7; Ez. ii 3; iii 5-6). This very term seems to have been greatly in favor with the editors of Jeremiah's prose sermons (Jer. vii 25; xiv 14-15; xxiii 21, 32, 38; xxv 4, 15; xxvi 5; xxvii 15; xxix 19; xxxv 15; xlii 5; xliv 4). Finally, from the exilic period on, prophets were at times designated as *malʾakim* (Is. xliv 24-28; Hg. i 13; Mal. i 1; 2 Chron. xxxvi 16; Ps. cli 4, LXX; cf. the Qumran recension).

There is, however, an additional aspect to be considered. Having determined that the Man of God, in line with classical prophecy, was conceived of as God's messenger, i.e. as a mortal angel, we may ask whether he was supposed to exist alongside heavenly angels or in

[1]) Cf. C. Westermann, *Basic Forms of Prophetic Speech* (E. T. by H. C. White), Philadelphia 1976, esp. pp. 90-128.

their stead. This question can be answered deductively by examining the attitude towards angels in other biblical texts [1]). Thus one finds that in all classical prophets, Zecharia excluded, angels are not mentioned as intermediaries [2]). The only exception, the mention of the *mal'āk* in Ho. xii 5 is probably intended to oppose a belief in angels. This corresponds to the anti-angelological trend in several books of the OT long ago detected by D. NEUMARK [3]). Deuteronomy regards prophets as the sole means of revelation: no angels, no dreams, no priestly instrumental divination (Deut. xviii 9 ff). In Deut. vi-vii the passage of Exodus xxiii 20-33 is quoted at large, but the figure of the angel, leader of Israel in the desert and in Canaan, which is so prominent in Exodus, has completely disappeared from Deuteronomy. Everything is done by the Lord who leads Israel by His immanence in the camp. No different is the attitude of the Priestly Code. In Ex. xii 13, P quotes Ex. xii 23 (J), but instead of mentioning the destroyer וְלֹא יִתֵּי הַמַּשְׁחִית לָבֹא אֶל בָּתֵּיכֶם לִנְגֹּף he talks about a destroying plague וְלֹא יִהְיֶה בָכֶם נֶגֶף לְמַשְׁחִית. The plague is inflicted directly by the Lord.

Apparently, the Man of God of 1 Kings xiii was also intended to replace the heavenly angels of the vulgar faith. This hypothesis aids in understanding the narrative. When the Old Prophet came forward claiming a revelation of a heavenly angel (vs. 18), the Man of God easily couldhave rocognized his partner's blatant lie. The Man of God was not merely deceived. He had already fallen into the snare of heresy, a belief in angels.

The same hypothesis explains the positive role assigned to the Old Prophet. He was prone to vulgar superstitions such as belief in heavenly angels, but since he did not belong to the elected group of God's human messengers and their disciples, this failing could not be reckoned a sin. *Nulla haeresis sine doctrina.* While lying, he did not do so to gain a profit, but rather to press the foreigner to accept hospitality [4]). Such good intentions did not merit punishment. The parable, then, has its own logic: the Old Prophet, who is a commoner,

---

[1]) In the following I summarize in brief excerpts from my dissertation, quoted *supra*, p. 157, n. 2.

[2]) D. NEUMARK, *The Philosophy of the Bible*, Cincinnati 1918; L. FINKELSTEIN, "The Pharisees: Thier Origin and Their Philisophy", *HThR* 22 (1929), pp. 185-261, at p. 235 ff. (Isa. lxiii 7, however, must be emended with the aid of the LXX); IDEM, *The Pharisees, I-II*, Philadelphia 1938, pp. 160-185; S. ZEITLIN, "The Sadducees and the Belief in Angels", *JBL* 83 (1964), pp. 67-71.

[3]) Cf. the preceding note.

[4]) The lie in the Bible does not appear to be condemned *per se*. Cf. 1 Sam. xxi 1-9; 2 Kings vi 19; Jer. xxxviii 26 f.

is retributed for his kind hospitality; the Man of God, who is God's elected messenger is punished for his heresy.

The late date of this story is supported by a number of arguments. The language is somewhat contaminated by late idioms: *mattat* [1]) instead of *mas'et* [2]) for the king's present; Rabbinical Hebrew *sa'ad* [3]) instead of Biblical Hebrew *sa'ad leb* for eating [4]). The theological expressions too seem to be late: *d^ebar YHWH* replaces *YHWH* as the source of the prophetic message [5]). Historical references to the reform of Josiah and to the cities of (the province of) Samaria prove that the story was not written before the end of the seventh century B.C.E. Actually, it must be of much later origin. The interest in Josiah's reform is only circumstantial, as the main issue is the proper conduct of the Man of God. In other words, the account of the events of the Josianic reform was here reelaborated with a new intention. Thus, the year 621 B.C.E. does not stand at the end of the literary history of this narrative but rather at its beginning. The altar and the grave were present at the time of the reform. An etiological story was told about them [6]). The parable was attached much later. Thus, the literary argument reenforces the linguistic and theologico-semantic arguments in establishing a post-exilic date of composition. The story can be described as a product of the fifth century, when disciples of the prophets in Judah discussed the function of the prophet in relation to his God. Their activity expressed itself in this parable, as well as in some redactional remarks in late books of the OT.

The prophetical parables appear to be a late development in the prophetical narrative. This conclusion depreciates their usefulness as sources for Israelite political history while simultaneously enhancing their value as documents of deep intellectual, theological meaning [7]).

---

[1]) Elsewhere; Ez. xlvi 5, 11; Prov. xxv 14; Qoh. iii 13; v 18.

[2]) Elsewhere: Gen. xliii 34; 2 Sam. xi 8; Jer. iv 5; Ben Sira xxxviii 2.

[3]) Bab. T. 'Erubin 53b; Debarim R. ix 1.

[4]) Gen. xviii 5; Judges xix 5, 8; Ps. civ 15.

[5]) The language is especially awkward in vss. 9, 17. Good Biblical Hebrew would run כִּי כֵן דִּבֵּר אֵלַי י׳׳ or כִּי כֵן צִוָּה אוֹתִי י׳׳. The present expressions approach the Targum's usage of מֵימְרָא דַיי.

[6]) Contrary to the opinion of J. Wellhausen, *Die Composition des Hexateuchs und der historischen Bücher des AT*, Berlin³ 1899, pp. 277 f., expanded by O. Eissfeldt (*supra*, p. 158, n. 3) which found the origin of the story in popular memories about Amos.

[7]) The cryptic character of OT parables is sufficiently explained by the fact that the teachings of the distinct religious circles were essentially not written but oral.

Thus, light is shed upon a fascinating phase of Israel's religious history.

More, however, is at stake. The present survey has shown — I hope — that some classes of prophetical stories belong primarily not to a naive oral but to a sophisticated written stage of creation. This conclusion, arrived at through an examination of some stories in the Book of Kings, also seems applicable to parts of the Torah-narrative, since we have demonstrated that two accounts of miracles performed by Moses are best understood in terms of simple and didactic *legenda*. Naturally, the next question is if, and to what extent, the literary classes of parables and *exempla* are present in the Pentateuch. Another field of Israelite literature may thus be affected by the study of prophetical stories. At the same time, within the prophetical narrative itself, the relation between the parable and other literary types such as historiography and martyrology requires consideration. The richness of prophetical narrative and its importance to the history of the religion of Israel are a challenge to biblical criticism [1]).

Therefore, the parables were incipiently accompanied by sufficient first hand instructions and information. This situation was not limited to the prophetic circles. Cf. M. TSEVAT, "The Meaning of the Book of Job", *HUCA* 37 (1966), pp. 73-106.

[1]) My thanks go to Rabbi Peter KNOBEL, Mr. Harvey BOCK and Mr. Burton CAINE who kindly revised the English style of this article and to Dr. Burke O. LONG who criticized it and made precious suggestions. The responsibility for the remaining errors and for those introduced later remains with me.

ADDITIONAL NOTE

Recent literature about 1 Kings xiii includes: M. A. KLOPFENSTEIN, "1. Könige 13", *Parrhesia, K. Barth zum 80. Geburtstag*, 1966, pp. 639-672; J. L. CENSHAW, *Prophetic Conflict, Its Effect upon Israelite Religion* (*BZAW* 124), Berlin 1971, pp. 39 ff.; A. JEPSEN, "Gottesmann und Prophet: Anmerkungen zum Kapitel 1. Könige 13", *Probleme biblischer Theologie* (*Fs. G. von Rad*) München 1971, pp. 171-182; E. WÜRTHWEIN, "Die Erzählung vom Gottesmann aus Juda in Bethel, zur Komposition von 1 Kön 13", *Wort und Geschichte* (*Fs. K. Elliger*), Neukirchen-Vluyn 1973, pp. 181-189; U. SIMON, "I Kings XIII: a Prophetic Sign, Its Frustration and Persistence", *Proceedings of the Sixth World Congress of Jewish Studies*, Jerusalem (in preparation). Having consulted these studies with interest and profit, I nevertheless stick to the interpretation offered above.

INDEX OF BIBLICAL REFERENCES